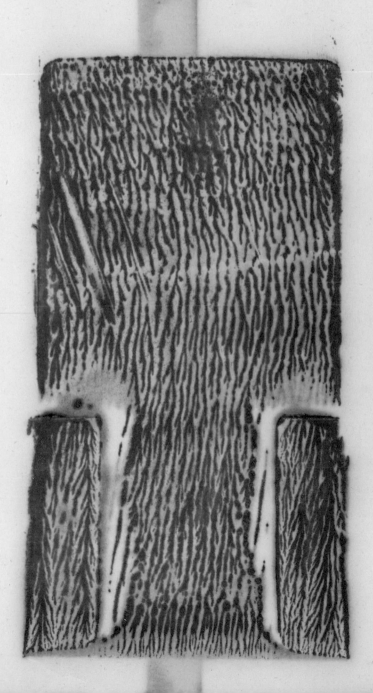

THE MADNESS OF ART

By the same author

The Madness of Art

A Study of Henry James

Walter F. Wright

UNIVERSITY OF NEBRASKA PRESS • LINCOLN

Publishers on the Plains

To "E. B."

FOREWORD

IN STUDYING the nature and range of Henry James's literary work it has seemed logical to begin with his concept of the relation of life and art, to continue with his major themes, and to conclude with the art of the telling. The novelist approached his writing with such devotion that he spoke of the artist's calling in religious metaphors. To use similar language in conveying his sense of virtual blessedness as he created his fictional worlds is, of course, not to identify James with any sectarian or other religious view of life. It is, rather, to focus on the novelist as a zealous craftsman, deeply immersed in life and unendingly surprised by the wonders achieved by art.

Critical study of James has increased steadily since his death. The present volume has drawn upon the findings of numerous scholars, whose books and articles are listed in the annotated bibliography.

To Professor Royal Gettmann I am indebted for criticism of the manuscript, and to A. B. W., as always, for assistance and encouragement. A grant from the University of Nebraska Research Council facilitated preparation of the manuscript.

CONTENTS

All creative art is magic, is evocation of the unseen in forms persuasive, enlightening, familiar and surprising, for the edification of mankind, pinned down by the conditions of its existence to the earnest consideration of the most insignificant tides of reality.

Joseph Conrad, "Henry James,
An Appreciation," 1905

CHAPTER ONE

THE NOVELIST'S PERSPECTIVE:
ART AS TRANSMUTATION

I. SUBSTANCE IN ACCIDENT

THOUGH HENRY JAMES called life "all inclusion and confusion" and art "all discrimination and selection," he did not mean that life and art were incompatible. On the contrary, the artist took what he found transitory and inchoate in actual life and transmuted it into the permanence of art. Or, to use James's own metaphor, life provided the yarns of varied colors from which evolved the figured carpets of the imagination.

To understand James as *artist* one must therefore begin with his feeling for life itself. Yet, despite abundant evidence to the contrary, not only in his less-known works, but in his major writing, his leaving America was interpreted by some early critics as a misguided or even guilty flight from the stuff of life which he should have drawn upon for his work. Even now some would identify James's proper spiritual heritage exclusively with the geography of New York and the neighborhood of New England. In leaving his native country and finding many of his themes abroad he supposedly, somehow, divorced his art from what should have been its primal sources in actual life.

It is true that both New York and New England had much to offer a novelist which James never used, and it is also true that on certain occasions the middle-aged James wrote with bitter rejection of the America which he then saw. Yet, although he could cry out with anguish at the thought of what he considered bleak, sterile, or vulgar in America, he was never inappreciative of the excellence of his numerous American friends; and in his autobiographical works, where he summed up his education for the writing of novels, he ruminated affectionately upon his childhood heritage in New York. Indeed, recalling both the scenes and his boyhood sensations in their presence, he was not merely tolerant of the gaudy New York streets, but maintained

1

unequivocally that his imagination had been nourished by them. More important, however, than his recognition of the education of his sensibilities in his American home was his confidence that, like certain of the Americans in his fiction, he had been the heir not just of contemporary America, but of *all the ages*.[1]

His trips with his family to Europe had meant no separation from life, but rather a feast of new things; and there was never to be a surfeit of his feasting. The letters which he later sent back to America, both for publication and for the private entertainment of his friends, show an intense zeal for making up, even in young manhood, for what he had already missed. He was not so innocent a culture-gathering tourist as his Miranda Hope, of "A Bundle of Letters," who grabbed culture by the armfuls; but he was nonetheless avid for experience. Sometimes, to be sure, he was romantically naïve, as when he rationalized the dirt of Florence and Siena into a necessary component of their picturesqueness. Sometimes he was a prisoner of his Murray or other guidebook. More often, however, he was concerned to immerse himself in the spirit of the place as fully as an outsider could achieve immersion, to feel the sensations which it evoked, to examine them in search of a unifying principle, and to give them concrete, harmonious embodiment in an essay or work of fiction.

There were places where life crowded upon the novelist's consciousness with such intensity that he felt himself blessed with its wealth of sensations and virtually overwhelmed by its magnitude and variety. Rome, Florence, and Paris—for it was always in cities that the richness was greatest—were among the major sources of inspiration, but most affluent of all for James was London. In his essay "London," written in 1888, he reaffirmed impressions set down in earlier letters. ". . . the British capital," he wrote, "is the particular spot in the world which communicates the greatest sense of life." It is, of course, apparent that, in his tribute to the life of London and in his comment that life is "all inclusion and confusion," James used the term with different connotations. Were it not for the selecting quality of the artist's sensibility and the alertness of his imagination to hints of harmony and unity, London

[1] For an account of James's life in New York see his *A Small Boy and Others* and Leon Edel, *Henry James: The Untried Years.*

2

would be a chaotic welter; but already an organizing principle has begun to work. The life is not entirely formless, and it is capable of being shaped into something yet more meaningful through analysis of its elements and their final synthesis in art.

The nature of that synthesis is manifested in James's own fiction. His interpretation of it is found in his commentaries on his own works and those of his fellow writers. At about the same time that he was giving his impression of London he spoke of the cultural significance of the works of an author in many respects unlike himself. In the writings of Pierre Loti he discovered "not simply the genius of an individual, but . . . that of a nation or of a conspicuous group," and he sensed a universality which could be described as a "world-drama." Clearly it was in Loti's depiction of the essence of a society that James found his merits as a novelist ("Pierre Loti," 1888).[2] Of the relation of an author's experience to his creative work he had written some years earlier. After speaking sympathetically of Musset's wild, passionate life, James concluded, "It takes certainly a great deal of life to make a little art! In this case, however, . . . that little is exquisite" ("Alfred de Musset," 1877). The nature of the distillation will concern us later; what matters at the moment is the sense of life itself—the life of a society in Loti, of a wandering spirit in Musset.

Recognizing early in his career, as Conrad was to recognize, that actuality is always seen through a temperament, James, as artist, was committed, nevertheless, to an unbiased search for reality. The distortion represented by optimism or pessimism was intolerable. However either came to take possession of an author's mind, it could only thwart his quest. Among the many strictures which James submitted concerning the novels of Zola and his Parisian associates was the complaint that they had established a jaundiced attitude toward their contemporary world and were unable to break free from their self-

[2] All dates are of initial publication. Except for "A Passionate Pilgrim," however, the quotations are from the final versions. Even when, as in certain of the novels, there was substantial revision of the phrasing, with consequent improvement of the tone, there was little alteration of the basic attitude. Similarly, though James developed greatly in understanding and in mastery of his art, there is amazing consistency between the broad concepts of life and literature in the early essays and reviews and the later criticism.

imposed dogma of pessimism. Balzac was James's master in many phases of his writing, but it was Turgenieff who best epitomized for him the ideal of impartial inquiry in the subjective realm of human passion. In an early tribute to the Russian novelist he generalized, "But the world as it stands is no illusion. . . . We can welcome experience as it comes . . . ." In that experience was inevitably a mixture—"mingled pain and delight." As if lecturing himself on his own responsibility as a young and as yet very imperfect writer, James added, ". . . but over the mysterious mixture there hovers a visible rule, that bids us learn to will and seek to understand" ("Ivan Turgenieff," 1874).

If a writer sought to understand, he would, of course, not end with an infinitude of facts. Always he would be generalizing and revising his generalizations as he obtained new glimpses; and whenever he felt confidence in his impressionistic sense of an experience, he could attempt its representation in art. The language which James used to describe fiction and the responsibility of the novelist reveals his concept of art as at the same time an immediate response to experience and a detached, imaginative synthesis. In "The Art of Fiction," 1884, he wrote, "A novel is in its broadest definition a personal, a direct impression of life . . . ." Its value, he continued, "is greater or less according to the intensity of the impression. . . . Catching the very note and trick, the strange irregular rhythm of life, that is the attempt whose strenuous force keeps Fiction upon her feet." In the same spirit, after objecting to optimism and pessimism as perspectives, he directed the writer of fiction to "try and catch the colour of life itself." Many years later, in the preface to *The Golden Bowl*, James was to make the bold assertion that the " 'taste' of the poet is, at bottom and so far as the poet in him prevails over everything else, his active sense of life." And, of course, the great message which his hero Lambert Strether gives to young Bilham in *The Ambassadors* is to live all he can.

Obviously, by living all one could and by giving an impression of life James did not mean floundering in multitudinous bits of chaotic experience. Even as Shelley expected the West Wind to speak through him in terza rimas, so James expected the novelist to give both the fresh sensation, untainted by sentimental coloring, and its ordered, disciplined arrangement in a tightly constructed story. But the sensation must come first. In speaking of George Gissing, whose talents he admitted were limited, James found him interesting because of his immersion in his subject; his was "a case of saturation" ("London Notes," July, 1897). Eight years later, in returning once again to his favorite topic, Balzac, James insisted that the novelist be steeped in his subject: "When saturation fails no other presence really avails; as when, on the other hand, it operates, no failure of method fatally interferes" ("The Lesson of Balzac"). In paying tribute to George du Maurier, James credited him with having so ably mastered and so long "interpreted . . . the social life of England that the interpretation has become the text itself" ("Black and White," 1889). Balzac was, for James, the foremost interpreter, for he provided a "distillation" of his environment; he had "preliminary possession" of "the natural and social air" ("The Lesson of Balzac"). As to taste, the reader of Gissing, Du Maurier, and Balzac will not incline to find them akin; but for James they had in common an absorbing interest in life. It must be recognized that James had no absolute knowledge by which to test their reliability as interpreters, and he may have been overgenerous, especially to Gissing. What concerns us is his never varying perspective, the standard he set for himself. Life *was* confusion, but *from* it one selected and transformed.

What one selected was always the human passions. "The moving accident," James wrote, "doesn't make the story . . . ; the human emotion and the human attestation, the clustering human conditions we expect presented, only make it" (Preface to *The Altar of the Dead*). Each of his novels and short stories has one or several human attestations. Perhaps they could all be grouped as expressions of the birth or death of a human spirit's consciousness of a significant experience. Some characters are, in a spiritual sense, awakened or reawakened into life; others become dimly, yet poignantly, aware of the life they have lost or missed. What James wrote of one of his heiresses of all the ages, Milly Theale, of *The Wings of the Dove*, is true only to a lesser degree of many other characters in his fictional world: "The idea . . . is that of a young person conscious of a great capacity for life, but early stricken and doomed" (Preface to *The Wings of the Dove*). Death itself was a touchstone for the testing of life. For Stransom, in

"The Altar of the Dead," the distinction between life and death is not a thing of burials—some who walk about are dead, and those for whom Stransom burns candles are intensely alive in his mind.

Human passions were to be encountered everywhere, in New York as freely as in Rome or London. Yet, for the novelist's education, there was a difference between emotions in a cultural void and comparable emotions in a civilization in which persons were conscious of a rich cultural heritage. Such a heritage James found primarily, though by no means exclusively, in Europe.

He admitted that in his early trips abroad he was still a tourist ("Macon," *A Little Tour in France*, 1889). But he was not necessarily less capable of entering into the life of Europe than he would have been of interpreting the life of America. Indeed, as Professor Anderson has shown, even late in his career James carried with him certain stereotyped impressions of the southern United States, having picked up his information from brief travel and from fortuitous associations with Southerners.[3] There was nothing about western Europe which made it more difficult to penetrate than James's own homeland; if anything, his reading and the conversations in his family's household made it even less remote than parts of New York City a few blocks from Washington Square. A man's cultural home is not a matter of mere geography; it is a clime of the well-fed imagination. As we find in the autobiographical writings, James did not segregate the historical information which he gleaned from older friends about New York from all that he learned, from books, paintings, visitors, and his own childhood trips, about Europe. Naturally, his knowledge was for a long time fragmentary and, at the same time, held in frameworks which inhibited full understanding. When Strether sees the actual countryside near Paris as if in a framed picture he once admired by Lambinet, he is doing what James admitted that he himself did. He remarked that, when young, he picked up impressions from picture books and that when he went to Europe he found he had been prepared, through the books, for the reality.[4] He had, of course, been both prepared and

[3] See C. R. Anderson, "Henry James's Fable of Carolina," and "James's Portrait of the Southerner" (bibliography, General Criticism).
[4] "Homburg Reformed," 1873; see below, page 75.

limited, in that he saw most easily what he was ready to see and, like Strether, tried to fit his new experience into the waiting frame.

Consequently, when we compare the impressions which in the 1870's James sent back to America, in personal letters and in reports to magazines and to the New York *Tribune,* with his later interpretations, we find less penetration of the social structure and the nature of daily life; but even from the earliest we are struck with an absorbing passion for the culture of the past. From the guidebooks he quoted the merits of a work of art or architecture; but much more, he noted the anecdotes connected with its history or the conditions from which it sprang. The facts ready at hand were not abundant, and James was not an antiquarian, still less an historical scholar. He did not arrange in precise fashion, either in space or time, his gleanings from a civilization that had once been. Rather, he followed a process for which he has provided his own metaphor. When he speaks of art as discrimination and selection, he pictures it as sniffing "round the mass [of life] as instinctively and unerringly as a dog suspicious of some buried bone" (Preface to *The Spoils of Poynton*). We may, if we wish, question the term *unerringly,* as any subjective approach to life is fallible. But it was much less fallible for the artist, James would maintain, than the most rigorous attempt at objectivity.

Let us look at the novelist's own words. In writing about the streets of Siena, in 1874, James remarked on "that vague, historic dusk . . . in which one walks and wonders" ("Siena"). Romantic, indeed intensely romantic, that desire to shut out for the moment the glaring daylight of the mere present and to become aware of distant shadows moving in loosely defined patterns in the semidarkness of the past! With the Palazzo Corsini, in Florence, as his immediate inspiration, James let his imagination take a philosophic flight: "In places that have been lived in so long and so much and in such a large way . . . the past seems to have left a sensible deposit, an aroma, an atmosphere. This ghostly presence tells you no secrets, but it prompts you to try and guess a few" ("Florentine Notes," 1874). The Palazzo is there in its physical actuality; it can be described with objective precision and discussed as an esthetic form. James was not indifferent to its appeal to the eye; in fact, it was with that appeal that he naturally began.

As he looked at a painting or a building, however, he was instantly lured into speculation about the past. The person who paid the cost of a given work of art or architecture might have been a boor, but there was a civilization in which the work had its origin, and there must have been, both then and since, at least a select few who could appreciate it. They would remain, perhaps, forever unknown or exist by names only; but to try to enjoy the work without regard for their enjoyment was to have but a single dimension to one's experience. The sensible deposit provided the breadth and height. Years later, in re-reading his stories for revision, James reiterated his historical passion and defined its major province. "I delight," he wrote, "in a palpable imaginable *visitable* past . . ." (Preface to *The Aspern Papers*). *Sensible* and *palpable* are synonyms for James. Most palpable, of course, would be that past just a little before one's own time, for one would normally bring to it the most numerous associations. But the imagination could leap generations when there were clues for the construction of an ordered world.

For what did the imagination look? First of all for symmetry, or for what James liked to call *tone*. If the imagined parts seemed to fit together, not so tightly as building blocks, but rather as shadowy forms might be found to harmonize, one could speak of the total effect as the tone. In his biography of William Wetmore Story, 1903, James reveals that Story's early letters were of interest to him because they helped him sense "the tone of the time." In the same study he spoke of Mrs. Procter as the "perpetuator, for our age, of the tone of an age not ours." He added, "It was her tone that was her value and her identity . . . ." That is, the special quality of her present charm was not her creation alone; a civilization had contributed to its making, and in the presence of the splendid elderly widow one seemed to live imaginatively in a visitable past.

James had always the romantic's view of times gone by. In the biography of Story, after telling of adventures described by Mrs. Story which involved the turmoil in an earlier Italy, he quoted "Old forgotten far-off things/ And battles long ago." A letter from Browning to the Storys conveyed "something of the charm of a document on the old romantic method of progression [travel]." And James commended

Story for being "frankly and forcibly romantic, . . . with a highly cultivated quality in his romance." The term *romance*, as James used it in the biography, is invariably associated with a sense of the past.

There is here a vast distinction between what James wanted and Story revealed, on the one hand, and mere revery, on the other. For James the re-creation of an earlier time was a disciplined act of the imagination. Though in his fiction the form which it took differed from that of Proust, the process was a no less orderly research into the tone of the past, into the essence of its atmosphere. And the tone, the atmosphere, were the composite of the qualities of men's minds. James regarded himself, consequently, as akin to the professional historian. "To represent and illustrate the past, the actions of men," he asserted, "is the task of either writer," that is, of the historian or of the novelist ("The Art of Fiction"). Again, unmistakably with the great corpus of Balzac's writings in mind, he wrote to Robert Louis Stevenson, in 1888, "I want to leave a multitude of pictures of my time, projecting my small circular frame upon as many different spots as possible and going in for number as well as quality, so that the number may constitute a total having a certain value as observation and testimony" (July 31). He was speaking of a history of his own time, but of a history inseparable from that of earlier times.

The inseparability comes from the fact that, for James, any present worth knowing brought with it a foreshortened manifestation of the past. The term *foreshortening* was important in James's vocabulary when he was thinking of the structure of his own fiction. There it referred to a method by which a scene, while presenting a new action, would give the essence of events that had gone before. In his approach to actual life he meant much the same thing. In describing the two forces in France which tugged at him in opposite ways for his attention, he saw the conflict as between one's "liberal instinct and what one may call the historic, aesthetic sense, the sense upon which old cathedrals lay a certain palpable obligation" ("A Little Tour," 1877). He found nothing wrong with the liberal instinct if one was concerned with the present and the future and defined life merely in terms of material progress and social justice. For James, however, these were not sufficient. In the materialistic changes which were occurring in

American cities he found ruthless disregard for the historical heritage. In Europe, though materialism was less crass than in America, liberalism was nonetheless in danger of denying the past. In contrast, the cathedrals preserved it in foreshortened form. One saw them in the present, but one saw them, too, as epitomes of history. They were, to use James's own phrase, examples of "the fine foreshortened past" (*William Wetmore Story*).

To experience history most fully and, indeed, almost palpably, James not only laid the scenes of many of his stories in earlier periods, but created a number of characters who became his agents in the historical exploration. Significantly, nearly all his men and women through whose consciousness he established his perspective for the recapture of bygone times are Americans, most notably Isabel Archer, of *The Portrait of a Lady*, Milly Theale, and Lambert Strether. In his preface to *The Wings of the Dove* James wrote, "I had from far back mentally projected a certain sort of young American as more the 'heir of all the ages' than any other young person whatever . . . ." Each of these persons, and perhaps even more the hero in James's unfinished book called explicitly *The Sense of the Past*, has to start with a present which has vestiges of history and, with a limited knowledge from books and by sheer sensitivity of imagination, to become the heir of a legacy—the foreshortened past.

Where would historical foreshortening most appear if not in the manners of men and women? Along with the misinterpretation of James's leaving America for Europe there has been a persistent misunderstanding of his interest in manners, as if they were somehow the antithesis of morals, or, more often, a superficial gloss in the absence of depth of feeling. Gilbert Osmond and Madame Merle, of *The Portrait of a Lady*, have been cited as examples of persons with excellent manners and wretched morals. Actually, all that James credited to each was a limited discernment in esthetics and a wish to conform to conventional standards. Osmond's manners are, in reality, execrable.

In the last stanza of *Modern Love* George Meredith wrote of the "faint thin line upon the shore" as our only means of reading the vast ocean force which cast the wave upon the beach. The thin line symbolized those hints in men's actions which suggest the passions beneath.

For James, manners, which included customs and habits of living, were the outward manifestation by which one sensed the quality of a man's mind or of a civilization. A New England puritan expressed his moral conscience through his ascetic manners, and the parasitic Osmond revealed the hollowness of both his moral and esthetic being through his gross lapses into pettish vulgarity. Manners, in the form of a rigid scheme of hard work, directed toward material progress, betrayed the American business world's inner aimlessness; the attempt to make a virtue of money-getting was bad morally, and the manners merely revealed the moral chaos.

There is never in James's fiction a contrast between the morals of one person or country and the manners of another. The contrast is between the spirit of the one and the spirit of the other. Morality, esthetic appreciation, and other precious qualities are James's concern, and there is much contrast involving these. But how does one identify them? Naturally, through their manifestation in men's speech and actions. There was, for James, no such thing, for example, as well-mannered selfishness. Whenever one of his characters is deficient, James does not tell us that, despite his perfect manners, he is really a bad fellow. We know that the Marquis de Bellegarde is cruel and egoistic because his manners expose him. And we enter into the moral state of the Prince and Charlotte, in *The Golden Bowl*, as we observe the nature of their adherence to what James calls the "forms" of proper conduct, or, in other words, their manners.

As we discuss therefore the significance of manners, we are accepting James's—and Meredith's—definition of the novelist's limitations and of his function. James could read the past only from the evidence still present. Similarly, he could read the minds of human beings and generalize as to the civilization which they represented only by what they said and did. To pretend to do more was to cease to be an artist and to lay claim to some kind of godlike insight. In practice it would mean the abandonment of all artistic concern for representation and the substitution of assertion of generalizations. For if James was dependent on manners for his clues as to the inner life of actual people, he was, as novelist, equally dependent on them when occupied with the imaginary persons in his books. But again, let us check the evi-

11

dence, for our own clues to the thoughts of Henry James are in what he wrote.

"Experience, as I see it, is our apprehension and our measure of what happens to us as social creatures—" thus did James define the boundaries of his interest (Preface to *The Princess Casamassima*). Rushing to cavil with so sweeping a statement, one may bring along the cohorts of semantics. There is, of course, the natural world in which human beings are not present, and there is the mystic awe of religion. The separating line, however, between one's interest in the world of nature or Western man's religious experience and one's social existence, however sharp semantically, is, in reality, not ascertainable. Like Donne, James was unable to separate himself from his fellow men. Whatever the subject of his contemplation, he saw with the help of others, and the search for his own identity meant, not the singling out and isolating of his own personality, but the seeing it in its social context. In the preface to *The Awkward Age* he maintained that the characters could be understood fully only in their relations to one another. It followed then that the novelist must be concerned with the nature of the relationships.

On this point James wrote, "We know a man imperfectly until we know his society;" and he added, ". . . we but half know a society until we know its manners. . . . manners lie very close to literature" ("Emerson," 1887). The view here enunciated became the central theme of his study of America in *The American Scene*, 1905–1907. In disagreeing with Howells as to the comparative stimulation for a novelist of America and of Europe, James wrote that an old civilization sets "a novelist in motion— . . . It is on manners, customs, usages, habits, forms, upon all these things matured and established, that a novelist lives—they are the very stuff his work is made of . . ." (Letter, January 31, 1880). Evidence that James was consistent in his preoccupation with "manners, customs, usages" can be gleaned from nearly every page of his works, both the fiction and the essays; and always stated or implicit is the awareness that one's present civilization is the product, in part, of the past. Things "matured and established" were much richer than things just taking form. Thus, in describing his impression of Santa Maria Maggiore in Rome, James stressed the "social atmosphere . . . the sense it gives you . . . of having been prayed in for several centuries by a singularly complicated and picturesque society" ("A Roman Holiday," 1873). Recalling his dictum that taste was, ultimately, one's deep sense of life, one can understand his statement that he liked faded records from the past, even when they showed imperfect esthetic judgment, "for they are what seems to bring us nearest to manners, and manners are, changing or unchanging, always most the peopled scene, the document to be consulted, the presented image and beguiling subject" (*William Wetmore Story*). In his exhortative lecture *The Question of Our Speech*, 1905, James summed up a lifetime belief: "The idea of good breeding—without which intercourse fails to flower into fineness, without which human relations bear but crude and tasteless fruit—is one of the most precious conquests of civilisation, the very core of our social heritage . . . ."

The limitations of America's social heritage were perennially James's concern. Once more we must consider major impressions. James knew a good many Americans who were not impelled by materialism and who cherished the things which he himself valued. It is certainly true, too, that by the nature of his temperament he undervalued what others, such as Howells and Emerson, found excellent in American life. We have to accept the fact that he was nourished extensively on the cultural traditions of England, France, and Italy and that he judged by what he knew. In an early sketch he half playfully admitted his bias in his castigation of Saratoga as an American vacation resort. Not all that he saw at Saratoga was bad, but what was good was somehow out of place. Of one attractive female vacationer he wrote, "She ought to sit on the terrace of a stately castle . . . and bandy quiet small-talk with an ambassador or a duke" ("Saratoga," 1870). In the same sketch he wrote, romantically and sentimentally, "There are few prettier sights than a charmingly-dressed woman, gracefully established in some shady spot, with a piece of needlework or embroidery, or a book. . . . The embroidery and the book are a tribute to culture, and I suppose they really figure somewhere out of the opening scenes of French comedies." What is here rather boyish and derivative can be traced in improved form through "Madame de Mauves," 1874, and

"Four Meetings," 1877, to passages in *The Portrait of a Lady*, 1880, and, yet later, *The Wings of the Dove*, 1902, and *The Golden Bowl*, 1904. Greater knowledge had refined the picture without altering the perspective.

In general, James found in American women the glorification of youth; the American girl, revelling in her personal freedom, even though her tastes were untrained, was supreme. The American man was preeminently the business man, who sweated in his city office throughout the summer, with furtive week ends at Saratoga or Newport, and at rare intervals, most likely after retirement, went on a pathetic pilgrimage to a Europe which he was unprepared to enjoy. Neither the girl nor the man ordinarily qualified as the heir of all the ages. Both belonged to "a country in which the social atmosphere, like the material, is extremely thin" ("Homburg Reformed," 1873). Many years later James was to praise Charles Eliot Norton for working to instill into American life what it most lacked. Norton was concerned with America's need of civilization—"the particular civilisation that a young roaring and money-getting democracy, inevitably but almost exclusively occupied with 'business success,' most needed to have brought home to it" ("An American Art Scholar: Charles Eliot Norton," 1909). Norton combined a New England sense of duty with a great love of the esthetic qualities of Europe. James was, of course, also an admirer of Hawthorne. He felt, however, that as a novelist Hawthorne had been unfortunately restricted by the milieu in which he worked. ". . . it takes such an accumulation of history and custom," he wrote, "such a complexity of manners and types, to form a fund of suggestion for a novelist." Had Hawthorne lived in Europe, James felt, "his sense of the life of his fellow-mortals would have been almost infinitely more various" (*Hawthorne*, 1879).

Once more we have manners, inseparable from foreshortened history, as the novelist's key to the human mind. One important manifestation of what James wanted was to be found in the social use of leisure. In America, he wrote, the social employment of leisure was "an undeveloped branch of civilisation." In contrast, England had many more persons free for "purely social purposes" ("An English Easter," 1877). The ideal rendezvous for the English leisure class was altogether unlike anything in America: "The most perfect" thing which the English "have mastered . . . so that it has become a compendious illustration of their social genius and their manners, is the well-appointed, well-administered, well-filled country house" ("An English New Year," 1879). *Compendious* is very close in meaning to *fore-shortened*, for there is once again the implication that what is present suggests much beyond itself which one reads from inflections and nuances, indeed whatever connotes a cultural history. James became intensely fond of English country homes. Allowing for his compli-mentary epistolary style, his letter to the Countess of Jersey concern-ing the use he had made of her home in "The Lesson of the Master" is indicative. He referred to his appropriation of "the dear old cubic sofa-cushions and objects of the same delightful order" (June 11, 1892). Much earlier he had written that "the walk to church from a beauti-ful country-house, of a lovely summer afternoon, may be the prettiest possible adventure" ("In Warwickshire," 1877). Everywhere in his European travels he found foreshortened expressions of tradition, most commonly in hotels and inns. Of a Liverpool waiter he remarked, ". . . could anything be so English as his intensely professional back? It revealed a country of tradition" ("London," 1888).

These examples are concerned with the social life of the leisure class and the consideration accorded that class by those paid to serve. James was not interested exclusively, however, in cubic cushions and walks to church. He came to know a fair amount about a very different aspect of English society. His hero, Hyacinth, of *The Princess Casa-massima,* "sprang up . . . out of the London pavement" (Preface to *The Princess Casamassima*). How had James learned what the pave-ments were like in the depressed sections of London? His account of how he had traversed them reminds one of how he had wandered through the cultural purlieus of Rome and Florence: "To haunt the great city and by this habit to penetrate it, imaginatively, in as many places as possible—*that* was to be informed . . ." (Preface). The ex-tent of the penetration is a separate matter. What concerns us here is that James did not confine his interest to one aspect of English life; and what matters even more is that he felt that he could interpret Hyacinth only by presenting the essence of his environment. There

15

was no knowing the predicament of the sensitive young man without seeing first of all the pavements from which he sprang.

The shop which supplied the golden bowl in the great novel was, according to James, an "image distilled and intensified" of many London shops (Preface to *The Golden Bowl*). In like fashion his characters and their actions were a distillation from all that a civilization had to offer. Particularly in certain early stories and in *The Bostonians* James distilled, or attempted to do so, from American life, but his most fruitful sources he found abroad.

If the origin of art's substance is to be discovered in fragments of life itself, if art draws upon history and manners for flesh to clothe its spirit, what then is that substance, that spirit? Its full nature defies description, for it is infinite. Its manifestations within James's own work are as varied as the separate experiences which he depicted. For our present purposes, however, a general definition is possible. Art—and for James art was, of course, pre-eminently fiction—had for its substance the imaginative experience of a sensitive mind.

The definition rules out action for action's sake. It also ruled out, for James, something not so elementary. His strictures upon a number of his contemporaries illustrate what he deplored. Gautier, he remarked, "cared for nothing and knew nothing in men and women but the epidermis" ("Théophile Gautier," 1873); the evil portrayed by Baudelaire began "outside and not inside" ("Charles Baudelaire," 1876). Twenty-six years later James was still protesting; D'Annunzio's *Il Piacere* failed to convey its intended meaning for lack of "inwardness" ("Gabriele d'Annunzio, 1902," 1904). In the meantime he had lamented that Daudet, Maupassant, and the Goncourts were too much concerned with the world of the senses rather than "the deeper, stranger, subtler inward life, the wonderful adventures of the soul" ("Pierre Loti," 1888). Flaubert did better, but in *L'Education sentimentale* he had too inadequate a vehicle for his vast intent: "It was a mistake . . . to propose to register in so mean a consciousness as that of such a hero so large and so mixed a quantity of life . . ." ("Gustave Flaubert," 1902).

James had no quarrel with the French novelists for being preoccupied with sexual passion; indeed, his own novels are repeatedly so concerned. But he did not want it by itself. Nothing original or indi-vidualizing could be said in a study devoted to any human impulse if it alone was portrayed. There must be a significant mind to give direction to or be affected by it: "What the participants [in sexual passion] do with their agitation, in short, or even what it does with them, *that* is the stuff of poetry, and it is never really interesting save when something finely contributive in themselves makes it so" ("Ga-briele d'Annunzio, 1902"). The term *finely contributive* is typical of James's thought. The adventure, for the novelist, could be only so meaningful as the consciousness of the adventurer. It goes without saying that this consciousness must actually exist and function in the story rather than have its fineness asserted by the author.

"There is no such thing in the world as an adventure pure and sim-ple," James wrote; "there is only mine and yours, and his and hers—it being the greatest adventure of all, I verily think, just to *be* you or I, just to be he or she" ("The Lesson of Balzac," 1905). The you or I is, of course, not just anyone; sensitivity is presupposed. With it adven-ture becomes possible, and what would otherwise be crude action, stemming from blind passion, takes on a distinctive character. It does not lose its universal aspect by rising beyond animality; rather, it achieves universal significance as the imagination seeks out its mean-ing. When speaking of the "stuff of poetry" James was thinking of the lyric quality of fiction—a quality expressed in the tone which pervaded the narration and the dialogue. That tone, which would depend on the author's attitude, would convey the sense of adventure with which he looked at life. How James looked is seen both in his fiction, where it appears obliquely, and in his autobiographic confessions. In speak-ing of the Rome known to Story and later to himself, he remarked that "no Rome of reality was concerned in our experience," that "the whole thing was a rare state of the imagination, dosed and drugged . . . by the effectual Borgia cup" (*William Wetmore Story*). Again a thoroughly Romantic view! Rome was to be drunk, not in half draughts, but by the brimming cup. Wishing, perhaps, that he were, at least for the moment, Italian, James once wrote, "It takes a great deal to make a successful American; but to make a happy Venetian takes only a handful of quick sensibility" ("Venice," 1882).

17

For the American, as he was to demonstrate, a very special sensibility was needed for a full life, the materials on which it could feed being so scarce. Story had such a gift, possessing "the right sensibility, . . . a universal curiosity, a large appetite for life . . . a talent that yearned for exercise" (*William Wetmore Story*). His act of leaving America "was not of the violent sort . . . ; but it was conscious and intelligent, arriving at the pleasure and escaping the pain, a revolution without a betrayal." In so characterizing Story's journey to Europe James was also describing his own. There was before him a freedom of exercise for the imagination, in contrast to a feeling of restraint or of lack of nourishment at home. In short, going to Europe was adventure—again not for everyone, not for example, for Jim Pocock, of *The Ambassadors*, or for various middle-aged business men in lesser stories, but very much for those with sensitivity. In fact, in the preface to *The Portrait of a Lady* James stated that he conceived of Isabel's coming to Europe as an adventure of the mind; and for Strether every moment abroad intensified his insight into a new world of the imagination.

Inseparable from adventure in the form of drinking from the Borgia cup was the moral pilgrimage, which, to shift the metaphor, was the other side of the coin. Morality was for James no simple matter of refraining from doing deliberate ill. Above all, it was not mere conformity to conventions which would encourage self-denial. Any such restraint upon one's conduct could become a negation of adventure. James not only objected to stoicism because it destroyed the possibility of free use of one's human capacities ("Epictetus," 1866); he also rejected that type of puritanism which defined pleasure as evil or the temptation toward evil. In his short story "The Third Person," 1900, the puritan Susan is unable to help the ghost of a smuggler by anonymously paying the duty on the goods he succeeded in smuggling into England so many years before. Since he was finally caught and executed, his last adventure was left incomplete. He can rest only after the more understanding Amy completes this last adventure for him by crossing the Channel, buying a Tauchnitz, and, at the loss of a few pence to the exchequer, smuggling it into England. The story is, of course, symbolic. Life was properly an adventure, and never more so than in the moral realm.

To accept Amy's act as moral, even though it violated the law, is to say that, not unlike Antigone, she saw an immediate social responsibility that transcended mere legal claims. A man had tried to carry out a perilous undertaking, and in the one unlawful act of her whole life she had participated in his excitement; she had taken a risk which, for a lady of the most respected reputation, was as great as his. In short, she had intensely lived, and at the same time she had thought, not of herself, but of him. Her escapade, in the Jamesian sense, had been very moral indeed.

We are to think of morality in James, therefore, as part of one's concept of life as a creative adventure in a social world—a world in which there is no real distinction between past and present. To conceive of a condition in which the individual would have the maximum freedom for self-expression was to think immediately of his indebtedness to his fellows, both living and dead. Amy owed a duty to the ghost, who was still acutely alive in her mind. There were things a person must do to be true to the past; and if he did not do them, he failed to live. In "The Altar of the Dead" any man who neglects his dead is regarded as having robbed himself of spirit, as having, in fact, committed spiritual suicide. Without loyalties, both to the living and to the dead, life became a mad whirling in a nihilistic void. With them one could build a coherent spiritual universe. Morality was, in other words, at the center of all one's thinking. It was a recognition of a debt and, at the same time, an appreciation of one's own capacity for creative contemplation. To act morally was to draw upon a cultural heritage and with its help to make choices which would give the greatest creative freedom. If one happened to be a woman of limited experience and talent, that freedom might find its highest expression in a bit of sacrificial smuggling. If one happened to be a novelist, it would lead to the giving of life to this charming adventuress and to all her scores of imaginary associates within whose passions the novelist himself most intensely lived.

When we turn, for concreteness, to James's evaluation of the substance of literature, we must therefore interpret his moral comments

19

in the context, not only of the paragraph in which they occur, but of the whole corpus of his fiction and of all that is known about his way of life. To do otherwise would be at times to make him appear to support positions maintained by the unperceiving, the morally righteous, and those who look upon literature with wrathful fear. A good example of our need for caution is his complaint that Baudelaire "has, as a general thing, not plucked the flowers—he has plucked the evil-smelling weeds" ("Charles Baudelaire," 1876). We need not pretend that James was unerring in his objections to other authors. In looking in vain for one quality he would seem at times to have missed virtues which were present. Certainly he was not by temperament inclined toward affinity with Baudelaire. What disturbed him, however, was no single passion or theme in Baudelaire's poems, but the lack of a strong unifying principle which would make the passions assume their places in a vast human experience of which they were only a part. As we noted above, James would permit the naked presentation of whatever emotion came into a human mind, but he demanded a perspective which emphasized what the mind did with it, once it had come. And what he expected the mind to do was to sort self-pity and other divisive feelings which set an individual apart, from the feelings which identified him with the best minds in his cultural heritage. Evil, as James saw it, was in the yielding to disintegrative forces, whereas art should be on the side of discipline and order.

At about the same time that James was unhappy about Baudelaire he labeled Charles de Bernard second rate because "he had no morality. By this we of course do not mean that he did not choose to write didactic tales, winding up with a goody lecture and a distribution of prizes and punishments. We mean that he had no moral emotion, no preferences, no instincts—no moral imagination, in a word" ("Charles de Bernard and Gustave Flaubert," 1876). In the dramas and novels of his French contemporaries James found "an incredibly superficial perception of the moral side of life. It is not only that adultery is their only theme, but that the treatment of it is so singularly vicious and arid" ("The Parisian Stage," 1873). The viciousness was a result of the superficiality. Had the writers seen into the depths, they would not have settled for commonplace cynical stereotypes. There was little or no adventure for the reader of their works because they themselves had declined to make a creative adventure of writing.

"To deny the relevancy of subject-matter and the importance of the moral quality of a work of art" was, James insisted, "very childish." He went on to say, "The crudity of sentiment of the advocates of 'art for art' . . . [reveals] a well-seated provincialism of spirit" ("Charles Baudelaire," 1876). Ironically James himself has been blamed for insufficient stress on morality merely because his books are not reducible to moral certainties. In emphasizing subject matter and moral quality he was in no way subordinating art to an ulterior purpose. Doubtless one could so define "art for art" as to make it include what James himself wanted. He was using the term, however, with specific reference to a group of writers whom he found superficial, and he found them so simply because they did not really accept the challenge of art; they did not seek to draw upon the resources of human experience and to build with them an architectural order. As artists they had narrowed rather than expanded the scope of their imaginations and had chosen a lesser technical problem where more difficult ones invited.

In contrast was Turgenieff, a disciplined, painstaking artist with a devotion to art. *The Memoirs of a Sportsman* James had cited as an adequate answer to provincial spirits: "It offers a capital example of moral meaning giving a sense to form and form giving relief to moral meaning" ("Ivan Turgenieff," 1874). In an early comment on Petrarch, James wrote, with no qualifying phrases, ". . . there are half a dozen stanzas in Wordsworth that speak more to the soul than the whole collection of his *fioriture*" (*A Little Tour*, 1884).

The moral view required, first of all, a full acceptance of the conditions of life. Whatever perspective shut out any aspect—be that perspective stoicism, cynicism, optimism, pessimism, materialism, or narrow puritanism—limited the world in which one imaginatively lived, and it permitted, at best, the construction of a shallow order for one's universe. The effect was identical for the writer as a man and as an artist, for what was art itself but a search for the greatest ordering of the vastest conceivable universe?

The moral aspect of life confronts us in every single work by James.

Isabel Archer hardly expected to find it in Europe; indeed she tried for a while to pretend that it need not exist. Strether was burdened heavily with it at the beginning, without, as yet, a point of view which would let him see it as an adventure in its own right. For both, of course, as for Fleda Vetch and many others, it became a major element in their education. James stated the issue perhaps most inclusively in the preface to *What Maisie Knew:* "No themes are so human as those that reflect for·us, out of the confusion of life, the close connection of bliss and bale, of the things that help with the things that hurt, so dangling before us for ever that bright hard medal, of so strange an alloy, one face of which is somebody's right and ease and the other somebody's pain and wrong."

Behind the moral theme expressed here was the conviction stated above that experience is what happens to us as social beings. Life, as distinguished from the mere chronology of events, was inevitably a matter of morality. And morality was not a simple thing with convenient placards to label good and evil. The very determining of what was good and what was evil was an exciting adventure, the most disciplined of all adventures for a sensitive mind.

II. THE MINISTRANT

IN OUR CONCERN for judging the finished work we sometimes forget that it came into being only because a given mind, with a background of impressions and a quality all its own, selected and shaped, gave emphasis and tone, and set the completed portrait in its frame. Joseph Conrad once spoke of the author of a work of fiction as the figure behind the veil. James, like Conrad, was interested in that figure, and he too wanted the veil, for he was indifferent to the commonplace externals of an author's existence. His own autobiography omits and selects as rigorously as does his fiction, and his biography of Story gives us, not a full account of his career, but the essence of his pilgrimage. If the face had been ravaged, as was Musset's, by human passions, James wanted to know the nature of their violence, to glimpse the inner turbulence from which the artistic substance erupted. But it was the experiencing of emotion by a mind of intellectual grasp and refined sensibility that interested him, for only then, as with Musset, would the resultant art be "exquisite." "There is one point," he wrote, "at which the moral sense and the artistic sense lie very near together; that is in the light of the very obvious truth that the deepest quality of a work of art will always be the quality of the mind of the producer. In proportion as that intelligence is fine will the novel, the picture, the statue partake of the substance of beauty and truth" ("The Art of Fiction," 1884).[5] Elsewhere he spoke of "the kind and degree of the artist's prime sensibility, which is the soil out of which his subject springs" (Preface to *The Portrait of a Lady*). And again, "Tell me what the artist is, and I will tell you of what he has *been* conscious. Thereby I shall express to you at once his boundless freedom and his 'moral' reference" (Preface). For *moral* we could substitute *philosophic*, keeping in mind James's statement that experience is what happens to us as social beings. The artist's moral reference was his sense of how things fitted together in a social universe.

We are constantly reminded by James that, instead of inhibiting, of making one fearfully shun pleasure, the moral view of life opens upon the most sublime vistas for the imagination. In his poem addressed to Terence, Housman enunciated one function of literature, to introduce the reader to aspects of life which, without the wisdom supplied by poetry, could shatter the soul. The increasing doses of poison had presumably enabled Mithridates to tolerate quantities which would kill an inexperienced person. James would have admitted the truth of Housman's analogy, perhaps, but his own approach to existence was positive, whereas all Mithridates secured was inurement. To keep Housman's metaphor, and James's too, Mithridates got no thrill from drinking of the Borgia cup, but only ability to survive. For James, a novelist did have to drink to survive, but if he drank he should get also the keenest, most intense reward: ". . . if you haven't, for fiction, the root of the matter in you, haven't the sense of life and the pene-

[5] In "John S. Sargent," 1887, James wrote, "There is no greater work of art than a great portrait." He never fully separated the task of a portrait painter from that of the novelist. Both were concerned with the tone of time—with an attitude and an ordered mood.

23

trating imagination, you are a fool in the very presence of the revealed and assured; but . . . if you *are* so armed you are not really helpless, not without your resource, even before mysteries abysmal" (Preface to *The Princess Casmassima*). The last two words are strong indeed, and they were not used lightly. Life uninterpreted was, for James, an unbearable mystery. Yet the very imagination which made one aware of the abysmal extent of the mystery was capable of penetrating it and making endless discoveries. In fact, if it were not for the initial mystery there would be nothing to penetrate, nothing to discover. One started with acceptance of all life, and with frank recognition that it is "confusion." It was not merely an artist's duty to bring order; it was also his boundless opportunity for adventure.

If an artist possessed sensibility and a discerning imagination, he must then accept as the province of his art what his experience provided. Not that he could not try to select to some degree by choosing where to live, what to read, and what to seek out. But when such conscious efforts had been made, there was still an incalculable amount of experience which was not of the artist's deliberate, conscious choice: ". . . one never really chooses one's general range of vision—the experience from which ideas and themes and suggestions spring . . . . The subject thus pressed upon the artist is the necessity of his case and the fruit of his consciousness . . ." (Preface to *Lady Barberina*). It is to be noted that there is the force of experience as a compulsion, but there is also the conscious appreciation, which itself influences experience at the same time that it draws upon it.

For James, people could be classified according to what they had imaginatively appreciated. There was always at work in the world a spirit antagonistic to the sensitivity which the artist represented. Its antagonism arose from bafflement before the abysmal mystery and resulted in aggressive destruction of what could not be understood. Materialism was the most obvious manifestation, but there were other forms too. The predominance of vulgarity, the "rule of the cheap and easy" was not a passive thing which would leave one alone. It was something which must be resisted, because otherwise it would claim its fee—no less than the soul itself (Preface to *The Lesson of the Master*). James saw educated, cultivated minds throughout the world as sharing a "felt difficulty and danger" from the forces ignorantly hostile to excellence (Preface to *Lady Barberina*). The hostility could destroy blatantly from without or insidiously by corrupting the artist's soul. The more the artist was "enamoured of perfection" the more poignant was his awareness of the enemy (Preface to *The Lesson*). A number of James's fictional heroes, perhaps most strikingly Ralph Limbert of "The Next Time," must struggle to achieve artistic excellence in the midst of callous indifference or opposition. How strongly, indeed bitterly, James felt on the subject is shown in his repeated reference to his being asked to write in a more popular vein for the New York *Tribune*. As he put the matter wryly in "The Next Time," "you can't make a sow's ear of a silk purse!"

Among important writers, as we have seen, there were several whose spiritual limitations disturbed James. He deplored D'Annunzio's vulgarity, which exhibited "the weakness of his sense of 'values'" ("Gabriele d'Annunzio, 1902"). And he lamented Zola's lack of taste: "When you have no taste you have no discretion, which is the conscience of taste . . . ." Zola's books showed no evidence of "the finer vision of human experience" ("Émile Zola," 1903).

What James wanted he found in certain other authors, notably Thackeray, George Eliot, George Sand, and Turgenieff, of whom he wrote, "It is into the conscience and the mind that we enter, and we think of these writers primarily as great consciences, and great minds." Of course he found it too in Balzac: "When we approach Balzac we seem to enter a great temperament—a prodigious nature" ("Honoré de Balzac," 1875). Of George Sand he wrote years later, "She herself lived with all her perceptions and in all her chambers—not merely in the showroom of the shop." She had tone, and tone was indispensable for the salvation of the soul ("George Sand," 1897). Another who kept a suite of inner chambers was Robert Browning. The one Browning performed man's ordinary duties in the world; but there was a second Browning: ". . . this inscrutable personage sat at home and knew as well he might in what quarters of *that* sphere to look for suitable company" (*William Wetmore Story*. Cf. also "The Private Life").

If a writer were endowed with inner chambers, if he did not shrink from life, yet had the capacity to retire and reflect, he could trans-

25

form the confused elements of experience into the substance of art. We have referred to Meredith's comparison of life to the ocean's force and the faint thin line it casts upon the shore. James used a somewhat parallel metaphor and drew additional implications: "The power to guess the unseen from the seen, to trace the implication of things, to judge the whole piece by the pattern, the condition of feeling life in general so completely that you are well on your way to knowing any particular corner of it—this cluster of gifts may almost be said to constitute experience . . . . If experience consists of impressions, it may be said that impressions *are* experience" ("The Art of Fiction"). The process superficially resembles the well-known one of drawing conclusions from facts and then applying them to new facts, actual or imagined; but it was, for James, no simple exercise of elementary logic working with scientifically accumulated data. It represented a fusion of logic and feeling, making use of every talent which the novelist possessed. A writer was limited by the quality of his imagination and experience, that is, of his significant sensations. Yet he could hope that the fruits of his artistic contemplation would have universal implications. Their nature, their special tone, would be that of the mind which brought them forth, and their range would be the measure of its vision.

III. THE TRANSFORMATION

First there is the plethora of things which happen to exist or to have existed. Long before an author has begun to think as a creative artist he has inevitably begun to discover relationships among these as they have crowded upon his consciousness. Even the most imperceptive of James's characters participate in the game of finding connections. They differ from the novelist most of all in the limitation of their imagination and of their power to feel. In contrast, the characters of insight and sensibility live lives which, in their orderly excellence, almost seem to be works of art. In this respect they resemble James himself as a private citizen, a member of a social group and the heir of a social past. James differs from the best of them—from Lambert Strether and Milly Theale and Fleda Vetch—not as a moral, social being, nor as an intense perceiver, but as a novelist. Through arduous practice, with a typical number of failures in his early experiments, James had learned how to write.

The mind is at best an unruly genie, refusing to confine itself to one thought or method at a time. It follows most irregularly the rigorous patterns which it shapes for its own discipline. Yet for the purposes of analysis one can differentiate the images, the preoccupations, the habits of deduction by which it is most significantly possessed. For James the conscious artistic process began with the discovery of a possible subject. The hint usually came as an accident—the hearing of a chance phrase, startling to the imagination because it suggested a story; the learning of an unusual combination of incidents whose causal relationships lay hidden; the sudden feeling that a type of person must have a special kind of experience, hence his own kind of story; even the sense of a place as somehow putting the storyteller under obligation. Such discoveries were somewhat fortuitous, and yet they could come only to the person who was prepared to recognize them. Wordsworth would have granted them only to the poet who had *thought* long and deeply. With perhaps little difference in total meaning James would have used the verb *felt*. If the author had immersed himself sufficiently in a civilization, he would be alert to every clue to its interpretation. But he would also, of course, have had to develop the practice of thinking and feeling in an artistic manner. James's autobiographic writing implies that he early recognized such a habit. Though in his reminiscences he is looking back from the vantage of long years of novel writing, his recall is probably in the main correct. He records that he began, while young, to think of actual persons and situations as if they were before him on a dramatist's stage; not as they were, but as they could be when modified and made more nearly universal (*A Small Boy and Others*). In later years, whenever he heard an intriguing anecdote, James almost instantaneously started it on its way toward transubstantiation in art.

Upon a woman's death her servant had told the bereaved daughter that her own loss was greater than the daughter's; the latter had lost a mother, but she had lost everything (*The Notebooks*). In retelling the story the daughter had obviously recognized its universal impli-

27

THE MADNESS OF ART

cations. So immediately did James, and from the recognition came, in due time, another servant, of the male sex, whose life and death symbolized something very different and perhaps yet more universal, the plight of all sensitive spirits in a world where sensitivity is attacked by the forces of brutality. Or again, a mother and son quarreled messily about some furniture, and the anecdote brought forth Fleda Vetch, whose existence was not even suggested in the original incident. And again, the novelist heard that Jane Claremont was still living obscurely in Venice and cherishing some letters of Byron and Shelley. The facts at once appealed to the kind of imagination that valued Mrs. Procter for her "tone" of an earlier generation; after many accretions had attached themselves to the original subject, there came into being a story permeated with the tone of time, but with a new theme altogether.

As a writer must use one or another metaphor to help him with his thinking, James employed, among various others, the concept of the growth of a plant. He did not belabor it, and he freely shifted to other images, but his narratives began for him as "germs." The anecdote, however short or long, was not quite itself the germ. The mind of the novelist created the living cell; the actual fact merely set the mind to work. And the plant, in the beginning, was of indeterminate nature, the novelist sometimes having not the faintest clue as to what its final flowering would be. To be sure, there was usually a traceable resemblance between the original incident and a superficial plot summary of the final story; but the theme might undergo major revisions, and all the nuances, which were what really mattered, came only with repeated contemplation.

Since we have the published notebooks, it is a simple chore, in many instances, to compare the germ and the harvest. In the earlier years, and to some extent later, the first, and perhaps only, entry was as crude as the inital stimulus, but it still served as a reminder. In the preface to *Roderick Hudson* James mentioned the fact that a writer of fiction consults his notes. In that to *The Princess Casamassima* he wrote that "'notes' had been from the cradle the ineluctable consequence of one's greatest inward energy." Again, speaking of several stories, he remarked, in passing, that "the habitual teller of tales finds these things in old note-books" (Preface to *The Altar of the Dead*).

A number of the notebook jottings merely recorded a hint or an impression. Those that were longer commonly stopped short of significant meaning.[6] The note that led to "The Liar," for example, was an exercise in ingenuity with a trivial ending. That for "The Real Thing" gave only the donnée, which at the time James believed was his theme, but which proved to be only a point of departure for the portrayal of the real thing. In one entry we can get a glimpse of the novelist's mind at work. Beginning with a farcical incident, based on actual fact, James set down a plot summary in which a wife, whose husband refused to do so, went downstairs at night to confront a burglar and afterwards contemptuously refused to tell her husband what had occurred. The motif would at best make a short, short story, with novelty only insofar as it might be ornamented with wit. But even while working it out, the novelist saw that his initial concept would not do. He never achieved a version to suit him, but before he quit talking to himself in the notebook he had decided to transform the husband from a coward to a person to be respected and the wife to an imperceptive antagonist. How the new roles were to be made convincing is not apparent in the fragment, but neither is it evident in the notes how the transformations of other stories were to be achieved. What took place between the germ and the fruition James described in his preface to *The American*, where he used another metaphor as a symbol. After getting the donnée for his story and playing with it for a while to test its capacity, he turned to other things. The idea, however, did not vanish irretrievably: ". . . precisely because it had so much to give, I think, must I have dropped it for the time into the deep well of unconscious cerebration: not without the hope, doubtless, that it might eventually emerge from that reservoir, as one had already known the buried treasure to come to light, with a firm iridescent surface and a notable increase of weight."

Without entering into a controversy on the formative power of the unconscious, we can, nevertheless, plot the general pattern of the

[6]Critics have sometimes erroneously drawn on the notebooks as if they represented James's final intent.

mental adventure by which the motif was given its iridescence and its accretion of weight. In the same preface James noted, "There always has been, for the valid work of art, a history." That history, as we have seen, had to begin even before the novelist became aware of his subject. It consisted of the process going on unendingly in his mind as he reflected upon all that he had seen, read, and heard. The mind was always at work remoulding the world that the novelist had come to know. When a donnée suddenly presented itself, it was at first a foreign interloper, to be accommodated as quickly as possible without any major upheaval of the author's cosmos. But James soon learned that, if given a chance, it would refuse to be relegated to a subordinate position. The notebook fragment was intended to preserve it from becoming lost before it had begun to exercise its power. Once it asserted itself it would develop brilliance and magnitude. The growth was magical enough, as the ways of the imagination were always magical for James. Yet it was not without a history that could be recorded. When the theme, in its elementary nature, had impressed itself upon James's consciousness, all his preparation for receiving it became part of its own history. He brought to *The American* what he knew of Paris, of Americans in Europe, and more important, of life as bliss and bale. From this moment the story of Christopher Newman began to take shape as a world in its own right, rather than as a small part of an existing world, and pertinent impressions from the world into which it had intruded joined themselves in new patterns around it. Moreover, new experiences found their places in this fictitious universe.

To what degree the revolution was unconscious in the early stages one can but conjecture. One can be sure that, to the extent that it was conscious, it was at first casual and ill-understood. Yet it was not without direction. If at the beginning the author did not see his novel in its architectural structure, if indeed he was still improvising till the very end and then again improvising in the later revision, there was, nevertheless, a discriminating agent at work from the outset, without which the treasure, when dredged up from the well, would have proved to be dull, corroded iron. That agent was the artist's sensibility.

In discussing Flaubert's approach to his subjects James wrote that the novelist "has on the one side to feel his subject and on the other side to render it . . . . The more he feels his subject the more he *can* render it . . . . The more he renders it the more he *can* feel it . . ." ("Gustave Flaubert," 1902). With Flaubert the emphasis was on the rendering. For James the feeling of the subject came first, and it controlled the selection and discrimination. Feeling of a somewhat different sort accompanied the rendering, and of a yet different kind was the fulfillment of successful composition. But what concerns us at the moment is that before James could convert a commonplace donnée into a subtle story a great deal of feeling had to take place. Of course, as we have indicated, feeling for James was not basically different from thinking. It represented the impression which one had of the relationships of things, an impression which, if orderly, had a dominant tone. If an incident or situation was irrelevant to the tone, it was rejected. Obviously, the vaster the novelist's reflective experience the greater would be the range of the separate impressions which must be sorted and synthesized before he could be contented with his ultimate tone.

After the "unconscious cerebration" and the tentative, probing tests to see in which general way the story should go, came the sketching of the major features of the design. James concurred in the truism that "all art is a simplification" (Letter to R. L. Stevenson, December 5, 1884). As we have seen, one began with life itself. But, as we have also seen, James later wrote that life was "all inclusion and confusion" (Preface to *The Spoils of Poynton*). He added that "life has no direct sense whatever for the subject and is capable, luckily for us [novelists], of nothing but splendid waste." Again he called literature "an objective, a projected result" and life "the unconscious, the agitated, the struggling, floundering cause" ("The Lesson of Balzac").

Now, with so sharp a distinction between mere life and art, we must come back to their proper relationship. In his essay on Trollope, James accused the "votaries of art for art" of a "narrow vision of humanity" ("Anthony Trollope," 1883). Elsewhere he wrote, "Art is essentially selection, but it is a selection whose main care is to be typical, to be inclusive. . . . the province of art is all life, all feeling, all observation, all vision" ("The Art of Fiction"). The relationship was in what art

31

did with life. In the same passage in which he called life "inclusion and confusion" and art "discrimination and selection" he indicated that art was "in search of the hard latent *value* with which alone it is concerned" (Preface to *The Spoils of Poynton*). The value was not inseparable from life, but it was also not inseparable from the artistic process. It was what art created from that which was offered by life. In one of his numerous protests against the formlessness of Dostoievski and Tolstoi, James gave them credit for genius and experience, but called their works "fluid puddings." "Strenuous selection and comparison," he wrote, were "the very essence of art;" and he continued, ". . . form *is* substance to that degree that there is absolutely no substance without it. Form alone *takes*, and holds and preserves, substance —saves it from the welter of helpless verbiage . . ." (Letter to Hugh Walpole, May 19, 1912). Of the relation of subject and form James had elsewhere remarked, ". . . if it be the subject that makes the interest [in a painting], it is the composition that makes, or that at any rate expresses, the subject" (*William Wetmore Story*).

We start then with a novelist's feeling for life, continue with admission that art is a simplification, and end with the assertion that substance is created by form. Along the way we find protests that life is wasteful and, on the other hand, that art for art is neglectful of life. How to reconcile the paradoxes? First of all, we must remember that, for James, portraits, because they best represented life, were the most interesting form of painting, and that in the picture of Andromeda and Perseus the clothed Perseus meant more to him than the nude Andromeda because of the historical associations which were more inclusively suggestive of life (*William Wetmore Story*). Art, to James, was representation. He specifically called the novel "an effort at *representation*" ("The Lesson of Balzac"). Whereas Zola gave only "an extraordinary show of representation imitated," Balzac was a true portrait painter in words.

The representation is of life, and yet it is a simplification of it. Why then is it not superficial? Because it sacrifices nothing of value in its search for order. Indeed, it rescues the value. Life persistently invites us to accept shallow and inconsistent interpretations. Rule-of-thumb morality, like the Ptolemaic concept of astronomy, generally seems to work, and so we try to live by it. We readily attach labels by which we can know that one kind of action is good, another bad; and, adhering to the code, we lead tolerable lives. The type of story in which a clearly identifiable virtue triumphs over an unmistakable vice is not a simplification of life. Before we judge it to be one, we must remember that it merely imitates our customary habits. Like our usual labels and ways of thinking, it does not really, artistically, simplify at all, but repeats the confusion. By simplification James meant something altogether different. It was simplification to have a man discuss repeatedly with a woman the unique fate which he sensed must be awaiting him like a beast in the jungle. It was simplification to have another man wander at night through the upper rooms of an apparently haunted house, to let another escape to the great good place, and to permit yet another to be reborn in an age that was past. It was simplification to use two volumes to bring to a happy ending the romance of Amerigo and Maggie, a romance which in its general plot could have been narrated in one-fifth the space. It is life that is complex, because we must forever tinker, adjust, and revise to make our rules of thumb work. They do not really serve us as we should like them to, and so we modify here and there, first making exceptions and then patching up the rules to try to include the exceptions. Art, for James, was simpler because it was concerned with essential principles. To the extent that it was successful there would be no exceptions, no need for incessant tinkering.

How did form contribute to its success, or, indeed, create subject? Obviously not just any form would serve. Some of the brief plot sketches in the notebooks are as superficial and hackneyed as those in popular fiction. The forms of James's early works and of some of his later plays are hardly better. But in the stories which represent him at his best the art is the agent of the simplification. Again, for the sake of analysis we must separate processes which were going on simultaneously in the novelist's mind as he wrote. We can speak of certain principles or perspectives with which James approached the creation of a work of fiction.

First of all is the importance of character. Usually James's earliest, and often exceedingly primitive, glimpse of his subject came to him

33

as an incident or situation, though a few stories began with a vague image of a character. But however the impulse came, he immediately blocked out the action in reference to its effect upon character. The primary necessity therefore was the creation of one or more persons who had acute sensibility. They need not be the ostensible protagonists; in fact, they might seem to avoid importance. But there could be no meaning apart from the meaning for them. In short, James proceeded to construct a world as they saw it. Only by so doing could he explore reality.

To the urbane gentleman who was Henry James the elements of life were much as to any other urbane gentleman. Some things were convenient, some frustrating; some flattered the ego, and some lashed it. The letters, in their frank expression of vexation, reveal that James suffered the usual annoyances and that, for excited moments, he could, like anyone else, be unphilosophic, self-centered, and stripped bare of his sense of humor. To say that, even so, he lived outwardly a life more ordered and thoughtful than many is still to admit a wide discrepancy between James the social creature and James the writer—a discrepancy exactly like that which he saw in Robert Browning and recorded in "The Private Life," in which the writer-hero lives an ordinary existence socially, but his true life in the hidden chambers of his imagination. It was only when James had conceived of a character possessed of a sensitive mind, equipped with a personal history, and confronted with a fundamental situation that he could best order and refine his own feeling and thought.

The writing of a work of fiction was the deepest possible experience of his spirit because only by seeing through the consciousness of a character could he comprehend any action in its fullness. For James there was no such thing as an action in the abstract. An action was a complete, rounded-out experience of the mind, and its quality was the quality of that mind. One did not enter deeply into experience, for example, by considering abstractly whether a person should feel free to injure another's feelings. If the wounding were blatantly wanton, the answer would, by definition, be no. But what if the motivation were not unkind? Or what, too, if the possible victim were, himself, a thoughtless inflictor of pain? Moreover, what of the effect upon the person who was tempted to perpetrate the act? To seek a meaning-ful answer one would have to leave the realm of the abstract and deal with the specific circumstances. Once we begin, there is really no stopping until we have a cast of characters, an engagement to marry, some valuable old furniture, and "at the heart of one's complexity an irrepressible *appreciation*," in short, Fleda Vetch (Preface to *The Spoils of Poynton*).

We should pause to stress the fact that we do not need to become entangled in a net of words. Was James an absolutist or a relativist? Could he be an absolutist if he dealt only in specific cases? Suffice it to say that there are types of actions which are always evil in James's works and others which are always good. But an action was properly a vast and subtle thing. Similarly, there are characters who can, in crude fashion, be labeled evil or good. But putting so general a desig-nation upon them and their conduct would not advance one's own perceptions. Truth, beauty, goodness existed for James as he saw them in concrete embodiments. Fleda and others of her type were such embodiments.

In *Roderick Hudson* it is Rowland Mallet who has appreciation, though the story narrates the history of Roderick; the "centre of inter-est" is in Mallet's "consciousness, and the drama is the very drama of that consciousness" (Preface to *Roderick Hudson*). In *The American* Newman is "the lighted figure," not quite the same as Mallet, and yet a person whose fate elicits our sympathy because we see it as it must seem to him. In *The Portrait of a Lady*, though James did at times briefly shift his point of view, he generally adhered to the method, which he afterwards described in the preface, of placing "the centre of the subject in the young woman's own consciousness" and being concerned with "her relation to herself." The last phrase takes on its full meaning when we remember that Isabel has an ideal image of conduct for herself and that the relationship involves her shaping her actions in accord with it. The image is not a fanciful thing; it is Isabel very much as she has acted in the past.

For such characters as Mallet and Isabel, James also used the terms *registers, mirrors*, and *reflectors*. Thus he spoke of keeping the "reg-ister" of Amerigo's consciousness in the first half of *The Golden Bowl* and of Maggie's in the second part. No single metaphorical image will quite express all that James intended. Essentially he meant that, while using third-person narrative so that he could from outside describe circumstances with a bystander's objectivity to set the conditions of his story, he depended on a character's thoughts, whether spoken or silent, for the meaning which he found in the incidents. Hence, in the second half of *The Golden Bowl* we see through Maggie's help both her herself and the others. By shifting for a short scene to Mrs. Assingham we see how events appear to her, and we know her to be a reliable witness on everything that does not require profound discernment. We thus have some objective facts—Mrs. Assingham's misinterpretations do not confuse us—and are then ready to see what Maggie makes of them. What she makes is, of course, the consequence of her experience and her sensibility. As we imagine with her, we work our way through what seems phantasmal complexity, and at the end we are rewarded with clear-eyed simplicity.

When we think of James's limited point of view, involved in his employment of registers, we must, of course, remember that there is no such thing as a totally omniscient approach to one's story. Scott and Thackeray and Dickens, for example, always set restrictions upon their direct consciousness of their narrative substance. James merely went further than they in limiting his point of view. For him characters were "interesting only in proportion as they feel their respective situations" (Preface to *The Princess Casamassima*). Those whom he called mirrors or registers were "intense perceivers, all, of their respective predicaments" (Preface). Hence his concern to see life as they saw it. If they were registers, they, too, must be limited in perspective, even in perceiving their own predicaments.

The logic of having them limited is obvious enough at the mere story-telling level. As James remarked, "It seems probable that if we were never bewildered there would never be a story to tell about us . . ." (Preface to *The Princess Casamassima*). The logic, however, is equally important in the search for truth. If, as in *The Princess Casamassima*, a young man is the son of an aristocrat who has been murdered by the boy's mother, if indeed, on the one hand, he has intense sympathy for the poor, among whom he has lived, and, on the

36

other, he senses the lure of aristocratic glamor, he obviously has a dilemma. One can quickly reach a rule-of-thumb recommendation for his case, involving compromise or renunciation. If the young man himself saw his situation clearly, he, too, could weigh the issues and patch up a solution. Yet, despite the fact that Hyacinth Robinson is a highly intelligent person, quite capable of seeing the broad features of his circumstances, he cannot resolve his problem. He is bewildered. Why not let him see his dilemma clearly and permit him a safe escape from it? The reason is that, whereas the broad outline given above superficially states his condition, the real conflict is composed of images that come into his mind, apprehensions or even terrors, glimpses that suggest ecstasy, and a fuguelike sensation of all these and many other feelings. He is perplexed by the "mysteries abysmal" which confront him. As we enter his consciousness, we soon come to realize that life *is* bewildering. Then, with the help of that particular consciousness, we begin to identify types of images, of feelings, even of understanding. Our own education in sensibility has begun. How the characters themselves felt was what mattered for James. He was concerned with appreciation, and he saw a character's "feeling" as his "doing" (Preface to *The Princess Casamassima*). The character must have enough ability to know and feel without appearing too knowing. Or, to put the matter differently, he must confront a problem which is of magnitude for him; were he more knowing, we should find him uninteresting until he confronted a more intricate circumstance.

Marcher, for instance, in "The Beast in the Jungle," is an intense perceiver, as intelligent as James could make him. If we want to cry out at him, "How blind you are," we hesitate for fear we have underrated his dilemma. In one sentence we can state abstractly what course would be preferable in circumstances broadly like his, and at the end we can still hold to our view, because such a course would have been better for Marcher. But had we not followed his lonely wandering, our feeling at the end would be as superficial as that at the beginning. Marcher's predicament has become ours; his bafflement is ours. If we refuse to waver from our initial conviction and end with it reconfirmed, we are nonetheless aware at the conclusion of much that we did not see before, of some things which we perhaps wilfully avoided recognizing. We have had to live for a little while in a nihilistic mind whose nihilism was not of its own choosing.

There could be yet a different limitation of a character's perspective, such as we find in the narrator of "The Aspern Papers." It is through his consciousness that we see the two women as well as his feelings about them. He is a keen observer of things around him, noticing minute clues and nuances and supplying us with an abundance of factual evidence. He is, in short, an excellent register of what happens and of many kinds of meaning which attach themselves to the events. Yet we see poignantly what he perceives dimly or not at all. His inability, despite his intelligence, to enter into the romantic thoughts of Tina leads to his committing unpardonable evil. At the same time, it reveals the excellence of what he has missed. Precisely in the limitations of the narrator's consciousness is the creative value of the story as a search for truth. The truth comes to us the more completely as we see it transcending the very consciousness which reports it to us.

In *The Awkward Age* there are registers of various degrees of sensitivity and of equally varied perspectives. We see each of several characters in his separate state of bewilderment. Nanda's consciousness is, of course, the most interesting because she senses for herself a much more inclusive world than that which satisfies her mother or Vanderbank or their coterie. In this dramatic novel perhaps more than in all but a very few of James's other works we find registers dependent on registers. It would have appeared simpler to tell what each character really meant when he said something, so that one would know immediately, for example, when Mrs. Brookenham was saying what she believed and when she was speaking for effect, and then to tell how another character interpreted her words. Thus we should have the objective facts and the interpretation, too. James would be communicating clearly; we should have no doubt as to what happened and what it meant. Instead, we have a bit of social gossip as told by Mrs. Brookenham, and we have to puzzle our minds with the question of her accuracy. We turn to Vanderbank for his equally involved response to her words. Then we have the question of what Vanderbank's interpretation of them means to Nanda, and we get her reaction only through her words to Vanderbank. We soon conclude that she is a girl of nobility of character, but the very nobility prevents her stating blunt, cruel truths. Are we being entertained with a guessing game, a parlor amusement? Of course not. The full discussion of James's purpose in the novel must wait until we can consider together a group of stories which especially share the methods of *The Awkward Age*. For the moment it suffices to say that in the novel James was trying to do all the things recommended above. What a fact meant to Mrs. Brookenham was in part a product of what she saw it as meaning to another; and, by the time a story had come to Nanda, with accretions from many sources, and she had brought to bear upon it her feelings about herself and about Vanderbank, her own words were the final statement of its meaning. To have reported to us by author's comment to insure our getting the point would have been bad not just because it would have been a resort to crutches, but because it could not possibly have told all that James succeeded in telling. Or—to remember the order of the process—because, had he settled for such a method, James would not have penetrated so deeply into the mystery. The registers were indispensable. Even the smallest and most distorting mirror or reflector contributed something, and the intense perceivers were registers of the subtlest discriminations.

It is difficult to discuss almost any aspect of sensibility without coming back to Strether. In his preface to *The Ambassadors* James spoke of Strether's "note" as "the note of discrimination, just as his drama is to become, under stress, the drama of discrimination." Whence came such a character as Strether? In one sense he was purely autobiographic at the same time that he was a dramatic fiction. In *Notes of a Son and Brother*, James wrote that in seeking as a hero for a story "the man of imagination," he "had in a word to draw him forth from within rather than meet him in the world before me, the more convenient sphere of the objective, and to make him objective, in short, had to turn nothing less than myself inside out." What was drawn forth in the case of Strether was a way of seeing life, of feeling, of appreciating.

Complaint has been brought against James that his characters, especially in the later works, are less real than those of some other authors, that they live off the "tops" of their minds, that they talk and talk about themselves and their situations as people do not talk in actual life. There is no need to defend all the characters in the later novels or to rule out other ways of telling their stories. It is not necessary to assume that James's limited point of view is per se superior to Scott's or Thackeray's commentary on the action. At the same time, the Jamesian method is not to be judged by its degree of resemblance to traditional methods or its imitation of actuality. It was for James one means of exploring reality, through the examination of a character's consciousness of it. The consciousness itself registered reality with limited fidelity, and the nature of its registering was the mark of its own identity. For James as a thinking being, whatever helped in the exploring was precious, and all else was irrelevant. Sometimes, as in *The Awkward Age* or *The Sacred Fount*, one or another character seems to exist only insofar as he is preoccupied with a mental problem. Yet he is not an allegorical abstraction or the mere vehicle for asserting a theme, for he possesses individuality of imagination and feeling.

Given the necessary registers and the general concept of his story, James had not yet done with the question of perspectives. As he wrote in the preface to *The Portrait of a Lady*, "the house of fiction has in short not one window, but a million." With every new scene came a fresh set of possibilities for presentation, and whatever plan was followed had to provide the maximum flexibility without compromising the art. In the early *Watch and Ward* James went freely behind various characters, commented on their feelings, and made things happen to them at his convenience. The deficiencies of the novel are indeed glaring. In part they represent commonplace moral views and shallow psychology. A limited point of view, however, would almost certainly have helped the author escape from the most sentimental and sensational effects. Being at liberty to know anything he wanted to know about each character, he recorded only the obvious—and this because, moving quickly from character to character and through a rapid series of incidents, he developed no situation to the point of significant meaning. The limited points of view which he later came to impose upon himself encouraged the slow unfolding of his story as it could be comprehended, bit by bit, by the characters themselves. Such unfolding meant that the novelist stayed with each incident until he had explored, with the character, its subtler implications and its relationships with numerous other incidents. Hence, what at first would seem a restraint upon the novelist's vision is seen to be instead an extension of that vision.

In James's middle and later years, H. G. Wells provided the primary examples of what should be avoided in art. Particularly disturbing to James was Wells's use of the autobiographic point of view. "Save in the fantastic and the romantic," he wrote Wells, "it has no authority, no persuasive or convincing force—its grasp of reality and truth isn't strong and disinterested" (Letter, March 3, 1911). James's stricture must be taken in its context, for he himself had used first-person narration effectively. Omitting such stories as "Four Meetings" and "The Real Thing," where the narrator is only an intelligent observer, we still have "The Aspern Papers," where the narrator is central in the action; and, if we admit "The Turn of the Screw" and *The Sacred Fount* to the kingdom of the fantastic and the romantic, they have a persuasive, convincing force. But it was not their kind of autobiography that James was protesting, for he built into each story safeguards against the omniscient tendency of traditional autobiography as practiced by Wells. What James wanted was the type of window upon reality which he used in such a work as *What Maisie Knew.* The artistic interest which he found in Maisie was "to make and to keep her so limited consciousness the very field of my picture while at the same time guarding with care the integrity of the objects represented" (Preface to *What Maisie Knew*). Not only did one see with the help of a special consciousness, in this case that of a highly sensitive, precocious, and yet naïve young girl, but one had a defined, limited frame within which all was ordered. It is not inconceivable that Maisie could have told her own story, for there have been recent examples in which children have done so; but certainly the method which James followed did give form to the action at the same time that it revealed what Maisie saw and knew, and distinguished this from what she merely saw but James and we were enabled to know.

Perhaps James's most unusual justification of a limited perspective concerns his portrayal of Milly Theale. Milly was seen mainly through the other characters because of "her painter's tenderness of imagination about her" (Preface to *The Wings of the Dove*). How "precious" the implications of such a view! But Milly *is* precious, in the proper sense of the word. She is very real, but she has a fragile, ethereal spirit. She is not to be exposed to the glaring brightness of day, which does no harm to Kate Croy's image, but would be cruel to Milly's evanescent charm. Kate was struggling with problems of logic and ethics. Milly, in contrast, was beset by no serious moral or rational doubts. With her rarefied imagination and exquisite sensibility, she lived in a lyric world of the feelings. The beauty of her universe could best be suggested by the showing of its effects on a diverse group of characters, including Kate. Every scene in the novel, even when Milly was absent, had to contribute its suggestion, either by her felt presence as she dominated the minds of others or by the implied contrast between her values and those of the persons present. The portrayal of Milly was one of the most noteworthy examples of James's method, by which he saw the true image the more distinctly by seeing it at times reflected.

There were other significant examples, too. In the preface to *The American,* James stressed the importance of Paris as his scene, but he added that he had to stand away to get the proper picture of the city. He went on to generalize: "The image has had for the most part to be dim if the reflexion was to be, as is proper for a reflexion, both sharp and quiet; one has a horror, I think, artistically, of agitated reflexions." He was speaking of the general reflection of life in a novel, but the same principle applies to the portrayal of certain characters themselves —persons such as the unnamed woman in "The Altar of the Dead," May Bartram, in "The Beast in the Jungle," and Alice Staverton, in "The Jolly Corner," as well as Milly. For of these persons one could say, as James said of actual life, "the affair of the painter is not the immediate, it is the reflected field of life . . ." (Preface to *The Princess Casamassima*). With each of them we do, at times, have a sense of the immediate, but much more we have images to recall; for the influence of their words lingers and becomes more meaningful as the stories ostensibly turn to other things. Hence the paradox that the limiting—the dimming—has resulted in an intensifying of the portrait, in the lighting up of its essential features.

In discussing the nature of the characters and the use of limited perspectives for their presentation we have inevitably been concerned to some extent with the narrative structure as well. Many of James's discussions of form really involve both character and narrative in that the consciousness of the characters is, as we have seen, a delimiting frame, and, at the same time, the story is about an action. He was thinking of both, though perhaps more of the action, when he made his pronouncement: "Really, universally, relations stop nowhere, and the exquisite problem of the artist is eternally but to draw by a geometry of his own, the circle within which they shall happily *appear* to do so" (Preface to *Roderick Hudson*). *Appear* is a modest term, as James was really concerned with having much more than the semblance of order and completeness. In actual life, of course, one has always to draw circles as soon as he begins to interpret. The novelist's problem was not basically different. His circle would be constructed in accord with his definition of his subject. The vaster the subject in its emotions and its social involvements, the more difficult its encirclement.

To turn specifically, however, to narrative structure—we may well begin with the now-famous metaphor in James's letter to Mrs. Humphry Ward. He complained that she presented her subject too immediately, "so that a wait to begin to guess *what and whom the thing is going to be about* doesn't impose itself: the ante-chamber or two and the crooked corridor before [the reader] is already in the Presence" (Letter, July, 1899). The value of the corridor and the antechambers for ordinary suspense is obvious enough; circus performers save their best acts for the climax. But what is pertinent to suspense in a novel is pertinent also to its truthfulness. Mountain climbers in the Karakorams and Himalayas have remarked that great mountains should be approached on foot; the sense of their magnificence is cumulative. One's sense of wonder, instead of being suddenly startled, is repeatedly stimulated by mountains which are increasingly spectacular. Then, when the last ridge has been passed and there looms up the most splendid of all, the mind is ready to appreciate because it now has a feeling for mountains. So with a novel. If the author were to try to unload his whole subject at once, the reader would be unprepared to make anything of it. In fact, the author himself would have failed to do so because only by the slow approach could he himself see his subject in its implications.

43

Thus, again we come back to the recognition that what is good form in art is good because it provides a profound approach to reality.

Keeping in mind that, for James, form was always the ordering of an author's thoughts and feelings, and that it was as author that James most richly lived, we can understand his distress upon reading the works of writers whom, to a degree, he admired, but who showed laxness as to structural form. Contrasting George Sand with Balzac, he noted that the former's novels had "style" but no "form," whereas Balzac's had "not a shred of style," but "a great deal of form" ("George Sand," 1877). In another discussion of George Sand, James remarked that her work was too fluid, "and the sense of fluidity is fundamentally fatal to the sense of particular truth" ("George Sand, 1899"). *Fluidity* is a general term to describe a series of events which do not seem to have an inevitable relation, either because there is no sense of cause and effect or because there is no central focus or harmony of tone.

Of a basically similar kind of narrative deficiency James could find numerous other examples, the most striking, perhaps, coming from the pen of D'Annunzio, who persistently exasperated James. Not only were D'Annunzio's characters shallow; there was no structure in their histories: "Presented each as victims of another rapacious person . . . there is no process, no complexity, no suspense in their story; and thereby, we submit, there is no aesthetic beauty" ("Gabriele d'Annunzio, 1902"). In short, D'Annunzio insisted on strong emotions by the mere assertion that the circumstances produced them, without, however, being concerned with why the circumstances themselves should have come to exist. One was not to be allowed to scant the logic required for a valid narrative sequence. The result of arbitrary calling up of incidents without the artistic preparation for them, which is implied by "suspense," could be only sentimentality.

If the sentimentality in D'Annunzio took the form of violence, that of the popular women writers in England was no less inartistic merely because it was more subdued. James leveled a general charge against the contemporaneous British novel, whose careless form he blamed upon the fact that it was dominated by women—"a sex ever gracefully, comfortably, enviably unconscious . . . of the requirements of form" ("Gustave Flaubert," 1902). *Gracefully* is more than a courteous term; it allows for certain legitimate lyric passages which might chance to spring from even the most loosely coordinated incidents. Such passages could exhibit feeling and style, but they could not atone for the lack of a dominant structural principle. Though graceful and perhaps delicately pretty, they could not attain to the passionate force which only a tense dramatic action could create. They were at best casual and scattered, badly motivated and accidental. Where gracefulness was not present the result was rose-colored sentimentality.

What James wanted was a method of composition which, while letting the imagination of the author range freely in the creation of individual scenes, was guided by a strict insistence on the logic of the total narrative structure. The function of a novel being to narrate events which would have significance because of their effect upon character, what it told, though intricate and subtle, must be dominated by one major action, to which all else must directly contribute. There were other writers besides George Sand whom James admired for one or another reason, but whose novels he, nevertheless, considered deficient in structural logic. In one of his best known critical pronouncements he grouped together *The Newcomes, Les Trois Mousquetaires,* and *Peace and War* (*sic*). He respected all three, but he labeled them "large loose baggy monsters, with their queer elements of the accidental and the arbitrary." He recognized the power of the books to capture a reader's attention, but asked what they "artistically *mean.*" To define his question he added, ". . . I delight in a deep-breathing economy and an organic form" (Preface to *The Tragic Muse*). In a very general way he was saying that in all three novels, as in George Sand's, some incidents occurred only because the authors decided to have them happen; they were not inevitable parts of a framed picture, with its artistic boundaries within which every action should be related thematically and causally to all the other actions of the story. In one sense, far more takes place in each of the three works than in any novel of James's middle or later period, but only because the implications and relations of events are brushed in swiftly or not at all. It was in these, on the contrary, that James was interested. It was valid relationships that gave a novel organic form.

At the same time that James was disallowing certain approaches to narration he was himself experimenting endlessly with new ways of telling a story. Summing up his experience in the preface to *The Ambassadors,* he wrote that "the Novel remains still, under the right persuasion, the most independent, most elastic, most prodigious of literary forms." *The Portrait of a Lady* and *The Ambassadors* were, James believed, his best examples of architectural proportions (Preface to *The Portrait of a Lady*). Just as a good picture is one which restrains what would willingly ignore the dimensions of the frame, so a great work of architecture is one in which the forces which would fain crush or push asunder the walls are held in restraint, so that the casual viewer sees not the discord between the parts, but the unity, the perfect symmetry of the whole. The trouble with the three novels of Thackeray, Dumas, and Tolstoi is, of course, that they are not constructed as towering cathedrals, but are rather more, wandering buildings, with each room interesting in itself, but with only a limited play of force against force; they always spread onto new foundations to house what does not fit into the central edifice. In good art, James maintained, the artist restrains the tendency of his subject to burst free in order to express itself. He achieves his end by foreshortening, which permits expression, yet economy and unity of impression (Preface to *Daisy Miller*).

We have dealt with foreshortening in reference to James's feeling for the past, where it meant compression and subordination. In a novel it meant the same. Nothing was really sacrificed by it. The essence of a situation, one aspect of the total subject, was retained and presented insofar as it pertained to the scene at hand and to the main subject. All else was omitted as being irrelevant, and what was given was not attached as a separate chamber, but became an integral part of the organic whole. The discerning reader could perceive that what was a foreshortened part of one story might be conceived of as a central part of another. One could, for example, imagine a tale devoted to Madame Merle of *The Portrait of a Lady* or to Madame de Vionnet of *The Ambassadors.* To the extent that the reader sees how each part wants to break free and make a story of its own he is aware of the disciplined art which keeps the novels from bursting asunder.

Again and again in James's critical writing we come upon passages concerned with what it is that holds a novel together and yet makes for variety among its elements. In his essay on Pierre Loti, James went so far as to assert that the unifying principles of a work of art were the primary concern of author and critic: "The study of connections is the recognised function of intelligent criticism." It was because of his interest in the connections, the relationships, that James became so much excited about his experiments in the drama. A play, he maintained, has its own logic of cross relations. In a play "no part of [the action] is related to anything but some other part—save of course by the relation of the total to life" (Preface to *The Awkward Age*). The qualification at the end reminds us that literature was not for James an idle game; but its subordinate position, as an obvious point, indicates that for the novelist it was the relationships within the work that were the measure of his creative power.

We have been using the term *action* and speaking of the proper causal or thematic relation of the events. By a shift in perspective we can more explicitly consider what James regarded as a major excellence of his later works. In his summing up for the New York edition he spoke of the "charm of the scenic consistency, the consistency of the multiplication of *aspects* (Preface to *The Tragic Muse*). He could have said *actions* in that a multiplicity of separate incidents is involved; but *aspects* is more precise. As soon as the reader tries to define one action in *The Tragic Muse*, of which James happened to be speaking, or in any of the other late novels, he finds that he cannot easily stop. True, in a general way the things that take place in the career of Nick Dormer are distinguishable from those that happen to Peter Sherringham, but only if one strips away all the nuances. In all that occurs one feels that he is merely looking at different facets of one large, varied, yet unified whole. Again, the multiplying is no mere game, no counting up of the number of ways in which the subject could be viewed. It was, for James, the inevitable result of concentration on the nature of his material. The shift from one aspect to another was sometimes so subtle that the transition was hardly discernible. Sometimes it meant turning to a new cast of characters and an apparently new subject, only to reveal in due course that they represented a different aspect of the same theme.

47

Every one of James's better novels illustrates his application of his theory. The most obvious illustration is perhaps *The Awkward Age*. The novelist saw this highly dramatic story as having a central subject with "lamps" around it, each lighting one feature of that subject (Preface to *The Awkward Age*). He also saw the novel in terms of architecture and painting. So described, it was "all dramatic and scenic—of presented episodes, architecturally combined and each making a piece of the building; with no going behind, no *telling about* the figures save by their own appearance and action and with explanations reduced to the explanation of everything by all the other things *in* the picture" (Letter to Miss Henrietta Reubell, November 12, 1899).

The relationships in *The Awkward Age* confront even the most casual reader, if a casual reading of the book be possible. Titles of divisions and groupings of characters in scenes, together with the thematic strands in their conversations, keep the emphasis upon Nanda and yet reveal the cross currents affecting the others. In *What Maisie Knew* the movement of the heroine from one household to the other, from one type of adult evil to another, introduces a new aspect of her predicament. In a general way that predicament does not change radically from one scene to another until near the end; yet there is surprise, a semblance of abrupt upheaval, with every shift of scene. Consistency is maintained at the same time that there is startling variety. The structure of *The Ambassadors* or of *The Golden Bowl* may also be described in terms of aspects, of lamps lighting the subject, of framed pictures, or of architecture. In the former Strether is always prominent; in the latter the Prince is most in the foreground for one half, the Princess even more for the second. *The Wings of the Dove* is more varied. One cannot dismiss the felt presence of Milly from any scene, once she has been introduced, but Kate Croy and Merton Densher have their own tragedies, too. In describing his method in the novel James spoke of its "successive centres" and, with free range of metaphor, called what was presented in reference to the centers "*blocks* of wrought material" (Preface to *The Wings of the Dove*).

Not that the blocks are exactly proportioned in James's novels, nor that they are invariably used with economy. He himself recognized one of his temptations. "The first half of a fiction," he wrote, "insists ever on figuring to me as the stage or theatre for the second half"; and he added that the two halves were usually unequal (Preface to *The Tragic Muse*). Sometimes, upon first perusal the baffled reader has insufficient clues to the importance of an incident early in a Jamesian novel or comprehends the dialogue imperfectly simply because James was trying to keep the first part of his story mainly a preparation for what was to follow. In presenting a subject of profound implications which must be revealed slowly, the novelist had to risk obscurity in the early stages and pray that his work would earn a second reading. Sometimes, too, as he recognized in discussing *The American* and *The Wings of the Dove,* he felt compelled to omit or scant a scene which realism would seem to require, because it threatened to detract from his main impression. Whatever the choice he decided to make, however, James was always preoccupied with the essential form, the proportions and the connections in his novels. As the notebooks reveal, he came more and more to sketch the outlines of his actions, the functions of the characters, and the development of his themes before working on the details. In fact, as he wrote Wells, he talked to himself in "an interminable garrulous letter" (Letter, November 15, 1902). There must be no fluid puddings.

In concentrating on structure we have, for a little while, seemed to neglect tone. Actually, the garrulous letters are always concerned with the tone. Indeed, the way in which James felt his subject determined the aspects which it would come to have. We may start with the general attitudes represented by realism and romance and with the part played in a novel by lyric overtones, or what James called poetry. In labelling allegory "quite one of the lighter exercises of the imagination" (*Hawthorne*), and in asserting that "the air of reality (solidity of specification) seems to me to be the supreme virtue of a novel" ("The Art of Fiction"), James was not favoring realism over romance. Allegory was not typically romantic merely because it used supernatural machinery or ignored the common circumstances of life; in fact, a good romantic story must have, for James, an air of reality, even if, as in "The Third Person," it dealt with ghosts. The distinction between realism and romance was of a different nature. "The real," James wrote, "represents to my perception the things we cannot possibly *not* know,

49

sooner or later, in one way or another . . . . The romantic stands, on the other hand, for the things that . . . we never *can* directly know; the things that can reach us only through the beautiful circuit and subterfuge of our thought and our desire" (Preface to *The American*). In the same preface in which he made this distinction James indicated that the difference between the two was more perceivable after the fact than recognizable by the author at the time of composition, "though indeed," he added, "I have ever failed to see how a coherent picture of anything is producible save by a complex of fine measurements." He found the interest to be greatest when a novelist, not at the same moment, but in the same story, possibly in the same scene, used both realism and romance "by the law of some rich passion in him for extremes." In "Sir Edmund Orme" he deliberately chose Brighton as a familiar, realistic setting for his romantic theme. Brighton provided "the note I wanted; that of the strange and sinister embroidered on the very type of the normal and easy" (Preface to *The Altar of the Dead*). Since the story verges on the fanciful, it needed an air of reality to give its shadows substance.

To march through each of James's works of fiction and say here he is romantic, there realistic would be a fatuous and often impossible undertaking. Some mischief in criticism has stemmed primarily from misunderstanding of the realistic air with which he enveloped his romantic portraits. *Daisy Miller* was quickly taken for a more or less sociological study of the American girl, and James's insistence, in his preface, that Daisy "was of course pure poetry, and had never been anything else" is still not always accepted today. "The Jolly Corner," though romantic throughout, has been read as if parts of it were rather literally autobiographical, with the autobiography demonstrated by certain realistic details that loosely paralleled events in James's own life. And "The Turn of the Screw" will probably never cease being treated as a case study in neurosis or insanity, despite James's plea that it was a "fairytale, pure and simple" (Preface to *The Aspern Papers*).

If a portrait, whether romantic or realistic, was successful, it would have about it a quality of poetry. In James's criticism of fiction the word *poetry* is strikingly rare. In all his writing, fiction and nonfiction, there are few passages which remind one of the traditional meter of verse. Two notable exceptions are Dencombe's impassioned speech near the end of "The Middle Years" and James's lament upon the death of Minny Temple, in *Notes of a Son and Brother*. There are, however, endless examples of the essence of poetry, not only in the form of images and metaphors, but in the very ring of the words. James not only spoke his lines to himself; he insisted that the poetry in fiction came out viva voce (Preface to *The Golden Bowl*). It has sometimes been pointed out that reading aloud clarifies many a wandering, colloquial sentence in the later works. It is also true, and important, that it brings out the poetic feelings, without which plot could become commonplace and the architectural framework a mere uninteresting shell.

Important to the tone of a story was a sense of what we may properly call tension, though James employed other terms. Architecture, used as a metaphor for characterizing fiction, implies, as we have seen, the counteraction of forces—the expansive imagination, on the one hand, unruly in its natural tendency to defy all restraint, and, on the other, the artistic logic, with rigorous discipline confining imagination and imposing form. Repeatedly in our study of James's critical views we have been concerned obliquely with the reconciliation of defiance and restraint, and the later chapters will accept the paradox that each has meaning only in reference to the strength of the other. In fact, not merely as a writer of fiction, but as a person, James was habitually intrigued with the story to be found in a situation, and a story always involved a reconciliation of conflict.

To choose from the many examples in the nonfictional works, we might single out a passage in "From a Roman Notebook," 1873, a passage taken from life. James had been sitting near a nun in the Gesù, at Rome. He himself was not a Catholic and could not have accepted Catholicism as a religion, but he was a devout frequenter of Catholic churches. Of the thoughts of the nun he knew nothing; but he noted immediately after the incident, "Can a gentle prioress listen to a fine operatic barytone in such a sumptuous temple and receive none but ascetic impressions?" No story in the usual sense of the term is told here, and yet the picture is replete with a feeling of action. We do not know whether for the nun, assuming that she is as James chose to imagine her, the scene represents the beginning of the action—the sud-

den awakening to an experience that is startlingly new—or the middle—
with the violence of sensation threatening destruction of an ascetic contemplation—or an intense fusion of sensation and contemplation, won
after struggle. We do know, however, that it was with just such a kind
of inner tension as he imagined here that James gave dramatic reality
to his imaginary heroes and heroines—to Strether, to Milly, to Stransom,
to Hyacinth Robinson, to Fleda Vetch.

We have already discussed James's sense of the past as an empire
to be explored by the imagination. In this realm, too, there is a fine
dramatic tension; he was lured into the past by the sheer wonder of
its strangeness, and yet he could find meaning only in the familiar. In
speaking of the paradox in reference to writing about the past, James
remarked, ". . . the difficulty is, for intensity, to catch it at the moment when the scales of the balance hang with the right evenness"
(Preface to *The Aspern Papers*). This he hoped he had achieved in
his story of the old woman and her niece living into the present, yet
still in the romantic age of Jeffrey Aspern. The European sketches constantly imply the charm in the search for the strange yet familiar. In
summing up the atmosphere of Siena, for example, James wrote, "Siena
was long ago mellowed to the pictorial tone . . ." ("Siena"). The Siena
in which James was interested was of the past. The city which was
most familiar to its contemporary inhabitants did not concern him;
indeed, he would have remained a stranger to much of its present life,
even had he made an effort to penetrate it. He was actually closer to
the Siena of an earlier time because he could associate it with imaginative experiences dating back through the years, even as far as childhood impressions gleaned from picture books and the conversations in
his parental home. His quiet summary does not represent living in a
sentimental haze. Behind it is an intense, indeed passionate, feeling.
He had to have the past, with its wonder, its endless vistas for the
imagination, and he had, too, to contemplate it in relation to familiar
patterns until it assumed an orderly, coherent form. Phrases such as
"pictorial tone" and "the tone of the time" represent the synthesis
which he sought. His supreme study of the paradox involving the past
and the present was, of course, *The Sense of the Past,* in which the

hero lives in bewilderment in both worlds, but, according to the plan of the unfinished part, was eventually to achieve understanding.

The tension between elements within the mind found its expression in the artistic tensions in James's fiction. In a letter written in 1900 to Mrs. Everard Cotes he regretted that he could not discover in her novel a "tense cord." He continued, "*I* like a rope (the rope of the *direction and march of the subject,* the action) pulled, like a taut cable between a steamer and a tug, from beginning to end" (Letter, January 26, 1900). There could be a tautness only if there were something which resisted being pulled along. For James, the resistance was all the implications of the subject which must be included, implications which made difficult the moving from situation to situation by demanding their own full development, or what James called their "overtreatment." To present each aspect, each impression, with fullness and still to maintain a "march of the subject," a sense of urgent striding toward a climax, meant that each sentence must at one and the same time help with both functions.

Important in James's discussion of the problems he faced in securing both completeness and tautness and in related reconciliations were the terms *idea, anecdote, drama* or *scene,* and *picture.* Because of the fusion which he sought, the terms were sometimes employed overlappingly, and the term *scene* was not always synonymous with *drama.* In the critical juxtaposition of the words, however, all the others were contrasted with one or another of the connotations, sometimes quite diverse, of *picture.*

In speaking of *The Spoils of Poynton,* which was neither a short story nor a full-length novel, James contrasted *anecdote* and *picture:* "I rejoice in the anecdote, but I revel in the picture . . ." (Preface). The simplest form of anecdote would be a plot not much longer than some of the jottings which James made in his notebooks. As painting was, for the novelist, pre-eminently portraiture, the term *picture* represented for him the written equivalent, which would necessitate action, but action quite different from the simplest anecdotal; in fact, in its most extreme form a picture would be a portrait in a story that scarcely marched. A short story, James noted, might be either anecdote or picture—though obviously not in extreme form—but could not be both.

53

A nouvelle, such as *The Spoils of Poynton,* or a novel would be both. We must, of course, grant an oversimplification here, as even the shortest of James's stories contain elements of picture, though they are primarily anecdotal. What concerns us, however, is that James was always seeking a fusion, so that a line which expanded the picture also advanced the basic plot, and conversely, every anecdotal line, except the sparest summary of action to give transition, contributed to the development of the picture.

Again, James contrasted *idea* and *picture:* "Every good story is of course both a picture and an idea, and the more they are interfused the better the problem is solved" ("Guy de Maupassant," 1888). In its simplest condition an idea in fiction is some kind of conclusion expressed by anecdote; an action occurs and its meaning can be summarized in abstract language. But when the action is complex, a portrait evolves, and any attempt to do more than provide a convenient paraphrase of the idea leads ultimately to the complete repetition of the story. What does even so anecdotal, so pictorially limited, a story as "Four Meetings" or "The Patagonia" mean? Paraphrase is possible, but the full idea involves images, inflections, juxtapositions, and all the other narrative, dramatic, and lyric paraphernalia of fiction; even the omissions become part of the idea.

A frequent contrast in James's criticism balances *drama,* or *scene,* against *picture.* The latter has here a somewhat different connotation from that elsewhere, covering what is described or narrated; and drama represents the dialogue in which the conflicting elements in the situation are discussed. Here, again, it is almost impossible to conceive of a complete separation of function. The description or narration is meaningful only if it specifically introduces issues or if it implies them obliquely by limiting the range of the subject; on the other hand, dialogue inevitably narrates. But each has its special technique, and each offers its own advantage. Consequently, we find James writing, in his preface to *The Wings of the Dove,* of "the odd inveteracy with which picture, at almost any turn, is jealous of drama, and drama . . . suspicious of picture." He was writing with the memory of his dramatic years, when he had experimented so much with scene. Though he himself appears never to have admitted the fact, the weakness of his most ambitious plays, such as *Guy Domville,* was their lack of picture; the drama was too much in a void. But in the great novels—*The Wings of the Dove, The Ambassadors,* and *The Golden Bowl*—there is ample picture, and the drama itself helps provide it. In his preface to *The Ambassadors* James wrote with critical justice that what is not scene "is discriminated preparation, is the fusion and synthesis of picture." By *discriminated* he meant directed toward scene. And in the preface to *The Wings of the Dove* he quite frankly stated his satisfaction with what he had achieved: "Beautiful exceedingly . . . those occasions or parts of an occasion when the boundary line between picture and scene bears a little the weight of the double pressure."

Admittedly preoccupation with the paradoxical principles of narrative composition did not begin with James. Nevertheless, he advanced substantially criticism of the art of fiction, with emphasis on the nature and reconciliation of conflicting forces, of double pressures of whatever sort. For him there was always the concern for what life offered, yet the contrary demands of form; there was the tense, often precarious, balancing of realism and romance; prose must be precise and logical, but there must be also the poetic overtones; and the shift from narration to drama and back again was a matter of meticulous comparison among the conflicting choices that presented themselves. "Beautiful exceedingly" could be used to describe a great many passages, not only in his own works, but in those of his predecessors, novelists who too rarely left behind them a single line of literary theory. Some of his best critical statements were made in specific reference to the works of one or another of the authors he had admired. Those in his prefaces discussed his own works, but all have universal significance. One can, for example, apply them to so erratic a genius as Sir Walter Scott, who, at his worst, descended to inartistic exposition or unconvincing narration, but who gave us, too, dramatic narrative which bore unmistakably the "weight of the double pressure."

Let us look at essentially the same substance from a different aspect, which will exhibit the tense relationship of theme, character, and action.

The various themes and the symbols which typify them will concern us in later chapters. For the present we can limit ourselves to a major theme, the conflict of commandments which recurs in novel after novel and which sometimes had for James its own special symbols. The one commandment was "Live all you can!" The other was "Renounce, renounce!" The symbol of the first was often Europe; of the second, America, and particularly puritan New England. We should hasten to say that we are speaking only of those instances in which the geographic terms were used as symbols. In his later years James himself sought to play down the geographic distinctions. In writing to William James in 1888 he joined America with England: "I can't look at the English-American world, or feel about them, any more, save as a big Anglo-Saxon total" (Letter, October 29, 1888). In his preface to *Lady Barberina* he went further to state that the contrast between America and Europe in *The Wings of the Dove* and *The Golden Bowl* was not essential, that "the subject could in each case have been perfectly expressed had *all* the persons concerned been only American or only English or only Roman or whatever." Nevertheless, the commandments would have been relentlessly present, and James found the symbols effective, as he had found them throughout the years.

One of the most explicit statements of the conflict occurs in 1874 in "Florentine Notes." After speaking of carnival time in Italy, James asks his reader to picture a young American, male or female, "by a remote New England fireside . . . reading in an old volume of travels or an old romantic tale" about a carnival. The young American senses the charm and excitement of Italy. He himself lives near "a white wooden meeting-house." As he reads, he forgets his surroundings, gives rein for a brief while to his longing, and "determines, with a heartbeat, to go and see it all—twenty years hence!" In "Four Meetings" James took such an American as close to Paris as Le Havre and brought her back still clinging desperately to the tatters of her original illusion. In "Europe," flight across the Atlantic symbolizes for Mrs. Rimmle's daughters escape from a witch's evil spell, which would deprive the women of their right to live. In a number of other short pieces which have for their subject the American girl, the American retired business man, or the serious young American professional man in Europe, the geographical symbol is pertinent. If these persons are not always conscious of how much they have renounced, they have, nevertheless, been unprepared for the commandment to live.

As we have seen, James projected Isabel Archer's going to Europe as her adventure, the adventure of an impressionable mind in a new civilization. Isabel is not a puritan, but she has the virtues of a puritan ethics, and she comes to shape her life with appreciation of both commandments. In the preface to *The Spoils of Poynton* James spoke of the "international fallacy," but he went on to cite "A London Life" as among a dozen or so tales concerned with "the supposed 'international' conflict of manners; a general theme dealing for the most part with the bewilderment of the good American, of either sex and of almost any age, in presence of the 'European' order." As illustrated in this story and in a number of others, the European order is defective, indeed evil, when the command to renounce has been defied. Confronted with such a circumstance, the American in Europe finds himself in an alien universe. Writing specifically of the American girl who, having lived under the one commandment, seeks to obey the second by venturing abroad, James generalized, "In the heavy light of 'Europe' thirty or forty years ago, there were more of the Francie Dossons and the Daisy Millers and the Bessie Aldens and the Pandora Days than of all the other attested American objects put together . . ." (Preface to *The Reverberator*).

In *William Wetmore Story* James made a great deal of the contrast of Europe and America and of the tension which they represented for Story. He spoke of the American "who has bitten deep into the apple" of Europe and then been forced "to take his lips from the fruit." The American apple is not bad, but it is "a totally different apple" and for different "teeth." This realization, remarks James, has come to thousands. Elsewhere in the biography he calls Europe the "real *fontaine de Jouvence*, the true and sovereign preserver." For Story, with his high seriousness, to have stayed in America would have meant to follow mainly the one commandment. In Europe he did not defy it; rather, to reuse James's phrase in a new context, he felt the double pressure. What Europe was to mean to Milly Theale, to Maggie Verver, and to Strether was yet subtler and more inclusive than what happened to Daisy, to Christopher Newman, and to Isabel. But for these three, too, there was to be, in one form or another, the problem of reconciling the two conflicting commandments.

Character, for James, determined action, and action illustrated character ("The Art of Fiction"). If we add what we have been implying, that character and action are to be interpreted in terms of theme, we then have a three-way relationship in which no one of the three components must be sacrificed for the others. In his article on Trollope, James wrote that "character in itself is plot, while plot is by no means character." Such a statement needs qualifying, as James had in mind a character confronted with a predicament and inspired by motives which would impel him to act within a limited field of choice. Indeed, it is sometimes not easy to say whether a given story came to James as a vision of a character or as the recognition of a situation which suggested a theme. In discussing the lack of adequate motivation in Maupassant, James commented, "It is as difficult to describe an action without glancing at its motive, its moral history, as it is to describe a motive without glancing at its practical consequence" ("Guy de Maupassant," 1888). Here James stresses character, but he also evaluates the motivation in moral terms, and morality brings one around to theme. In speaking of the early history of *The American* James indicated that the theme shaped itself into the question of what such a man as Christopher Newman would "do" in his predicament. There could be no theme, of course, apart from the determination of what kind of man Newman was. In *The Portrait of a Lady* James began with "the conception of a certain young woman affronting her destiny" (Preface). Again, theme and character are inseparable, and *affronting*, like *do*, assumes that the theme will exist in the action. Elsewhere James emphasized the importance of theme. We find him saying, for example, that the characters in a novel "are interesting . . . as subjects of fate . . . in proportion as, sharing their existence, we feel where fate comes in and just how it gets at them" ("The Lesson of Balzac").

In other pronouncements James emphasized action. Recalling that the donnée for *The Spoils of Poynton* was given him in the form of incidents from actual life, he continued, "The germ, wherever gathered, has ever been for me the germ of a 'story' . . ." (Preface). In reference to *The Ambassadors*, which depends on the character of Strether and certain general concepts of life which may be called theme, James wrote that an author's "interest in the story *as such*" is ever, obviously, overwhelmingly, the prime and precious thing" (Preface).

When one starts to examine a James story in terms of action, however, he has to think in terms of the theme. What takes place, for example, in "The Liar" or in "The Aspern Papers"? One set of events, if the reader is interested only in the hero's ingenuity, but something very different if he begins with a belief that to tamper recklessly with the souls of others is evil and then reads the stories as variations on that theme. Similarly, if one tries to classify characters by types, he must come back to the themes. There is no other character like Crapy Cornelia or Nick Dormer, but there are other characters who confront variations of their destinies. Theme therefore becomes the discriminating principle for discussion of James's works. Theme alone would give us mere skeleton allegory; and so, even while we are preoccupied with it, we must remain acutely conscious that the theme does not tell the characters what to do, that they act according to their own motives. But when they have so acted, we find resemblances in their destinies; and when we try to describe these resemblances, we end up with themes.

So far we have been talking mainly about the figure in the carpet as it is made up of bold lines and contrasting colors—a figure which might be described in terms of values, masses, balance, and all the other elements that go to make an artistic synthesis. It is time to turn to the craft of composition. Again, we cannot here exhaust all James's views on the subject or examine the countless examples of good craftsmanship in his works. We can single out only illustrative comments.

Even before James had mastered the traditional methods of storytelling he was aware of the importance of craftsmanship in fiction. In the attack on Gautier's portrayal of life he gave him credit for having learned to do well what he wanted to do; his work demonstrated, for James, "that a man's supreme use in the world is to master his intellectual instrument and play it in perfection" ("Théophile Gautier," 1873). In writing on Balzac, more than thirty years later, James gave precedence to what he considered the two greatest difficulties for a novelist, both primarily in the province of craftsmanship. The first concerned "that mystery of the foreshortened procession of facts and figures, of appearances of whatever sort, which is in some lights but another name for the picture governed by the principle of composition" ("The Lesson of Balzac"). Earlier we noted the *raison d'être* of foreshortening; here James is thinking of the artisanship involved in its attainment. The second difficulty was "that of representing, to put it simply, the lapse of time, the duration of the subject: representing it, that is, more subtly than by a blank space or a row of stars, on the historic page." Sometimes in meeting the two difficulties in his better works James used narration, with touches of description; sometimes he employed dialogue or very brief sketches of images that floated through a character's mind. Almost never during the later years did he resort to exposition or summary. The choice of methods was not an easy one. Even when he was lecturing himself, "Dramatise, dramatise," he still had to keep working at a scene until he had felt his way both through the general substance to be included and through the manner in which, at the same time, he could be most complete and yet most concise, in which he could elaborate the nuances and yet make his story march. The style which he finally developed was the reward of endless experimentation with the tools of his craft, and he had to invent and refine them for his need.

The ideal he sought was a unified total impression, an artistic whole. He knew, however, that such a creation was the consequence not only of a bold conception, but of attention to each detail. To indicate his standard of craftsmanship he spoke of "all the weaving of silver threads and tapping on golden nails" (Preface to *The Princess Casamassima*). It takes more threads of silver than of coarser stuff to make a square foot of tapestry, and some critics, like William James, have preferred the rougher brand. They have complained about the circumlocutions, the long passages of talk, and the unfamiliar word order—with its parentheses, interruptions, half statements, and involved syntax—to be found in *The Ambassadors* and to be matched or surpassed in *The Golden Bowl*, not to mention the obtuse obscurity of *The Sacred Fount*. Against William's charges Henry offered no rebuttal except the wry comment that he almost feared William's liking any story of his. There is, of course, no absolute answer. Certainly "The Cask of Amontillado" is one of the most economical stories in all literature, and assuredly

James's later style is far removed from Poe's. Moreover, not every revision of the texts for the New York edition was an unqualified improvement. Yet the ruling principle in James's experiments in the craft of the telling was economy.

We have noted the novelist's comment that he delighted in a "deep-breathing economy." We have seen, too, his distress at the formlessness of *War and Peace*. He attacked the epic novel not only for its structural laxness, but for its deficiencies in detail, its "denial of composition, selection and style." Tolstoi had a "mighty fund of life, but the *waste*, and the ugliness and vice of waste, the vice of a not finer *doing*, are sickening" (Letter to Hugh Walpole, August 21, 1913). Since he read Tolstoi in translation, we cannot be sure as to his use of the word *style*, but, clearly, he found Tolstoi's narrative method cumbersome. By *waste* he meant elsewhere, and probably here, the careless use of subject, by which the author failed to develop all the nuances which distinguish the work of a sensitive writer from that of the mere narrator of events. Economy involved both the conception and the *doing*.

"Working out economically almost anything," James wrote, "is the very life of the art of representation; just as the request to take on trust . . . is the very death of the same" (Preface to *The Lesson of the Master*). Here economy certainly refers to the fullest use of one's subject. James approached the same question in a different way when, writing of his method in *The Spoils of Poynton*, he remarked, ". . . but where a light lamp will carry all the flame I incline to look askance at a heavy" (Preface). With much the same perspective he cited "The Two Faces" as an "example of the turn of the *whole* coach and pair in the contracted court, without the 'spill' of a single passenger or the derangement of a single parcel" (Preface to *The Aspern Papers*). The small lamp and the contracted court both required "overtreatment" and careful attention to foreshortening. The test of one's artistry was to take an unpretentious subject and, by unfolding it, perhaps through the consciousness of a sensitive but equally unpretentious character, to discover a complete world which, however small in size, would symbolize all the elements of a cosmos.

IV. THE SACRED MADNESS

FOR JAMES CREATIVE COMPOSITION was very closely synonymous with living itself. If, because of illness, he was unable to write, he felt helpless and lost. When, in the autobiographic works, he tried to recapture his boyhood and youth, he was as much the creative writer as in any of his fiction. The autobiographic pages are imaginative interpretations, and the emotional tone which pervades them comes from the author's feeling of suspense, as he was anxious to find what would suggest itself to his mind as he wrote. Events had occurred, but what did they, after all, mean? What could they mean? As he recalled and examined, he lived among more facts than he could conveniently use. His problem, however, was more than merely selecting what might be typical; it was a literary matter of creating a life that would have a unity of design, that would indeed be an historical portrait of the man then at work on the biographic task.

When he was engaged in the revision of his works for the New York edition, the rereading was as thrilling as the initial composition. He found some things that were bad, but he was also delighted that, with revision, so much could still meet his exacting tests. The rereading was a dual experience in that it also meant looking again into past motives, past impressions, past habits of living and thought (Preface to *Roderick Hudson*). There are occasional slight discrepancies between the factual record as given in a letter or notebook at the time of initial composition and the statement of facts as James recalled them when writing a preface; there is often a great difference in their interpretation. In writing of *The American,* for example, James recalled Paris from the vantage of a lifetime of reflection, and the city took on a meaning which he had not known at the time he was writing his novel there. It was now inseparable from that creative adventure, and his interpretation in reference to the experience was in itself a new adventure in the synthesis of impressions. In the preface to *The Golden Bowl* James called his rereading a "re-dreaming," that is, a re-creating of the story. Indeed, every aspect of reworking his materials became an exciting creative opportunity.

In the preface to *The American* James hailed the "constructive . . .

creative passion" as "the rarest boon of the gods." It was, for the novelist, "the great extension, great beyond all others, of experience and of consciousness; with the toil and trouble a mere sun-cast shadow that falls, shifts and vanishes, the result of his living in so large a light."

In calling the activity of the imagination an extension of experience James was defining it as the greatest source of knowledge, which in turn was the aim of life. To create being to know, the more exacting one's search to know, the more exacting was one's demand upon his art. James could equate difficulty with freedom and seek greater difficulties as the vineyard in which to work. Whatever, he wrote, makes the "art of representation . . . arduous makes it . . . infinite" (Preface to *Roderick Hudson*). Again, he asserted that "free selection" involves "free difficulty," and he continued, "This is the very franchise of the city [of art] and high ambition of the citizen" (Preface to *The American*). One is reminded of Joseph Conrad's satisfaction with *Nostromo* because, of all his works, it presented the greatest technical problem. In a letter to Howells in 1908 James confessed, "I find our art all the while, more difficult of practice, and want, with that, to do it in a more and more difficult way; it being really, at bottom, only difficulty that interests me. Which is a most accursed way to be constituted" (Letter, New Year's Eve, 1908). There have been critics who would gladly have said amen. But James meant something much more philosophical than his words would at first seem to imply. For *difficulty* we could substitute paragraphs of explanation, since it really meant the seeing of one's subject in the most inclusive manner, discovering the most significant relationships and subtlest nuances, and achieving a synthesis which would be a model of economy.

What mattered, for James, was the fact that the difficulty was of one's own choosing, unless we accept the argument that the novelist's own temperament would not let him rest. Because he chose his subject for artistic exploration and was free to experiment as to method, James could speak of "that priceless freedom which is to me the thing that makes it [the novelist's art] worth practising" (Letter to Howells, January 2, 1888). In the preface to *The Aspern Papers* he wrote, "The historian, essentially, wants more documents than he can really use; the dramatist only wants more liberties than he can really take." The exercise of the power of choice increased the novelist's awareness of the possibilities of the imagination, compounding thus his interest in the difficulties of his craft. "The artist," James averred, "has but to have his honest sense of life to find it fed at every pore . . . with more and more to give . . . in proportion as more and more is confidently asked" (Preface to *Lady Barberina*).

Though accepting its popular connotation as strength to endure, James early rejected stoicism as a philosophy and insisted that life must be regarded as an opportunity to cultivate one's capacity to understand and feel: "Stoicism, then is essentially unphilosophic. . . . It fosters apathy and paralyzes the sensibilities. It is through our sensibilities that we suffer, but it is through them, too, that we enjoy . . ." ("Epictetus," 1866). In his study of Hawthorne, James identified enjoyment and art: "There are a thousand ways of enjoying life, and that of the artist is one of the most innocent. But for all that, it connects itself with the idea of pleasure. He proposes to give pleasure, and to give it he must first get it." The enjoyment of which James was speaking was, of course, fraught with philosophic implications. The pleasure of the artist was really a state of understanding. There could be only limited satisfaction in sensation if the imagination did not take command. In art it was most fully in command, sorting, arranging, intensifying, and, if successful, bringing forth a disciplined vision of reality. There was no genuine pleasure from art except as one followed the ritual with exacting attention to every detail. Pleasure came as a by-product, with the perception that reality had been penetrated imaginatively and that the penetration represented the ultimate mastery open to the human mind. Impassioned knowledge was the artist's goal.

Not final knowledge, of course, but that which invited to new vistas was the seemingly infinite range open to the imaginative artist. James stated explicitly that the sense of wonder, which grew with increasing knowledge, was his sole concern. As a novelist, he wrote, he had "seen this particular sensibility, the need and the love of wondering and the quick response to any pretext for it, as the beginning and the end of his affair" (Preface to *The Altar of the Dead*). He continued, ". . . since the question has ever been for me but of wondering and, with all achievable adroitness, of causing to wonder, so the whole fairy-tale side of life has used, for its tug at my sensibility, a cord all its own." We shall have to return to James's use of *fairy tale* in discussing "The Turn of the Screw." It suffices here that the term would include *The Faerie Queen* and "The Rime of the Ancient Mariner," *The Golden Bowl* and *The Ambassadors*. A good fairy tale represented a fusion of logic and passion.

"What a man thinks and what he feels," wrote James, "are the history and the character of what he does; on all of which things the logic of intensity rests" (Preface to *The Princess Casamassima*). Action, for the artist, consisted of the expression of significant, ordered thought and feeling: ". . . to 'put' [i.e. represent] things is very exactly and responsibly and interminably to do them. Our expression of them, and the terms on which we understand that, belong as nearly to our conduct and our life as every other feature of our freedom; these things yield in fact some of its most exquisite material to the religion of doing" (Preface to *The Golden Bowl*).

James saw life as a passionate intellectual quest. ". . . no education," he wrote, "avails for the intelligence that doesn't stir in it some subjective passion . . ." (*A Small Boy and Others*). In speaking of the challenge offered his imagination by London, he remarked that he determined early to "take" its "great things" on a high plane in "the aesthetic, the 'artistic,' the romantic in the looser sense, or in other words in the air of the passions of the intelligence" (*The Middle Years*). In his tribute to Turgenieff he wrote, "He has an eye for all our passions, and a deeply sympathetic sense of the wonderful complexity of our souls" ("Ivan Turgenieff," 1874). In the sternly disciplined art of Turgenieff the passions were inseparable from the intellectual insight; the writing itself was an intense intellectual experience accompanied by subjective passion.

At the age of seventy-two James wrote, "It is art that *makes* life, makes interest, makes importance . . ." (Letter to Henry James, Jr., July 10, 1915). He was restating what he had been saying or implying all his life. Several years before, he had written, "Poor is the art . . . that . . . is not far more pressing for this servant of the altar [i.e., artist] than anything else, anything outside the church, can possibly be. To have been the tempered and directed hammer that makes the metal hard; if that be not good enough for such a ministrant . . . we shall not know him by the great name" ("George Sand, 1899"). In the preface to *Daisy Miller* he reaffirmed his dedication; what the artist values, he exulted, "is not the variable question of the 'success,' but the inveterate romance of the labour." Writing was first and always a romance of adventure for the imagination. In the preface to *The Spoils of Poynton* he became almost mystical and called art a "madness; the madness, I mean, of a zeal, among the reflective sort, so disinterested."

Perhaps James's greatest and most poignant tribute to his art is the passage in which a novelist whose habits are very like his own bids farewell to both art and life. Dencombe, of "The Middle Years," has known all the romance of the labor. He has experienced frustration and has won command of his art only with the exhaustion of life itself. There will be no second chance, now that mastery has at last come. As Dencombe relives his adventure, he can account for some things. He knows that his task began with a zeal to understand and that it has exacted a relentless discipline. There is, however, a strange, mysterious magic about art which transcends his understanding. Its nature he will never know; its power may be infinite: "We work in the dark —we do what we can—we give what we have. Our doubt is our passion and our passion is our task. The rest is the madness of art."

CHAPTER TWO

A MAJOR THEME:
THE FORCES OF DARKNESS

I. BLINDNESS IN THE MIDST OF LIGHT

THE DARKNESS of which Dencombe spoke was a realm in which the philosophic imagination must inevitably wander. It was vague and formless except as shape was given to its shadows by the creative mind, and its extent was boundless.

There were other kinds of darkness, however, which were limited and definable. These were not inevitable, but they were always present. James lamented their existence, for he was aware that they were not philosophically inherent in human life, and yet they were psychologically so enveloping as to be inescapable. At the same time that he deplored them James found in them part of the substance for his art; for whatever the materials at hand, whether good or evil, the imagination could find full play in exploring their nature and fitting them into a proportioned, orderly edifice. Moreover, even as the opposite sides of the medal were bliss and bale, so there was a relation between the forces which oppressed the human spirit and the force with which it resisted and sometimes triumphed over them.

Those accustomed to language that does not appear in James's fiction have sometimes assumed hastily that he was overdelicate in depiction of the seamy, the sordid, and the horrifying. But it was not timidity that motivated James; it was a concern that violent overt expression not be mistakenly accepted as a substitute for the portrayal of the underlying crassness or savagery which impelled men toward evil. He was also guided by his sense of the relative importance of evils and their pertinence for the artist. Mere bestiality had no place in his art. Its existence was a shock to any mind which was not itself bestial, and no art was needed to emphasize its horror. In fact, for James, it was of exceedingly limited artistic importance because it did not involve the question of what the mind did with its passions.

There is a great deal, however, in James's works that pertains to spiritual negation—a subject not immediately horrifying, usually not even sensational, but for the philosophic imagination a cause for pity and fear. Sometimes the negation is the expression of a demonic impulse, however disguised; and it may then become the primary theme of a story. More commonly it amounts to blind submission to false gods or to what Conrad would have called a flabby devil. If it be of this second type, its victim does not wilfully set out to be destructive; yet, in his instinctive, egoistic efforts to survive, even to prevail, he may tragically destroy. This second kind of negation is seldom the main preoccuption of a story, but it is, nevertheless, a prominent antagonist. Sometimes it is expressed by one or two persons in a story; very often it is represented by society in general or by a segment.

Significantly, although James found more of his examples of spiritual blindness in American society than in European, the evils he deplored were international. Whatever their avatars, they represented enslavement to the trivial, the false, or the ugly. The most diffused of all oppressions to the sensitive mind was *commercialism*. Rarely presented by itself, it commonly appears in James's works as part of a manifold expression of cultural sterility or barbarism. James admitted that he knew nothing of the American business man plying his money-making trade. He also drew attractive portraits of men who, having won large sums of wealth through their enterprise, were now sensitive questers after values in a different realm. It was not the individual business man working at his speculations that James chose to study. Indeed, he never drew a full-length portrait of such a man. He had a conviction, however, that, in the mass, the world of commerce tended to destroy sensitivity of feeling and to restrict the freedom of the imagination. It had, he felt, developed its own religion—glorifying material progress, power, newness accompanied by barrenness, and, worst of all, a puritanical attachment to duty. Its willing devotees had created a tradition of hard work—not the kind of freely elected difficulties James as artist cherished, but a conventional ritual, to violate which was heresy.

Direct or implied criticism of the commercial world occurs in many of James's works, and it becomes sharper toward the end of his career. A few examples in addition to *The American Scene* can typify the rest. In "The Point of View," 1882, in which, to be sure, the characters unintentionally expose themselves as well as what they criticize, they also at times speak unmistakably for James. Miss Sturdy considers American men to be "better than the women," but she remarks that they "are extremely busy," and she adds that they are "professional, commercial." A rather reliable French observer writes of the "platitude of unbalanced democracy, intensified by the platitude of the spirit of commerce." Again, he remarks that America is "very big, very rich, and perfectly ugly." Though an American defends his country on other counts, James lets these strictures go unchallenged.

An oblique light on James's perspective appears in a casual remark in his sketch of the Pont du Gard, in *A Little Tour in France*, 1884. He admired the "manly beauty" of the structure, but also noted in it "a certain stupidity, a vague brutality." He generalized that it was representative of Roman work, "which is wanting in the nice adaptation of the means to the end. The means are always exaggerated . . . ." Whether or not the cavilling is just, it accords with James's abhorrence of waste; and it illuminates, too, what he felt to be a defect of American commerce, its emphasis on power, even sheer brute force, to achieve its ends. Not unlike the effect of Roman architecture was that of "loud longitudinal New York," marked by the demolition of the old and cherished, for the advance of mere efficient newness ("Europe," 1899; "The Jolly Corner," 1908). With the passing of the years James looked back, not only with nostalgia for the tone of social life of an earlier New York, but with a feeling that even commerce, in its stress on modernity, had lost something which it had once possessed.

Indeed, the thesis of *The American Scene*, 1905–1907, insofar as it includes business, is that the ills were increasing. Wealth begat vulgarity in giving it augmented opportunity for expression. Speaking of New York City in *villeggiatura*, James wrote, "Here was the expensive as a power by itself, a power unguided, undirected, practically unapplied, really exerting itself in a void that could make it no response . . . ." Again, he protested, "No impression so promptly assaults the arriving visitor of the United States as that of the overwhelming preponderance, wherever he turns and twists, of the unmitigated 'business-man' face." By now less distressed than earlier by the hardness of American women, he found them to be of a "markedly finer texture than the men," and among other things, "less commercialized." He spoke of the "note of vehemence" of New York life as "the appeal of a particular type of dauntless power." Tall, new buildings destroyed the significance of old ones and yet seemed to be only transitory, await-ing destruction in favor of yet newer ones. The demands of commer-cial efficiency simply crushed out the past. One was conscious of "the air of hard prosperity, the ruthless pushed-up and promoted look worn by men, women, and children alike." ". . . the great black ebony god of business," James asserted, was "the only one recognized." "To make so much money," he again lamented, "that you don't 'mind,' don't mind anything [including prices and rude manners]—that is absolutely, I think, the main American formula." The most devastating of his com-ments was reserved for southern drummers. There were a good many things which he disliked in his brief acquaintance with the South, and some appear to represent preconceived notions; but his special antip-athy was for the drummers, who were "as to facial character, vocal tone, primal rawness of speech, general accent and attitude, extraor-dinarily base and vulgar."

Christopher Newman, though he still thinks in the images of the world of commerce, is not a business man once his story begins, and Adam Verver's dilemmas no longer concern the amassing of wealth. In the unfinished *The Ivory Tower*, however, the old Titans Gaw and Betterman have had no life apart from their business. Rosanna Gaw sees her now retired father "steeped up to the chin" in commerce. Betterman's fires are now becoming extinguished, and before his death he develops a vague sense of having missed life perhaps altogether. To young Graham Fiedler he confesses, "I've *been* business and noth-ing else in the world. I'm business at this moment still—because I can't be anything else." Then he adds wistfully, "The question isn't of your doing, but simply of your being." Perhaps a more exact word than *being* would have been *appreciating*, but the contrast is clear. For James there was romance of adventure in the kind of doing which was a means to understanding, but what had laid waste Betterman's life was purposeless aggression in a tangled wilderness, where beasts fought, not to enjoy, but merely to conquer.

As to James's concept of society in general—sometimes the picture which he gives is varied, and one has the impression, as in *The Princess Casamassima,* that the characters move among shifting scenes in which others are working out their separate destinies. In such instances society is the vast, complex milieu which represents the composite of many individual lives. But society is also, for James, very often a general pattern of life to be illustrated by the conduct of type characters or to be castigated in the mass for its deficiencies. In such instances there is a contrast between the sensitivity of the individual hero or heroine and the crudity, or, to use James's term, the vulgarity, of society. The sensitive spirit, at times James himself in the sketches or autobiographic writing, is affronted by the absence of culture or, worse, by some positive display of bad taste or impertinence. Society so represented changes little for James and, after a while, comes to be virtually a stereotype. Indeed, a chronological examination of his works reveals no basic difference in the strictures upon society between the early 1870's and the 1900's, even though his understanding of man's relation to his social world developed significantly during those forty or more years.

Naturally, knowing America best and not finding in it the picturesqueness which in Europe helped to compensate for dirt and untidiness or even to dispel their presence entirely for James, the novelist most easily found his examples of vulgarity or cultural sterility in American scenes or among Americans abroad. In the contrast between America and Italy in "At Isella," 1871, he admitted that the American imagination had to work hard at creating charm and antique grace in modern Italy, but the narrator in the story finds fragments on which his imagination can build. In contrast, he speaks of his American homeland as "barren of romance and grace." In "A Passionate Pilgrim," of the same year, the American Searle contrasts England and America. In the latter he "found a world all hard lines and harsh lights, without shade, without composition, as they say of pictures, without the lovely mystery of color." Searle is speaking of the country itself, but the country suffers from the fact that, unlike the English with their long history of bringing art to nature, the Americans still live in an unformed land and have, if anything, accentuated the harshness by their architecture.

A few years later, in *An International Episode,* 1878, a story that strikes hard at society on both sides of the Atlantic, James introduced a long descriptive passage showing how New York must seem to a stranger from Europe: "Of quite other sense and sound from those of any typical English street was the endless rude channel, rich in incongruities, through which our two travellers advanced—looking out on either side at the rough animation of the sidewalks, at the high-coloured heterogeneous architecture, at the huge white marble façades that, bedizened with gilded lettering, seemed to glare in the strong crude light, at the multifarious awnings, banners, and streamers, at the extraordinary number of omnibuses, horse cars, and other democratic vehicles, at the venders of cooling fluids, the white trousers and big straw hats of the policemen, the tripping gait of the modish young persons on the pavement, the general brightness, newness, juvenility, both of people and things." [1] The scene is not wholly bad; there is life in the garishness, and in looking back to a somewhat earlier time than that of the story, James averred, in his autobiography, that the streets had quickened his imagination. Yet the tone differs markedly from the gusto which Mark Twain would have manifested. It is of no consequence that the street is hardly unworthy of the two tradition-bound Englishmen who are forced to traverse it.

During the short period 1878–1884 James seemed especially preoccupied with the dominance, for good or bad, in American society of women and children, particularly of the American girl. In *An International Episode* Mrs. Westgate repeats the aphorism that there are "only two social positions worth speaking of—that of an American lady, and that of the Emperor of Russia." Her sister Bessie and Daisy Miller, of 1878, are fine American girls, in whose careers we tend to forget the type and sympathize with the individual. Blanche Evers and Angela Vivian, of *Confidence,* 1879, are revealed, also, to be individuals; but at the beginning Blanche appears to be "simply the Amer-

[1] This passage is much altered in detail from the original version, with a general sharpening of the criticism.

ican pretty girl, whom [Bernard] had seen a thousand times," and Angela, for a time, dominates her mother in what James considered typical American fashion. In "A Bundle of Letters," 1879, Miranda Hope, from Bangor, is the best of the entire international lot in Paris because she is thoroughly alive; but though James found her refreshingly amusing, he still made her a caricature. In "The Pension Beaurepas," 1879, there is the repulsive American Mrs. Church, dragging her daughter around Europe in search of a good marriage, and there are also the American Rucks, mother and daughter, who pull Mr. Ruck as by a halter. In "The Point of View," 1882, Miss Sturdy, who enjoys satire, begins with attacks on American vulgarity at Newport, continues with ridicule of American speech, and winds up with a ludicrous picture of the dominance of children in American life: "But the little boys kick your shins, and the little girls offer to slap your face! There's an immense literature entirely addressed to them, in which the kicking of shins and the slapping of faces carries the day." In "Pandora," 1884, James gave a portrait of the "self-made girl" which is both satiric and compassionate. The self-made girl was culturally superior to her parents and fully conscious of that fact. Her cultivation was "perhaps a little too obvious," acquired mainly by reading and demonstrated by her literary allusions. She had been to Europe and probably had got into society there before she did so at home. At all times she was or wished to seem in full mastery both of herself and of her family. In "Pandora" she is called "the new type" and "the latest, freshest fruit of our great American evolution." James felt sorry for her, as she had no heritage, and he, of course, deplored a civilization in which she was the finest product.

Five years after *An International Episode* James again attacked the ugliness of life in New York, drawing his evidence heavily from the meaninglessness of the architecture. In "The Impressions of a Cousin," the mildly satiric Miss Condit, speaking of Fifty-third Street, writes in her journal that "the vista seems too hideous: the narrow, impersonal houses, with the dry, hard tone of their brownstone, a surface as uninteresting as that of sand-paper; their steep, stiff stoops . . . ; their lumpish balustrades, porticoes, and cornices, turned out by the hundred and adorned with heavy excrescences—such an eruption of ornament

and such a poverty of effect!" In the same year, 1883, James referred
to the American Mrs. Headway, of "The Siege of London," as coming
from "a country where everything is new and many things ugly." In
"Pandora" the Capitol at Washington, which Pandora thinks "very
fine," exhibits crude architectural taste. The German Count Otto,
from whose point of view the action is seen, may, like the others quoted
above, have less patience with things American than some of the sensitive Americans in the stories of the same period, but his impressions
of the Capitol seem intended to represent James's own: "In the lower
house there were certain bedaubed walls, in the basest style of imitation, which made him faintly sick." In "A New England Winter,"
1884, it is Boston that comes in for satire. Florimond, whose artistic
judgment seems to be reliable, finds in the Boston shops "the stamp of
the latest modern ugliness." In 1908, in "The Jolly Corner," James
once more returned to his attack on New York architecture, and in
1910 he gave a bleak, dismal picture of the city in "A Round of Visits."
In his autobiographic reminiscences he was as unreservedly caustic
on American life as forty years before. Typical is his recall of Saratoga as it was in 1870. His accusation scarcely differs from his various
earlier protests about Saratoga and Newport when he speaks of "the
great hot glare of vulgarity of the aligned hotels of the place and
period" (*Notes of a Son and Brother*).

That sensitive persons should spring from such an environment made
their genius, for James, the more remarkable. In transplanting Jeffrey
Aspern from Byron's England to America, in "The Aspern Papers,"
1888, James felt that he was making his fate the more poignant: ". . .
at a period when our native land was nude and crude and provincial,
when the famous 'atmosphere' it is supposed to lack was not even
missed, when literature was lonely there and art and form almost
impossible, he had found means to live and write like one of the first
. . . ." Though the words are those of a character who is later to commit evil from lack of moral understanding, like much else in the story
they are meant to be factually reliable. In the same year James contrasted two men as representatives of their respective countries. The
English Sir Rufus Chasemore, in "Two Countries," is prejudiced and
not very imaginative, yet he has "an air of having been more artfully

74

fashioned in conformity with traditions and models." In short, his social heritage has helped a mediocre person to rise above mediocrity. The American Macarthy is a better fellow, and yet he "looked unfinished." Actually, as James revealed in his autobiography, he knew personally a surprisingly large number of Americans who had sensibility and who were "finished." He was determined to believe, however, that they all suffered from the milieu in which they lived. So it is, too, with his fictitious Americans. Consciously or unconsciously they have missed out on what they might have found or do come to find in Europe.

In his preface to a number of the stories discussed above, James admitted, years after their composition, that he had deliberately contrasted America and Europe (Preface to *Lady Barberina*). The contrast was not exclusively unfavorable to America. In fact, the strictures on Europe in these stories and others, though less frequent than those on America, were often equally sharp. They were also equally patterned, so that their chronology matters little. In "Homburg Reformed," 1873, James did not hesitate to admit the preconceptions with which he viewed Europeans as racial types. He merely insisted that his observations abroad had not changed them: "I think that . . . you are very likely to find a people on your travels what you found them described to be under the mysterious woodcut in some Peter Parley taskbook or play-book of your childhood. The French are a light, pleasure-loving people; ten years of the boulevards brings no essential amendment to the phrase. The Germans are heavy and fair-haired, deep drinkers and strong thinkers; a fortnight at Homburg doesn't reverse the formula." Generally James disliked the Germans. He disapproved of their art ("Darmstadt," 1873), and he seldom drew a pleasant portrait of a German, the chief exception being the composer Heidenmauer, of "Collaboration," 1892. The would-be philosopher in "A Bundle of Letters" is a sinister fool, the Germans at the pension in "Fordham Castle," 1904, are "the vociferous German tribe," and those in "Covering End," 1898, are silly tourists.

The French fare better only in that there are more good characters who are French. The pensions, which James knew firsthand, are depressing. French aristocratic society has not only the wicked Bellegardes and other decadent families, but a false sense of aristocracy itself. In *The American* a fat, ugly duchess receives homage solely because of her rank; the Frenchman who passes for a man in "A Bundle of Letters" is the product of a decaying society; the American-French Proberts, in *The Reverberator,* 1888, are caricatures of what an aristocracy should be; and the attack of the young American Cockerel, in "The Point of View," covers the French, along with the English and Italians. "As for manners," Cockerel explodes, "there are bad manners everywhere, but an aristocracy is bad manners organised. . . . Of course you'll come back to the cathedrals and Titians, but there's a thought that helps one to do without them,—the thought that though [in America] we've an immense deal of pie-eating plainness, we've little misery, little squalor, little degradation. There's no regular wife-beating class, and there are none of the stultified peasants of whom it takes so many to make a European noble."

The British share some of the French defects, but have their own special type as well. Fatuousness and mental sterility are common among them. Bolstered by aristocratic heritage, they are vacuous as individuals. Lord Lambeth and his mother, of *An International Episode,* cling to the tradition of their rank despite Lambeth's being an agreeable nonentity and his mother's being a boor. Miss Vane, of "A Bundle of Letters," is insipid and bound by tradition. The society to which Brooksmith, 1891, must descend lacks even the pretense of intelligent conversation. Vanderbank, of *The Awkward Age,* himself no paragon of insight, can still speak bitterly of the obtuseness of his fellow Londoners: "London doesn't love the latent or the lurking, has neither time nor taste nor sense for anything less discernible than the red flag in front of the steam roller." The society into which Mrs. Medwin's clients seek introduction is so lifeless that it needs a disreputable adventurer to entertain it ("Mrs. Medwin," 1901). In *The Outcry,* 1911, society women kill time by gambling for high stakes. And in several stories, notably "Two Countries," "Brooksmith," and *The Princess Casamassima,* there are brief but damning pictures of squalor and ugliness.

These are the generic portraits which James made of what would inevitably confront one in America or in Europe. He found more to contrast than to compare, and yet on both sides of the Atlantic there was much to deplore. His pictures were not subtle, not much individualized. Rather, they were sketched in broad strokes suitable for the backdrop on a stage. In the works from which the examples above have been taken the ills are explicitly present. In others they are a felt presence, an implied contrast to the ideals of characters who try to live imaginatively and creatively in a world which knows not those ideals.

One particular species of blatancy, again found internationally, was a special affront to James because it infringed directly on the province of the artist. His own bitter confrontation with the standards of journalism rankled in his memory for the rest of his life. He wrote of it in his letters and returned to it in "The Next Time," 1895, where the narrator, in speaking of Ralph Limbert, is really speaking of James, too: ". . . such work as he has done is the very worst he can do for the money"; and with equal acerbity, ". . . you can't make a sow's ear of a silk purse!" The experience, of course, was his exchange of letters when he was being pressed to popularize his articles from abroad to the New York *Tribune* which appeared in 1875–1876.[2] A review of the correspondence suggests that James was somewhat more testy than he needed to be, but, in any event, the consequence was an intensification of his dislike for newspapers and popular journals. There were two aspects to journalism which offended him. One was the preoccupation with the ephemeral and half true, with which the quotations above are concerned. The other was the callous, sometimes ruthless, violation of privacy and the destruction of the shyly subtle and beautiful through the glare of publicity. Journalists would not live and let live. To James, they were vandals in their stupid search for novelty and their sacrifice of nuances for sensationalism. Excluded from his castigation, of course, were such persons as Densher and Strether, who were men of sensitivity.

The journalist is much the same, for James, from whichever hemisphere he comes. He begins to figure prominently in 1885, in *The Bostonians,* where Mr. Pardon—the name is ironically appropriate—will

[2] See Ilse D. Lind, "The Inadequate Vulgarity of Henry James" (bibliography, "The Next Time").

try any means to secure quotations for his articles. In *The Reverberator*, 1888, the journalist Flack is motivated by personal pique, but he is also eager to dispense titillating scandal about private lives. The editor of the *Promiscuous Review*, of "Sir Dominick Ferrand," 1892, is squeamish about the tone of literary work, but will publish with equal glee personal scandal or eulogy, so long as it has a journalistic appeal. The reviewers in "Greville Fane," 1892, are ignorant and stupid. In "The Death of the Lion," 1894, the *Tatler* is named for its function, to offer up tidbits about the lives of prominent men; in "The Next Time" the *Beacon* specializes in "tremendous trash"; in "The Figure in the Carpet," 1896, reviewers collectively present a "great blank face"; in *The Outcry*, 1911, it is the clamor of the papers that justifies the title.

The most sustained studies of journalism are in "Flickerbridge," 1902, and "The Papers," 1903. In the former the culprit is not a caricature. On the contrary, she is a clever, interesting young woman, to whom the hero, a portrait painter, is said to be engaged. What Addie cannot understand is that the antique charm of Flickerbridge and its mistress are not to be shared by the world. She has just enough power of appreciation to know that Miss Wenham is enveloped in the tone of time, but not enough to know that journalistic publicity is its deadly enemy. For Granger, Addie's contemplated sin is nothing less than the annihilation of the sacred private spirit of a person and place—for places have rights, too, for James. In his bitterness, Granger remarks to Miss Wenham, "We live in an age of prodigious machinery, all organised to a single end. That end is publicity—a publicity as ferocious as the appetite of a cannibal."

"The Papers" is an ingenious comedy whose journalist hero is a likable victim of his illusions of power. Because he is "mild and sensitive," he is capable of revulsion at his profession and, at the end, of reformation. The heroine, naïvely romantic, for a long time holds to her sentimental illusion that Fleet Street is "life"; but before the end even she can cry out, "Damn the papers!" Much more than mere journalists, the two are typically bewildered human beings wandering among illusions, and James has fun with them in a story that has serious undertones. The real subjects of his satire are the silly publicity seekers, who want the journalists' services, so that the story is a sharp rebuke to a publicity-crazed society.

One of the most impassioned diatribes in all James is his attack on newspapers, in *The Question of Our Speech*, 1905, in which he lashed out at "the mere noisy vision of their ubiquitous page, bristling with rude effigies and images, with vociferous 'headings,' with letterings, with black eruptions of print, that we seem to measure by feet rather than by inches, and that affect us positively as the roar of some myriad-faced monster—as the grimaces, the shouts, shrieks and yells, ranging over the whole gamut of ugliness, irrelevance, dissonance, of a mighty maniac who has broken loose and who is running amuck through the spheres alike of sense and of sound." The journalists themselves were, of course, merely the representatives of a society which devoured what they wrote—a society which would sacrifice the Miss Wenhams, the Jeffrey Asperns, indeed all persons, dead or alive, who were newsworthy.

The crudity of an imperceptive society was always most oppressive to the creative artist. Not only was the artist especially aware of the ugly and blatant; he was most often a victim of aggression. Brooksmith, who has the soul of an artist, Limbert, and poor Gedge of "The Birthplace," 1903, must endure sordidness, nagging, or sentimental stupidity.[3] In the portrayal of the struggling Limbert, James became vehement: "Within doors and without Limbert's life was overhung by an awful region that figured in his conversation, comprehensively and with unpremeditated art, as Upstairs. It was Upstairs that the thunder gathered, that Mrs. Stannace [his mother-in-law] kept her accounts and her state, that Mrs. Limbert had her babies and her headaches . . ." ("The Next Time"). Gedge must suffer, not only from the selfishness and cowardice of Mrs. Gedge and the sentimentality of a silly public, but rather more from the self-righteous commercialism of his chief employer, who demands corruption in the name of piety and figures for Gedge as a "beast-tamer in a cage" who will make his future "spring at him."

[3] The extent to which the worldly Mrs. St. George actually helped to corrupt the "master," in "The Lesson of the Master," is obscure, but certainly she was no inspiration. As usually, the emphasis in the story is different from that in the notebook entry.

The subtle insidiousness of the aggression endured by the artist is illuminated in "The Middle Years," 1893, and "Broken Wings," 1900. Dr. Hugh is treated affectionately by the Countess as one of her "little lambs," and he tells Dencombe that, though "she exacted perpetual attention, it was impossible not to like her." Yet, without pushing the inferences, one perceives that she is worse than indifferent to art, that she is defensively hostile to anything, including art, that threatens her little matriarchy. In "Broken Wings" the unpopular artist Straith and Mrs. Harvey, who writes literary notes, are "at the bottom of the social ladder." Welcome at week-end parties because they are clever, they finally come to recognize how dearly they pay as guests. "We can't afford the opulent," remarks Straith, and he continues, "But it isn't only the money they take." "It's the imagination," replies Mrs. Harvey. To her broken-off phrase "As they have none themselves—" Straith adds "It's an article we have to supply? We've certainly to use a lot to protect ourselves . . . . And the strange thing is that they like us." Mrs. Harvey sums up, "That's what makes it easy to cut them. They forgive." The patrons, as a matter of fact, are generous, meaning well enough according to their lights; but the breakaway of the two captives is a leap to the freedom of creative adventure.

If the imaginative person was at the mercy too often of a world not of his making, it was also true that he sometimes found himself acquiescing in its values. "The Great Good Place," 1900, provides perhaps the most penetrating example. George Dane has sought fame, not egregiously but unquestioningly, and he has allowed his life to become busied with a great welter of details. There is nothing very wrong with any one of the events with which his days are crowded, but the sheer accumulation is too much, and the spirit loses clarity of vision. The brother tells him that life has become "overscored and overwhelmed, still more congested with mere quantity and prostituted, through our 'enterprise,' to mere profanity." He speaks, again, of "the wild waters . . . of our horrible time." In his new world Dane is "without newspapers and letters, without telegrams and photographs, without the dreadful too much."

Traditions, habits of life, manners—as James wrote in his letter, cited above, to Howells—were of primary importance to the novelist. If a tradition were good, it represented a shared insight; through the generations its meaning had been refined, and the heir of all the ages could gratefully accept it. But a tradition was good, for James, only if it represented free expression of spirit. When critics have tried to force one or another of James's own stories into a traditional religious mould or to demonstrate that they can be pigeonholed under some traditional philosophical label, they have denied him the very freedom he demanded. He himself, to be sure, used general labels, as we have seen, and our immediate topic will again reveal him doing so; but he saw systems of thought and ways of living mainly as suggestions, perhaps precious ones, for his own thinking. We are, of course, not concerned here with each incident in his own life, with every spontaneous remark in a letter, or even with the notations, sometimes commonplace and stereotyped, which he jotted down as données for fiction. In protesting the ferreting out of biographical facts and in insisting that an author's real life was in what he had written, James was accepting the fact that much of his own life and much of his casual thinking accorded with convention. In "The Private Life" he made the point unmistakably that a great artist's outward life might represent conformity to the social code, with no particular hint of independence of thought. The true existence of the artist was not on display in the window of his shop. In the inner recesses of his creative thought he would make use of labels, of patterns, of conventional symbols, but with a spirit of inquiry rather than of mere acceptance. The conformity against which James protested was of a different sort.

Certain of the habits of thought to which he objected are rather obvious and of little philosophic importance; sometimes they appear in his fiction only as broadly drawn contrasts to the themes he is pursuing. In *Daisy Miller,* for example, social conventions are clearly objectionable. Though in any civilization Daisy could not have escaped eventual suffering, because one's yearning for experience inevitably meets circumstantial restraints, yet she could have had a somewhat happier life if she had not been the victim of trivial conventions. "I dare not, and so thou shalt not" is the commandment to which the earthbound adhere. Because of the example and opinion of others, they bow down and require others to do likewise before an idol in

81

which they find no reason to believe, but which they, nevertheless, fear. The precise nature of the conventions may change, but the fearsome idol does not relax its forbidding gaze. Winterbourne worshipped it as a skeptic and at Daisy's death was tempted to find a new religion, but he retrogressed. In *The Awkward Age,* twenty years later, Vanderbank was a more thoughtful skeptic, capable of detached examination of his fellow worshippers; but his reason yielded to the images and sensations which had taken possession of his mind. Though he got no real satisfaction from a way of life that he knew to be superstitious and corrupt, he could not escape the bewitchment of the idol's stare.

In a great number of James's other works conventional thinking on the relation of the sexes or on a character's family or social obligations contrasts with a more imaginative view stated or implied. In "The Patagonia," even as in *Daisy Miller,* it leads to mischievous gossip, at least contributing to the heroine's impulsive suicide. In "Collaboration," it takes the form of hereditary hatred of a national enemy; in "Owen Wingrave," that of obsession with family military tradition. Sometimes, as in *Guy Domville,* it amounts to pressure to become involved in the things of the material world.

Perhaps the most extensive examination of this last form of worldly oppression is in *The Tragic Muse,* 1889, where the world of art is engaged in a clash with the world of affairs. In the person of Nick Dormer's mother the hostility to art is sketched in broad outline; it is actually fear that inspires her. As Nick remarks, "She has inherited the fine old superstition that art's pardonable only so long as it's bad— so long as it's done at odd hours, for a little distraction, like a game of tennis or of whist." The widow of a politician, Lady Agnes is depicted as typical of those moral, practical persons who believe that the work of the world must be done and, having no clue to the understanding of art, are baffled by its impractical nature and become resentful in their helplessness to comprehend.

Julia Mallow, a more carefully drawn character, shares Lady Agnes' dread. She is beautiful, and she has a distinguished heritage, with traditions of statesmanship. If Nick marries her, she can help him achieve distinction politically, and she will surround him with traditional elegance. But much as she owes to the world of art, she is still bound by the conventional and demonstrably practical. She loves Nick, but, like a number of other young women in James, wants him to be her creation; she will make him successful if he will only abandon any serious interest in art and seek a career in Parliament. On one occa sion, moved in part by jealousy, she cries out, "I hate art, as you call it . . . but till this morning I didn't know how much." By the end of the novel she has come around as far as she can by letting Nick paint her portrait, and it appears that she will marry him without forcing him into a worldly mould. James respects Julia; she is intelligent and sensitive. The struggle that goes on in her mind is between the desire to be secure in established habits of thought and the impulse to be adventurous. While making furtive attempts to break loose and at last managing what is for her a major revolution, she reveals the colossal force of tradition, of convention, which resists change.

The dilemma of Peter Sherringham, Julia's brother, is much like hers, with the complication that he must maintain his career as a diplomat. Since he has no artistic talent, only a great fondness for the theater, he cannot be expected to throw away diplomacy for what would amount to idleness. He could, however, exhibit more understanding and tol- erance. Though he protests to Miriam that he loves her, he demands that she renounce the theater. She replies, "You admire me as an artist and therefore want to put me into a box in which the artist will breathe her last." To which he ingenuously responds, "You'd make of me the husband of an actress. I should make of you the wife of an ambassador." Reconciliation is impossible, and at the end Peter will marry Biddy Dormer, a gentle girl, of limited talent as a painter and, though sensitive to things artistic, not likely to interfere with the march toward an ambassadorship. But, like Julia, Peter has yielded some- what. Nick sums up the change, "The great trouble of his infatuation subsided, leaving behind it something appreciably deep and pure." That there should be some ascendancy of art over the world of prac- tical affairs is an affirmation on the part of James, for the arguments he has marshalled on the other side are very strong indeed. At the same time, there is a poignancy in Nick's choral summation.

What we have been discussing is, in one form or another, the encroachment of a profane world upon the precincts of the imagination. There was also, however, an altogether different danger, that of unimaginative self-denial, which would reject, not merely the profane world, but the entire realm of creative adventure. As we noticed earlier, James found stoicism an unacceptable philosophy; it excluded, not alone the irrelevancies, but the essentials of life. So it was with any philosophic or religious concept which denied complete freedom to the mind to be creative. Though fond of Catholic cathedrals, James would not accept monasticism; the retreat in "The Great Good Place" is not a traditional monastery. In *Watch and Ward,* 1871, Nora writes from Rome that the nuns in the convent "are literally buried alive; they are dead to the outer world." In *The American* Mrs. Bread says that the Carmelites are "really not human; they make you give up everything in the world you have—for ever and for ever." It was not devotion that disturbed James, far from it; as an artist he believed in immersion in one's work without reservation. But absorption in one's art was a joyous adventure, with the wonderful privilege of exploring one way of life after another, even the monastic. Intensity of imagination, working upon observation and experience, allowed the writer of fiction to live for a little while unreservedly in a world of his own creation and then to begin anew in another. It carried out its magical function by feasting, not by fasting.

There was no basic difference in point of view between the monastic exclusion and the puritanism which James deplored. Just as he did not choose to pursue Catholicism to its potential religious ecstasy, so he did not concern himself with the intensity of puritan inspiration as it might find expression in the poetic prose of a Jonathan Edwards. In James's works the puritans are not seekers of visions; they are hardly Christians at all. Now and then—for example, in Mr. Wentworth, of "The Europeans," 1878—puritanism takes the form of sturdy integrity and simplicity, even as the stoic spirit demonstrates traits that are praiseworthy. Generally, however, puritanism, for James, represents negation. In *The American* the Unitarian minister from Dorchester, who is essentially puritan, detests Europe as "unscrupulous and impure," and his approach to art is to find a "solemn message." In "The Europeans" the New England atmosphere suffers from oppressive puritan restraints. Charlotte Wentworth suppresses her personal longings: "I don't think one should ever try to look pretty." Gertrude, who is restive under the puritan shadow, protests, "And yet we are always repenting!" When Felix, the foreign portrait painter who eventually marries her, remarks that it is not what one does "that promotes enjoyment. . . . It is the general way of looking at life," Gertrude replies, "They look at it as a discipline—that's what they do here." Speaking for James, Felix philosophizes, "Well that's very good. But there is another way . . . to look at it as an opportunity." Much later Gertrude is still under the shadow: "Why do they try to make one feel guilty?" Even though Mr. Wentworth is a well-meaning person, Gertrude chides him: "You wouldn't let me be natural. I don't know what you wanted to make of me. Mr. Brand [the clergyman who first courted her and afterward Charlotte] was the worst." Her wedding to Felix will amount to a partial escape from bewitchment, but she will never be entirely free from her past.

The Baptist church in "Four Meetings" is a symbol of Caroline Spencer's ordeal. In the final scene the narrator goes "back past the Baptist church," whose portico, he has earlier remarked, "looked more like an old-fashioned bedstead swung in the air." Steeped in Hawthorne's studies of puritanism, James approached the subject, not to see what deep consciousness of sin might be brought to light in a human heart, but rather to describe what the puritan atmosphere did to chill the tone of life. Here, in "Four Meetings," Caroline is in spirit not greatly different from Gertrude Wentworth. She does not consciously accept puritanism; on the contrary, she tries to keep an illusion of an antipuritan Paris. Yet she is irrevocably within its oppressive domain. It was ugliness where beauty could have been created and denial where, as Felix said, there should have been search for "opportunity" that impressed James in puritanism.

In "The Art of Fiction" James wrote, " 'Art,' in our Protestant communities, where so many things have got so strangely twisted about, is supposed in certain circles to have some vaguely injurious effect upon those who make it an important consideration, who let it weigh in the balance." The same year, 1884, he provided an extraordinary illustration of his belief. In the wife of Mark Ambient, of "The Author of Beltraffio," he achieved a fusion of puritanism and Philistinism which was utterly hostile to art. Mrs. Ambient is pretty in a Gainsborough or Lawrence manner, but "with no more far-fetched note in her composition than a cold, ladylike candour, and a well-starched muslin dress." She is terrified by her husband's works because they are frankly true to life. Her own concept of a novel, the narrator tells us, "is a thing so false that it makes me blush. It's a thing so hollow, so dishonest, so lying, in which life is so blinked and blinded, so dodged and disfigured, that it makes my ears burn." She does not obviously display her fanaticism: ". . . it was only after a while that her air of incorruptible conformity, her tapering, monosyllabic correctness, began to affect me as in themselves a cold, thin flame. Certainly, at first, she resembled a woman with as few passions as possible; but if she had a passion at all, it would indeed be that of Philistinism." Though Mrs. Ambient would not have gone out into the forest with the acquaintances of young Goodman Brown, she is nonetheless a devout worshipper of evil gods. Her eventual sorrow, after the sacrifice of her son, does lead her to new insight, and she "even dipped into the black Beltraffio." The story is what James would call a fairy tale, with the husband, wife, and son both real and symbolic, the death of the boy being indicative of the price in experience that must be paid for understanding.

Finally, as we have seen in "The Third Person," James defined the contrast between the Hellenic and the puritan in unmistakable symbols. Susan's conscience money was fruitless; only Amy's daring bit of smuggling could pacify the frustrated romantic's ghost. "Live all you can" had been James's motto long before Strether pronounced the words to Little Bilham. What we have been examining indicates the massive forces in man's social environment and heritage which would deny him that birthright.

II. THE DEMONIC IMPULSE

THOSE WHO HAVE FOUND James wanting in representation of the baser emotions have overlooked scores of instances in which a demonic force within a character has led to tragedy for him or suffering for others.

It would be contrary to James's feeling for his subjects for us to make a Dantean hierarchy of the sins depicted in his works. At the same time, there are degrees of evil and, more important, of the subtlety in its portrayal. In all periods of his writing one can find characters who, however distressing the harm they cause to others, are rather simple embodiments of evil. Their rationalizations of their conduct, if any, are obvious, and so there is little or no interest in their self-deception. They act from motives not requiring, or at least not given, much explanation, and individually they rouse little philosophic speculation. Yet in their totality they represent a vast portrait of aggressive nihilistic force.

On the way through the crooked corridor toward the more subtle manifestations of evil we pass by a goodly number of persons whose conduct is of the stock and trade of melodrama and adventure stories. To begin with, there is the lustful murderess of James's very first published short story, "A Tragedy of Error," 1864, who plots her husband's death. There are also such persons as the tyrant husband in "At Isella," 1871, the desperate debauchee who kills himself in *Watch and Ward,* 1871, and assorted vengeful relatives or selfish lovers, as in "Gabrielle de Bergerac," 1869, "The Sweetheart of M. Briseux," 1871, and "Adina," 1874.

In the early stories the motifs are readily apparent. Simple jealous revenge brings the denouement of "The Romance of Certain Old Clothes," 1868; it will reappear stripped of ghostly trappings and made more horrifying in "The Two Faces," 1900, and more base in the conduct of Lord Mark of *The Wings of the Dove,* 1902. In the early examples there is sheer hatred and will to destroy. The cunning machinations of Max, in "A Light Man," 1869, the monstrous selfishness of Eustace, in "Master Eustace," 1871, the shameful vengefulness of Edgar, in "Guest's Confession," 1872, the paternal curse of Captain Diamond, in "The Ghostly Rental," 1876, the drunken brutality of

Crawford's wife, in "Crawford's Consistency," also 1876, are sensational and cheaply melodramatic.

The conduct of the Bellegardes, in *The American*, again of 1876, is more extensively presented, but even in the revised version the villainy is still elementary and in some respects contrived. The marquis is a heavy-handed, arrogant, theatrical sneerer. His mother, an adulteress and murderess, is more complex than the wife in "A Tragedy of Error," but her portrait is neither consistent nor profound. With Osmond, of *The Portrait of a Lady*, 1880, we have a villain of somewhat greater complexity, both as to motive and actions, though still drawn in general outlines and seen mainly from outside. We know that he actually has inferior taste in art, despite his managing to surround himself with its atmosphere, that he feels painfully his inferiority to Isabel, and that he seems not to comprehend his cruelty to Pansy. Since the story is not his, but Isabel's, we accept his portrait without demanding analysis of his mental frustrations, for we are willing to believe that such a deepseated will to destroy can exist and we need only to see its effect upon others. Similarly, in so late a work as *The Spoils of Poynton* we accept the reported aggression of Mona as the natural expression of envy by an inferior mind.

Along the corridor, too, are a number of egoists who do not wish to be cruel and have no concept of the evil they commit. The subtlest examples come, naturally, from the middle and late stories. Typical are the good-natured Jasper Nettlepoint, of "The Patagonia," 1888, whose irresponsible attentions to Grace Mavis lead to her suicide; the weak Owen Gereth, who brings humiliation to Fleda by his irresponsible expressions of love for her; and the morally indolent Chad Newsome of *The Ambassadors*. Their fellows can be found in Gwyther, of "The Two Faces," 1900, who asks the woman he has jilted to befriend his young wife, and in Tony Bream, of *The Other House*, 1896, whose moral softness leads to corruption and encourages murder. A variant of egoism is the vanity which impels a number of characters and, as in "The Beldonald Holbein," 1901, can lead to exquisite cruelty.

Somewhere along the corridor, not far short of the inner chambers, are the Moreens, of "The Pupil," 1891. The Moreens differ from such persons as Lyon, of "The Liar," or the narrator-hero of "The Aspern

Papers" in that their evil-doing is not accompanied by intellectual ingenuity; they get none of the excitement of a game of skill. They have a limited cunning and they must be held responsible for their conduct, but they are pitiable creatures, trying in their sordid manner to survive. They are, indeed, perhaps the most pathetic doers of ill in James's fiction. As we see them through Pemberton's thoughts they "were adventurers not merely because they didn't pay their debts, because they lived on society, but because their whole view of life, dim and confused and instinctive, like that of clever colour-blind animals, was speculative and rapacious and mean." There will be echoes of the Moreens in other characters who live rapaciously, among them the Brookenhams of *The Awkward Age* and Nan's family in *The Sense of the Past*. In the Moreens themselves even the pretense of honor sometimes gives way and their desperate shamelessness stands undraped. There is no hope for them; no light, not even through the death of their son, can come to them. What makes them the more appalling is one's feeling that through them moves a great destructive force impelling them toward evil. The force cannot be wished out of existence. Where there is no light of imagination, no means of creative self-expression, life becomes a jungle in which blind animal impulses run their course.

The most extensive and varied portrayal of the unrestrained will to destroy is in *What Maisie Knew*, 1897. As suggested by the title, the evil in that novel can best be studied in terms of what Maisie had to learn in her full initiation into reality. It is enough to point out at the moment that, bad as the Moreens happen to be, their animal instinct for survival is surpassed by the cannibalism of Maisie's parents and the sinister corruption of her stepparents.

The aggressions we have been illustrating have been against an external world. A very different kind is cynicism, which strikes outward because it first strikes home and is a form of intellectual and moral suicide. There are touches of cynicism in many of James's characters, particularly the journalists, but the most glaring examples are to be found among the artists. In "The Madonna of the Future," 1873, the foil to contrast with Theobald, who has artistic feeling but never completes his canvas, is the maker of satiric statuettes of cats and monkeys, who aspires to nothing better than his cheap productions and has settled for a philosophy to match: "Cats and monkeys,—monkeys and cats,—all human life is there!" Admittedly, the sculptor could not have done great work, but he has defiled such capacity as he possesses. The Gloriani of *Roderick Hudson*, 1875—whose portrait is modified in *The Ambassadors*—is less offensive than the cats-and-monkeys man, but his much greater technical skill is still prostituted. He "represented art with a mixed motive, skill unleavened by faith, the mere base maximum of cleverness."

Roderick himself reveals romanticism turned cynical. He cannot honestly face the person he is, a man of considerable talent, but not yet of genius. Instead of working patiently to learn, he resorts to theatrical self-condemnation, an inverted form of self-adulation. If he were not beset by his passions, he might, he believes, achieve greatness; and so, pretending to himself that it is his fate to suffer more than common mortals, he vents bellows of rage at the evil genius which is destroying him. Through his hero, Rowland Mallet, James displayed extraordinary patience with Roderick. When, in a burst of defiance, the latter asserts, "The Greeks never made anything ugly, and I'm a Hellenist; I'm not a Hebraist!" Rowland delivers no philosophical lecture to right the balance—even though Roderick is a very poor Hellenist and Rowland has the virtues of both traditions. One feels that James is interested in studying Roderick as a tragic figure more than in condemning him. Condemnation is simple enough; Roderick is brutal to his mother, borrows money from Mary after speaking contemptuously of her, and becomes a parasite on the affections of others while flaunting his superiority to all moral claims. He boasts of "a restless demon within," and Rowland finally, and reluctantly, recognizes his words as a "supreme . . . expression . . . of the high insolence of egotism." Yet even Rowland repents any ill thoughts toward Roderick when he is dead. James could have told his story in much less space if he had set as his aim merely the proving that such a view as Roderick's brings wretchedness and self-destruction. He would have been wholly an Hebraist, however, and an exceedingly narrow one at that. Though, even after revision, the story has some cumbersome and theatrical passages and Roderick's accidental death by a fall in the mountains has to be taken as an arbitrary symbol of his spiritual death and a convenient way of bringing about a final chorus, the tragic theme of the novel is significant, and one's final judgment on Roderick's career may well be expressed as "the pity of it."

Subtler and more obliquely presented is the portrait of the sentimentally cynical St. George, of "The Lesson of the Master," 1888. Indeed, the method of the story has sometimes caused it to be misread to make St. George the spokesman for the author—a spokesman whose inconsistent final act, his marriage to Miss Fancourt, is felt to becloud the portrait.[4] Such a misreading comes, as in other misinterpretations of James, from treating a story as if it were a static sketch and hence oversimplifying the action. To be sure, as St. George sees his life, it reminds one of that of Limbert, in "The Next Time," who suffers unmistakably the persecutions of the undiscerning. Moreover, much more than Roderick, the master utters sentiments not altogether unlike those to be found in James's nonfiction. But to say that St. George speaks for James and that James is inconsistent in letting him violate his own advice to Overt by remarrying is to make him an illogically conceived allegorical device, not a human being. As a matter of fact, he is consistently inconsistent throughout, as a sentimentalist always is. It does, of course, take a while for the true picture to reveal itself.

Mrs. St. George is obviously an unpleasant, worldly woman—her own words expose her—and so one is tempted to accept the bitter accusations which her husband makes against wives and children. Decrying himself as "the depressing, the deplorable illustration of the worship of false gods!" St. George is quick to rationalize that it is family pressures that have led him downward. Even so, he thinks of Miss Fancourt as a woman worth fighting for, and thus the seed is planted for a repetition of his supposed enslavement after he has once become free. His decline under family harassment has taken the form of living in an expensive house and riding in a brougham. In the midst of his comforts he calls his life a "kind of hell" and his sons "thriving consuming organisms." It is his family commitments that have converted his im-

[4] For example, in F. O. Matthiessen and Kenneth B. Murdock, *The Notebooks of Henry James* (bibliography, General Criticism).

pressive library-study into a "good big cage," where he turns out popular successes instead of masterpieces. In one of his bursts of revulsion he complains that one must make sacrifices for art and that he has made none: "I've led the life of the world, with my wife and my progeny; the clumsy conventional expensive materialised vulgarised brutalised life of London." Under St. George's lashing exhortations Overt is inspired to live ascetically in devotion to his art, but, as he learns more of the master he also develops in power to judge him. One letter from St. George is particularly revealing in that, in a sudden reversal, he praises his now dead wife: "She carried on our life with the greatest art, the rarest devotion, and I was free, as few men can have been, to drive my pen, to shut myself up with my trade." Upon Overt's return St. George is at first seemingly frank with him, but then cries out with sarcastic self-pity, "Consider at any rate the warning I am at present." Overt's silent reflection serves as a choral summary: "This was too much—he *was* the mocking fiend." Upon marrying Miss Fancourt, St. George ceases to publish altogether.

Like Rowland Mallet, Overt provides a touchstone. He has been overgenerous in his sympathy to St. George at the beginning. He has also been aware of the general validity of the master's charges, for he, too, knows the temptations and pressures of the world; he has even, for a moment, felt that it is good that art be paid for with broughams. But Overt comes to discover something in his working at his own art that makes no sacrifice of his renouncing worldly things, or indeed of his doing without Miss Fancourt, whom he has found conventional and naïve. St. George, on the contrary, has been destroyed, not by his family, not by the world, but by his own cynical wordliness.

Although James did not explicitly present the religious aspect of life in his novels, his interpretations of evil accord with religious motifs and with Christian ethics. As a novelist he was concerned with creative expression as the highest activity of the human mind and with the absolute sacredness of the soul. Whatever prevented creativity or the development of sensibility, be it cynicism or whatever, he considered tragic. Whatever violated the sacred freedom of another soul—its inalienable right to self-respect and self-expression—was supremely evil. To list the characters who tyrannize over others, whether from a desire to possess them and, like a god, to shape their destinies, or, from a base intent, to use them or to have sport by tampering with their souls, would be to include characters from well over half the stories. James accepted the fact that it is natural for people to want to influence the lives of others; he even remarked that Mary Garland would have liked to shape Roderick's personality and that Mamie Pocock would be unhappy for not having been permitted to mould Chad's. In story after story persons try to persuade others to do their liking, to become the creations of their own hands. There is a distinct chasm, however, between those who are well-meaning, even if unluckily injurious, in their attempts, and those who have lost normal human affinities.

As to the degree of their evil it would not be possible to distinguish between those who wish primarily to possess and those who wish merely to use, and, indeed, sometimes the two evils exist together. The first story that portrays a wicked would-be god is "Professor Fargo," 1874. It draws unconvincingly upon prenatal influences now no longer accepted and upon "animal magnetism," but taken symbolically, it has a legitimate motif. The charlatan Fargo achieves such power over a deaf-mute girl that she leaves her father to go with him. Hawthorne would have told the tale better by keeping it entirely in the realm of symbolic romance, and Thomas Mann, to judge by "Mario und der Zauberer," would have given it more dramatic intensity to make its horror shattering. James was still remembering Hawthorne, but trying to tell his story in a realistic setting and with realistic incidents, and it was to be some years yet before he mastered his technique. He was fully confident, however, of the truth of his romantic concept of the fiendlike impulse to possess and destroy an innocent human soul.

That impulse reappears in a new guise in *Washington Square*, 1880. Although Catherine Sloper tries to excuse her father's cruelty as stemming from his love for her dead mother, James is not concerned primarily with the doctor's motives. Sloper's love for his wife and his desire to protect Catherine from the worthless Townsend in no way explain the perverted pleasure he derives from his sarcasm or his contemptuous references to her. Fancying himself a scientific thinker, Sloper insists that Catherine know the truth about herself, that she is not brilliant and that she cannot expect to be wooed except for her inheritance. Under the relentlessness of his ironic contempt she is led to believe herself "ugly and stupid." The doctor even reaches back from the grave, by means of his will, to humiliate her. It is significant that James did not try to provide an analysis of Sloper's thoughts. The portrait is not a case study of a man who, from some pathological quirk, comes to seek vengeance for the death of his brilliant wife. It is simply a picture of perverseness, with the wife's death only the particular incident that lets it unfold. In short, the novelist is not concerned with demonstrating the psychological plausibility of the actions; he assumes it. Rather, his province is the philosophic aspects of moral evil on the part of Sloper and of human sorrow on that of Catherine. The distinction is significant because, though later Jamesian portraits of evil doers may include much more psychological motivation, none of the stories—including the controversial "The Turn of the Screw"—are primarily case studies. Professor Fargo, Dr. Sloper, and all their successors are, first of all, characters in "fairy tales" as James understood the term.

The fairy-tale quality of "Georgina's Reasons," 1884, is immediately apparent. Georgina, of upper-class New York society, swears her husband to secrecy concerning their marriage, puts her baby in the care of strangers so that its father never finds it, marries bigamously, refuses her first husband a divorce, and escapes only because he refrains from exposing her. Yet at no time do we learn her reasons; we know only the summary of what she has done. The story was clearly for James an *amusette*. The reader is free to invent whatever motivation he wishes. Whatever the psychological sequences he may imagine, he must always return to what matters—the fact that Georgina did do monstrous things, that she symbolizes in horrifying proportions the incomprehensible nature of the evil in our souls.

The Bostonians, 1885, has not escaped the case analysts, who are quick to point out a Lesbian attraction of Olive Chancellor toward Verena Tarrant. There is much in the novel that is in accord with such an attraction, but again the theme is about something else. What we do know beyond question is that, having used Verena's special talent for speaking to further her crusade for women's suffrage, Olive

94

THE FORCES OF DARKNESS

finally finds herself struggling for possession of Verena against Basil Ransom, who would make of her a feminine, noncrusading, domestic little wife. Romance and James are on the side of Ransom. Without encumbering the story with Lesbianism, one can still recognize in Olive's obsession a serious evil. If Verena were not dramatically rescued by Ransom, she would be in danger of loss of her very freedom itself; and, on the other hand, for Olive the girl's defection is "tragic."

"The Marriages," 1891, is a Hawthornesque story, but unlike "Professor Fargo," successfully given a realistic habitation. The excuse for Adela Chart's determining to prevent her father's marrying Mrs. Churchley is that the woman is grossly inferior to Adela's dead mother. But again James is not concerned with the psychological development of a special pathological condition. He is interested in the moral and philosophic consequences of Adela's decision and with the resultant tragedy. Obsessed with preserving the self-respect of the family, she takes control of her father's fate by telling lies about him. At the height of her machinations she has lost all awareness of the enormity of her sin: "I did right—I did right!" A choral perspective comes in her brother's reply, "You raving maniac!" Adela is finally redeemed when she learns of her father's generosity and suffering, but her atonement cannot bring back the past.

In "Europe," 1899, the circumstances are realistic, the theme and symbols again romantic. The aged Mrs. Rimmle has a past, of course, during which she can be presumed to have progressed, step by step, toward her condition at the beginning of the story, and during the intervals of the action she develops senility. James cares nothing about her, however, as a physician's exhibit, for she is really a witch. The narrator calls her tricks to keep her daughters from going to Europe, while repeatedly whetting their desire to go, the "mere conscious mischief of a subtle old witch." At the end, when she has completely lost touch with reality and believes that Becky, now dead, is in Europe and that Jane, now in Europe, is dead, he speaks of "the wonderful witch's white lips." Having begun with admiration for the tone of time associated with the Rimmle yard and house and for "the air of Puritanism reclaimed and refined" of the mother and her three daughters, he soon becomes initiated into the demonic perversion of Puritanism. The witchcraft makes no pretense of supernatural means; no devil is called upon in mysterious rites. Everything occurs in the light of day, without any violent disturbance of the outer calm. But we come to realize that the one thing that keeps Mrs. Rimmle alive, in fact the whole principle of her being, is her sense of a witch's power over her daughters. Even when Jane has escaped from the enchantment, the witch still has possession of her in her illusion. When one comes back to "Europe" from *The Sacred Fount*, he is struck with the realization that Mrs. Rimmle has really taken years of life from her daughters to add to her own. The horror of the story is in the fact that evil succeeds so magnificently —that when we leave aside all ordinary questions of morality and contemplate only the strange magic of her existence, the old woman is indeed wonderful.

The subtlest of all James's studies of the will to possess another's soul is "The Liar," 1888, which has had a fate of misinterpretation not unlike that of "The Lesson of the Master," though it has recently benefited from critical enlightenment.[5] In his notebook James began with an undistinguished idea: A man would be notorious for telling lies; his wife would endure the humiliation until finally he would lie so preposterously that she would hate him. Just how there could have been a convincing reversal in such a sequence of actions is not clear. The only element of suspense would have lain in the question as to when the revulsion would become overwhelming. In the plot of the story as it was written, on the other hand, the interest is not in when but whether Mrs. Capadose will reject her husband. Since she does not and since to the artist, Lyon, she has lost the power to choose—"So he had trained her"—the story was construed as a study of how evil, in the form of Colonel Capadose, could eventually corrupt and enslave. Such an interpretation merely compounds the evil allotted the Colonel in the notebook.

Actually, however, the finished narrative is about a very different subject. The notebook entry is concerned with Capadose, whereas, though narrated in the third person, the action of the story is seen exclusively from the point of view of Lyon; it is he alone that James

[5] See Edward Stone, *Henry James: Seven Stories and Studies* (bibliography, "The Liar").

goes "behind"; it is his thoughts and emotions that are explored. As Lyon is confident of his gift for reading character—he has found Mrs. Capadose "clear as a bell," and he tells her, "I could do you in the dark"—we begin by accepting both the facts which we learn through his words or thoughts and the inferences which he draws from them. Since he credits the Colonel with certain virtues, he is presumably an unprejudiced witness. Meanwhile, however, we do note that others, unlike Lyon, are tolerant of the Colonel's idiosyncrasy, which comes and goes like an illness; and James remarks outright, "If our friend hadn't been in love with her he would surely have taken the Colonel's delinquencies less to heart. As the case stood they fairly turned to the tragical for him . . . ." With Lyon we wonder why Mrs. Capadose married the Colonel, and particularly why, some years before, she refused the hand of the already promising young artist. Jealousy is human, and we do not blame Lyon for hoping to find some faint clue that she repents her mistake. The wish may not be noble, but the compassion is that would arise from a confession: "Oh, to hear that woman's voice in that deep abasement! Lyon had no harsh design, no conscious wish to practice on her sensibility or her loyalty; but he did say to himself that he should have liked to bring her round, liked to see her *show* him that a vision of the dignity of not being married to a mountebank sometimes haunted her dreams. He even imagined the hour when, with a burning face, she might ask *him* not to take the question up. Then he should be almost consoled—he would be magnanimous."

James lets us join Lyon in what becomes quickly a romance of adventure, an intrigue promising excitement. The artist will make of his portrait of the Colonel "a masterpiece of fine characterization, of legitimate treachery," and, now working "not only by instinct but on a plan," he encourages the Colonel to lie. His project gives him anxious delight, and when his treachery has apparently succeeded, he has unmitigated joy. From his concealment he has heard Mrs. Capadose's cry of anguish before the portrait: "What he has made of you—what you know! *He* knows—he has seen"; and he hears the Colonel's amazed "Damn him, damn him, damn him," and sees him slash the canvas in what seems to Lyon "a prefigured or rehearsed suicide." There is no evidence to

97

prove that, even now, Capadose can see anything wrong with the painting which he has so generously admired. His action is an expression of absolute trust in his wife and it is an unquestioning sacrifice for her. At the end, after the Colonel, to cover up, has told the only base lie we hear him tell, that another person must have destroyed the portrait, Lyon sees only its odiousness, not the fact that he has driven the Colonel to it; and when Everina tells a lie of her own to protect the man who has always loved her and even figuratively committed suicide for her, Lyon, though disappointed, still manages to convince himself that she is the victim of her husband's training. She is, for him, presumably still "clear as a bell."

It is the casual, sometimes ironically playful tone in which the machinations of Lyon are described, with the focus on the ingenuity of his adventure, that gives special intensity to the horror. Though Lyon has been tricked out of his sought reward, he is conscious only of frustration, not remorse. For him, it is still Capadose who is dishonest. The measure of his own evil is, of course, his abysmal failure to see it.[6]

Not only was it wicked to attempt to master another human soul; it was evil to inquire into or expose its inner chambers; and, once again with James, even the dead had rights. In "Sir Dominick Ferrand," 1892, the hero by mere chance is lured toward a seemingly justifiable revelation of the scandalous life of the late Sir Dominick. The evidence is before him in documentary form; but the pleas of his new friend, who has a premonition of danger, cause him to burn it. In the scenes that follow he learns that she is Sir Dominick's illegitimate daughter and that Sir Dominick was kind to her mother; hence the authentic documents, because of their incompleteness, would leave a false impression. The moral for biographers is apparent. More important, however, is James's larger view of his subject. Before he knows whether the publication of the documented facts would be fair to the dead man, the hero, after being tempted, comes to a verdict, mild in form, yet fraught with implication: ". . . it didn't matter that he was dishonest. Peter felt him sufficiently alive to suffer; he perceived the rectification

[6] We shall be concerned with a different aspect of "The Liar" in Chapter Three.

of history so conscientiously desired by Mr. Locket [the publisher] to be for himself not an imperative task."

In "The Great Condition," 1899, it is a woman's past that is sacred. Chilver refuses to ask Mrs. Damerel about her mysterious past, but the suspicious Braddle cannot bear not to know. It is insufficient for him that she seems to be a virtuous woman; if he is to marry her he must possess her entirely, including her past. Search for it takes him around the world, but leaves him empty-handed. As only misery could result if he found the evil with which he is obsessed, his inquiry itself is evil.

"The Real Right Thing," 1899, gives an extraordinary twist to the theme. Upon the death of a great writer his widow urges his publishers to bring out his life. The clue to the action is in the first scene, for the widow reveals, not only a sense of loss, but also a sense "of what she had lacked." By way of the crooked corridor we come in time to see that she expects the young biographer to give her back the husband who, because of her inability to understand, never really belonged to her in life. What the poor woman has mistakenly hoped, James implies, is that now she can have the man on her own terms, unbaffled by his genius. Though at first under the illusion of ghostly cooperation from Doyne, Withermore comes to see that the spirit will frustrate his attempt: "We lay him bare. We serve him up. What is it called? We give him to the world. . . . he makes us dim signs out of his horror." The rejection is tragic for Mrs. Doyne: " 'It would mean that he won't take from me'— But she dropped for despair. . . . 'Anything,' said poor Mrs. Doyne." Not even the dead can be possessed.

In portraying persons who ruthlessly sacrifice others for some gain for themselves James ranged from the commonplace to the ingenious. Mrs. Light, of *Roderick Hudson,* has borrowed money by making her young daughter show her beautiful face as security to the money-lenders; and later, by blackmail, she forces Christina into a wretched marriage. In "Mrs. Temperley," 1887, one daughter is sacrificed for another; in *The Sense of the Past* the rest of the family attempt to sacrifice young Nan. One story, "Lady Barberina," 1884, depicts a woman who typifies conventional attitudes and yet, like Georgina, is a law unto herself, depriving her physician husband of his profession simply by forcing him to live to suit her. Throughout the story her conventional attachment to her British heritage is emphasized, but it alone is not responsible for her dislike of America and her forcing Lemon to return to England. Lemon has loved Lady Barb for her classic repose of features and her suggestion of an old civilization, but, having tried to assert his independence, he finds himself her helpless victim. His beautiful wife has a "dense patient ponderous power to resist. She wasn't light, she wasn't supple, and after six months of marriage he had made up his mind that she wasn't intelligent—in spite of all which she would elude him." At the end Lemon rides obediently in the park with his wife and daughter, who exhibits "features that he already scans for the look of race—whether in hope or in fear." One is reminded of the later May Archer in Edith Wharton's *The Age of Innocence.*

"Fordham Castle," 1904, is a more romantic, symbolic fairy tale than most others, but not without realistic touches. The incidents are extreme in their improbability, and yet the human motives and emotions are valid enough. Sue Taker does not appear on the scene, for she is at the castle posing as Mrs. Sherrington Reeve, while her husband is not merely exiled to a pension at Geneva, but forced to give up his name and identity. The cruelty of Sue is echoed by that of Mrs. Vanderplank's daughter, who, not quite so heartless, does send for her mother once Sue has helped her get a lord for a husband. The wistful admiration which Taker has for his wife makes the more poignant his desolation. "Her baser part, her vulgar part," he feels, "has ceased to be, and she lives only as an angel." He assumes that she may be married or planning to marry. As for himself, after Mrs. Vanderplank is called to Fordham, "he felt as abandoned as he had known he should—felt left, in his solitude, to the sense of his extinction. He faced it completely now, and to himself at least could express it without fear of protest. 'Why certainly I'm dead.'" If the events seem strange, so too, James would say, is the bewitching power of an evil spirit.

James was a Hellenist in his desire to make of life an adventure, but he was an Hebraist, too, for he recognized that there was no escape from responsibility. At the same time, he was aware of the very natural human wish to escape, to live in some kind of elfland where one could have his pleasure and still pay no price. Tony Bream tries to, and so does Chad Newsome. Certain stories are specifically concerned with the attempt. In each there is a casual tampering with souls, sometimes even with a pretense of virtue. "The Path of Duty," 1884, is an ironic version of the draining of another's sacred fount. Having been in love with Lady Vandeleus before his marriage to Joscelind, Tester has renounced his love for Joscelind's sake. But now that Lady Vandeleus is a widow, the renouncing has only brought the two lovers closer together. "Yes, they are certainly in felicity," writes the woman narrator; "they have trod the clouds together, they have soared into the blue, and they wear in their faces the glory of those altitudes. They encourage, they cheer, inspire, sustain, each other, remind each other that they have chosen the better part. Of course they have to meet for the purpose, and their interviews are filled, I am sure, with its sanctity. He holds up his head, as a man may who on a very critical occasion behaved like a perfect gentleman. It is only poor Joscelind that droops." The story is comic, of course; but, then, hypocrisy *is* comic.

The hero of "The Solution," 1889, does repent his whimsical, sportive tampering, but too late. Tricking an acquaintance of "dovelike" character into believing he has compromised an unattractive girl, he comes to realize that he has entangled innocent lives. The victim gives up most of his inheritance to undo the harm, once he learns the truth, but the girl has nonetheless been humiliated. In the opening of the story the hero's annoyance with the girl's mother and the naïveté of young Wilmerding are sufficient enticements to have amusement at their expense. After the consequences have become apparent, however, he writes his own condemnation: "As I relate my behaviour to you it strikes me, at this distance of time, as that of a very demon." The awesome fact is that, at the time, it did not at all.

In form "Lord Beaupré," 1892, is an ironic farce. Firminger persuades Mary Gosselin to be vaguely engaged to him to protect him from designing mothers with marriageable daughters, and particularly from a cousin. Mary survives the experience to wed another, and Firminger, now a lord, has to pay for his sins by falling a marital victim to the cousin after all. Tragedy is averted, however, solely through Mary's tact and spirit, for Lord Beaupré had no intention originally of paying any price for his egoism. A more poignant and subtle version of a similar motif appears in "The Special Type," 1900, the plot of which was suggested to James by an actual incident. To secure a divorce Mr. Brivet must give grounds. Since he cannot compromise the woman who is the real reason for the divorce, he wants for his purpose a woman of a special type, "someone who could easily be squared." When asked whether eventually the woman "would be simply sacrificed," he prefers the term "remunerated"; "I should pay her enough to keep her down, to make her easy." His conduct is scrupulously proper; the two are never alone, and, of course, the conditions of the arrangement are clear. When the divorce has been secured, "his cheer was that of his being able to say to himself that he had got all he wanted precisely *as* he wanted: without having harmed a fly." At the end he is somewhat embarrassed because, having been promised that she can ask of him what she most wants, the special type chooses his portrait, which his fiancée has commissioned. For James, Hell was less often a place of conscious suffering than of complete absence of understanding.

In four of his works James provided particularly noteworthy examples of the ease with which one slips into the abyss of moral nihilism. The last of the four, *The Wings of the Dove,* 1902, has other elements that require a separate study. It suffices here that Kate Croy reaches a point where her sense of her relation to Milly is divorced from social and ethical reality. No possible system of moral philosophy can permit her to be kind to Milly at the same time that she is using her.

In that tricky comedy *The Awkward Age,* 1898, the poignant ending is by no means the only tragic part. Mrs. Brookenham is most diverting in her social ingenuity, and we become intrigued in the part she is playing, not always successfully, but with a high average of victory, and certainly with climactic triumph when at the end Vanderbank is more than ever hers. When we sort out the elements, however, we find some items that are sinister and even tragic. Mrs. Brook has recognized her daughter as her rival and has plotted with sheer mad cunning to remove her from the field; and, though she seems to live entirely in the little social empire over which she rules, she has actually lost all real feeling for her associates, except that of a gambler playing a desperate game to hold her artificial world together.

THE FORCES OF DARKNESS

"The Aspern Papers," 1888, gives a special turn to the screw. The narrator-hero is brilliant, amazingly observing, and convincing. His plan to gain possession of Jeffrey Aspern's letters to the now-aged Miss Bordereau promises an exciting adventure.[7] He must match his wits in a delicate, intricate contest against a wary opponent; besides offering a tangible reward, the game itself is a high form of sport, a splendid exercise of his talents. If one puts aside the moral issues, which the hero repeatedly attempts with some success to do, the story continues almost to the end to be a romance of ingenious adventure. But the moral issues are nonetheless present from the beginning.

James's technical problem was to give his hero "authority," to use his own term with which he characterized his famous governess, and at the same time to provide choral guiding comments that would not be too obtrusive. What the man says is at all times factually accurate; apart from moral considerations his inferences are, likewise, to be accepted, and even his occasional self-rebukes are in convincing language. The irony, however, comes in the fact that, though he accurately describes his evil conduct, he manages always to rationalize it and plunge still deeper, till finally he has reached a depth which he cannot describe because he has at last lost awareness of how far he has descended.

Significantly, the hero is a journalist, hence trained to observe and also, by James's concept of journalists, free from qualms about prying into the private life of a dead poet or destroying the tone of an earlier time as it might reveal itself in a still-living embodiment of an earlier age. Miss Bordereau, once the mistress of the poet Jeffrey Aspern, has letters which will help to give the public a portrait of Aspern, and it is his responsibility to print them. That he is about to go beyond what is legitimate is indicated by his admission that Mrs. Prest, a friend, "found my interest in my possible spoil a fine case of monomania." Other hints reveal the egoistic concern for the fame that will come to him, though he hastens to reassure himself that he has a duty to Aspern, a duty that justifies whatever he may have to do: "Hypocrisy, duplicity

[7] In the actual incident which was James's donnée, there was an implied betrayal of Jane Claremont by a Captain Silsbee, who tried to get the letters in her possession; but the substance of the story is James's own.

103

are my only chance. I'm sorry for it, but there's no baseness I wouldn't commit for Jeffrey Aspern's sake." When he begins by using a false name and pretending that he is in need of lodgings, the moral issue threatens; but in a letter to Mrs. Prest he brushes it aside with affable cynicism: "I'm prepared to roast all summer—as well as through the long hereafter perhaps you'll say!"

Juliana Bordereau is a queer, ugly creature, who has hidden herself away in Venice and even wears a "horrible green shade" over her eyes as if to shut out the present. The shade serves also as a mask: ". . . at the same time it created a presumption of some ghastly death's-head lurking behind it. The divine Juliana as a grinning skull . . . ." She has an "acquisitive propensity" and is a "sarcastic profane cynical old woman," a "subtle old witch." The description is factually accurate. Juliana is cunning in driving a bargain to get all the money she can from her lodger, and we learn in time that she is indeed subtle, even unscrupulous; for while the journalist is pretending friendship to get the papers, she is playing a wily game of her own to get the money and, better yet, a husband for Tina, her elderly niece. We may assume that she was no less calculating years before, when Aspern idolized her; she has never been a saint. The fact remains, however, that though we know only what he tells us, we see, as the journalist does not, that she still possesses qualities which she had when young, and that even the eyeshade is a clue to the Juliana whom Aspern knew. The poet overlooked whatever was earthy about her and let his imagination turn her into an ideal; and we may interpret the shade as implying that she has so cherished the memory of what he made of her that she wishes to protect it from anything that would destroy it. Beneath the grotesque skull which has replaced the beautiful face is the same Juliana, only more interesting now, for it becomes evident that she has achieved a miracle of preserving in a strange modern world the tone of a romantic past.

The journalist has only enough imagination to perceive that there will be human interest in the letters; he cannot see Aspern's Juliana in the grinning skull. If the story concerned only the two antagonists, it would be replete with irony, for the hero accuses Miss Bordereau of dishonesty because she does not naïvely fall victim to his carefully thought-out lies. But it would probably still move above the depths of tragedy, for though he can cause her annoyance and though he possibly hastens her death, he cannot touch her soul. When he tries flattery, she stops him short: "Don't try to pay me a compliment; I've been spoiled . . . ."

Tina, however, has no such defense against his plots when he discovers that, to win the old woman's favor, he must pretend great kindness to Tina. He has summed up her appearance as "long lean pale," and he considers her "stupid." He does try to associate her with a past age: "Her tone, hadn't it been so decent, would have seemed to carry one back to the queer rococo Venice of Goldoni and Casanova." She is indeed romantic, but her sweetness of character is of no particular time or place. The hero indicates his duplicity toward Tina in the very process of denying it: ". . . I had no wish to have it on my conscience that I might pass for having made love to her." But his lies to her continue, and his attentions revolutionize her world. Taken to the Grand Canal, an adventure which is a revelation to her, she utters "a murmur of ecstasy." In one of his self-chidings the journalist admits that he has felt "almost as base as the reporter of a newspaper who forces his way into a house of mourning." He comes to see that he is responsible for Miss Bordereau's "unholy flame; it was I who had put into her head that she had the means of making money." And when he confesses his deception to Tina, he is astonished that she does not call him "very base." But always self-excuses prevail. Recalling his stealthy entrance to Juliana's rooms in search of the letters, he later reflects that it was "the worst thing I did, yet there were extenuating circumstances." He still remembers her hissing at him "passionately, furiously: 'Ah you publishing scoundrel!' "

Then follows his supreme act of cruelty. His cowardice has led to his flight, and his obsession has limited his contrition: "It had been devilish awkward, as the young men say, to be found by Juliana in the dead of night examining the attachment of her bureau; and it had not been less so to have to believe for a good many hours after that it was highly probable I had killed her." With so mild a penitence, he cannot be expected, upon Juliana's death, to spare what is now easy

THE MADNESS OF ART

prey, and he is even willing to undergo Tina's condemnation, should she offer one, as a prelude to her further deception.

It would be erroneous to say that he succeeds in corrupting Tina. She has been loyal to Juliana, but she knows, too, that Juliana has wanted money for Tina's sake. What she does is not from corruption, but from helplessness. Having saved the letters from burning, she remarks timidly that Juliana might feel a difference in his having them "if you were a relation." The best he can later say for his conduct is that, in response to her unbaring of her secret, he showed her no "disrespect." No abasement could be more complete than hers: " 'I don't know what to do; I'm too tormented, I'm too ashamed!' she continued with vehemence. Then turning away from me and burying her face in her hands she burst into a flood of tears. . . . 'I'd give you everything, and she'd understand, where she is—she'd forgive me!' " Charteristically, Tina accuses herself undeservedly.

That the hero has been jarred by the revelation is proved by his strongest self-castigation in the story: ". . . there were moments when I pacified my conscience and others when I lashed it into pain." But the lower mind takes over once again. Giving a modern role to sleep, James suggests that the base desires are nourished in the subconscious; ". . . in the unconscious cerebration of sleep I had swung back to a passionate appreciation of Juliana's treasure." The conscious mind works out the details: "I mightn't unite myself, yet I might still have what she had."

There follows the nearest approach to Jeffrey Aspern's spirit of which the journalist is capable, though even it takes its origin in baseness. When he returns to the attack, he is astonished by Tina's beatific appearance: ". . . her look of forgiveness, of absolution, made her angelic. . . . It seemed to me I *could* pay the price." But the letters have been burned: "Yes; what was I to keep them for?" Though we are to suppose no change in Tina's sorrowful and forgiving countenance, "the transfiguration was over and she had changed back to a plain dingy elderly person." His sending her money under pretense of having sold the miniature of Aspern which she has given him is a hollow atonement. The final words, though perhaps artistically too obvious, sum up his moral state; "When I look at it [the miniature] I can scarcely bear my loss—I mean of the precious papers."

The positive evil is so great that one may forget to look for its origins. But when one does, he finds that the deceit and the violations of human souls, the very monomania itself stems from a lack of understanding which is in itself tragic. Juliana and Tina are intensely romantic, and a world of romance is presented to the journalist for his enjoyment. Had he possessed the kind of imagination needed to appreciate what was offered him, he would have abandoned his original intent, not merely because it was wicked, but because it was irrelevant.

The Other House, 1896, is an experimental novel, drafted first as a scenario for a play and later, in 1909, with no fundamental change in characterization or theme, converted from a novel into a play. Tony Bream's dying wife, who remembers her unhappy childhood with a stepmother, exacts from her easy-going husband a promise that he will never marry so long as their daughter lives. He is loved by two women —one a sweet, self-sacrificing girl, the other a *femme fatale* initially betrothed to another. To make him free to marry her the second woman drowns the little daughter. At the end, the husband is sure as to the murder, and others no longer have any doubts; yet the woman is not legally punished. Because the action, especially at the end, is so unlike what we expect, the story may seem puzzling. Rose Armiger, the murderess, blames Jean Mantle, her rival, for the drowning; yet Tony, knowing both of the murder and of Rose's malicious lies, tries to take the guilt on himself; Jean, who has openly expressed her hatred for Rose, nevertheless lets her go unpunished; and Vidal, whom Rose has treated shamefully and to whom she brazenly accuses Tony of the murder, consents to her final duplicity, the pretense that they are re-engaged. Rose is not contrite, only disappointed, and, though desperate, she still seeks to enjoy the power she believes she has over others.

This is not the way novels customarily end. It would seem that James, whose stories always involve social rather than legal matters, determined to make murder itself a purely social concern. The world of *The Other House* consists of a finite group of characters, and it is a closed universe. The intrusion of a policeman might bring quick justice as we normally desire it, but policemen are from an alien

107

realm. Then granting that no external agent is to take over and impose its concept of justice, why should not the inhabitants of James's little universe impose their own? Rose has murdered one of their number and has betrayed others. Why should they not, within the framework of their own society, administer the punishment within their power by casting her forth into exile? The fact is that she is already exiled; moreover, the others have to admit that they, too, are guilty.

Tony has always sought to evade unpleasantnesses. Even when his wife was near death he tried to be cheerful. Having taken the easier way out at the moment by promising not to remarry, he has knowingly let Jean come to love him and he has encouraged Rose's love, though she has been affianced to Vidal. Now, jarred by the sudden horror, he admits that he is to blame. Jean insists on sharing the guilt, for though she technically respected Tony's pledge, her affection for the child was an indirect claim upon him. In telling Rose of her love for Effie she has, in effect, declared herself a successful rival, since she can have Tony through the child, whereas Rose cannot. Though at the end the latter reflects bitterly that she has merely made it possible for Jean and Tony to marry, they see the horror of murder separating them. In concluding that Rose will be punished sufficiently by having to live, Tony is judging, not from her words, but from his own feelings. He is not capable of profound penitence; but he has been shocked into a sense of reality, and his customary cheer has forever departed.

Vidal, to whom Rose lies even while demanding that he share in her latest deceit—her announcement that they are re-engaged—tells Tony that he will do everything possible for her "but marry her." He has been more nearly guiltless than either Tony or Jean, and he is a slightly detached observer; yet he feels himself immersed in the horror that has occurred. As he comments to Tony, "I don't in the least know where I am, save that I'm in a black, bloody nightmare and that it's not she [Rose], it's not you, it's not anyone. I shall wake up at last, I suppose, but meanwhile—."

Even the doctor, who comes from his other duties in a world outside, shuts that world out for the occasion to accept complete citizenship in this nightmare universe, a universe in which he can neither share the truth with others nor yet condemn them. We feel confident that he believes with the others that Rose is a murderess. We know that he has no affection for her, and that he cannot have a high respect for Tony. Yet he tells Vidal that he must protect his friends and that he will therefore report an accident.

There are defects in the novel, and they are scarcely reduced in the play. Vidal's summary to Tony indicates what the story is about; yet there is a good deal of action which contributes only obliquely and meagerly toward that impression. The purpose behind all the activity is to suggest the intricate relationship of many actions, the fact that what each character does is an influence on each of the others. There could, however, be much more pointing up of the significance. Moreover, certain key incidents, such as Tony's meetings with Rose, are merely reported, not psychologically dramatized; so that we are left with a feeling that the crooked corridor has sometimes taken us a roundabout way and still has not adequately prepared us for the "presence" when we are suddenly before it.

The fault, put in a different way, is the imperfect fusion of realism and romance. The theme was essentially romantic; the story was to illustrate the author's belief in corporate guilt. The details were to provide realistic verisimilitude. Vidal's conclusion was implicit in the initial design; it did not evolve slowly from the evidence. And the realistic details had too many tangential implications which distracted from focus on the theme.

Allowing, however, for the limitations in the telling, one can still find significance in the author's intent. Each of the four principal characters, as well as the doctor and perhaps even one or two minor characters, is a part of the microcosm whose horror suddenly bursts upon them, and yet, paradoxically, at the same time each is tragically alone. In protecting Rose the others are really trying to break the isolation in which they find themselves. Each—even to a degree Vidal—has gone his own way, seeking his own ends, and certainly in the case of Tony and Jean, trying to disguise from himself his own nature and motives. They have influenced each other, but have been unable to achieve affinity. It is a supreme act of nihilism that suddenly reveals each to himself and to the others. They are still alone, more consciously

so than before, and at the same time more aware of the moral loneliness of others.

The Other House is indeed unusual in method, yet it is typical of
James in disclosing the ubiquity of the demonic impulses in the human
soul.

CHAPTER THREE

A COUNTER THEME:
EMANCIPATION BY
IMAGINATION

THE DARKNESS WAS EVER PRESENT, threatening to envelop. All worldly paths led toward its shadows, and there appeared to be in the nature of man an impulse to seek the center of the blackness. Sensitivity of feeling and imagination were the only means of escape.

As we have seen, for James living consisted of the appreciation of experience, or what he liked to call "awareness." One must cultivate the talent to enjoy perceptively and with discrimination. The only adventure that mattered was adventure of the imagination; and though pain could not be annihilated, it could be transmuted into poignant beauty by the sensitive, imaginative mind. Hence it was that, in story after story, James presented one or more characters uncommonly attuned for appreciation.

I. LIFE AS APPRECIATION

IT IS ABUNDANDTLY EVIDENT that, at an early age, James determined to cultivate his own sensibility. When he began to write fiction he tried to make various characters the vehicles to represent his own values. Since he had still to master the art of writing, the narrative technique was crude; and since he had not yet sharpened his analytic faculties, the characterizations and the representation of feeling were commonplace and usually sentimental.

If we were to accept as a mandate James's warning not to explore the sacred chambers of an artist's private life, we should perhaps have but a questionable right to examine the early stories, for they have more pertinence as biography than as art. But if we lay bare their

111

naïveté, we can argue for forgiveness on the grounds that we are trying to find the nature of the germ which grew into the flowering plant.

Take, for example, the thin, static picture of Miss Blunt as she is characterized by the more romantically named Locksley in "A Landscape Painter," 1866. The girl's name is not fortunate, for it does not adequately represent even the qualities of independence and frankness which it is intended to suggest. The young woman is significant because, though she exists mainly as her virtues are abstractly summarized, she foreshadowed Isabel Archer and other American heroines. We know what she is like because Locksley tells us in his diary: "She is, moreover, intelligent; she is probably quite reserved; and she is possibly very proud. She is, in short, a woman of character. There you are, Miss Blunt, at full length,—emphatically the portrait of a lady." The "full length" is amusing. When we learn the additional fact that Miss Blunt is musical, we see how derivative the picture is. James was not necessarily imitating bad novels; his reading appears to have been mainly in competent literature. He was merely unable to give dramatic vividness to the characteristics he had abstracted from his reading. And, of course, he did not yet comprehend all that could go into the testing of character to evolve a truly full-length portrait of an Isabel Archer.

The expository evaluation of Bingham in "My Friend Bingham," of the next year, is again derivative, though there is an attempt at novelty both in the plot and in Bingham's character. Having accidentally killed a woman's son, he wins the bereaved mother's love, presumably because she comes to perceive his excellence. "Bingham was *par excellence* a moralist," we are told, "a man of sentiment." Having formerly been melancholy, he becomes happy: "He is a truly incorruptible soul; he is a confirmed philosopher; he has grown quite stout." The last touch is interesting because it may throw light on the later characterization of Marmaduke in "Maud-Evelyn." Bingham never really becomes alive, and the psychological reversal necessary for the marriage is only asserted. Even the term *moralist* is without definite meaning, and we do not discover in Bingham much dramatic evidence of the reported sentiment. Yet the mood, the tone, associated with him hints

112

of the lives of many "poor sensitive gentlemen" whose histories were still to be written.

Severn, in "Poor Richard," of the same year, is another paragon of virtue and sensibility, though, like Bingham and Miss Blunt, he is dependent on expository summary for his portrait. He is reportedly a man of courage and conviction, and the sensitive Gertrude thinks "of her modest, soldierly, scholarly friend as of one whom a wise woman might find it very natural to love." In a story of the next year, "Osborne's Revenge," Robert Graham is so sensitive that he commits suicide because of his love for Miss Congreve. His friend Osborne appreciates his gentle ways: "It was his spirit, his affections, his sympathies and perceptions, that were warm and active, and Osborne knew that he had fallen sole heir to these." Miss Congreve is even more accomplished than Miss Blunt and Gertrude. She is, so we are informed, a fine actress, a good translator of literature, a student of Latin and Greek, a musician, and an artist. In her presence even Mrs. Radcliffe's young ladies would have seemed ignorant indeed.

"A Most Extraordinary Case," also of 1868, suggests the influence of the famous authoress or of others of her literary lineage, for there are passages which particularly remind one of her work. If so, however, James had been but a halting scholar; for though Mrs. Radcliffe did write as bad descriptions as anything in James's story, she did much better at her best. The hero, through whose awareness we perceive much of the action, is a pensive, even melancholy invalid, who under Caroline's nursing begins to convalesce, but upon learning that she loves another, loses his desire to recover and uncomplainingly dies. As for Caroline, James gives us a report of her size, the color of her hair, her complexion, and the quality of her lips, then continues, "Her forehead was broad, open, and serene; and her eyes of that deep and clear sea-green that you may observe of a summer's afternoon, when the declining sun shines through the rising of a wave." Seated at the piano, she "would discourse infinite melody. Mason's eyes rested awhile on the vague white folds of her dress, on the heavy convolutions of her hair, and the gentle movement of her head in sympathy with the music." Mason's feelings toward her are "patient, discreet, and modest,—almost timid." Here we have a faint hint of what was to become one of James's subdued portraits of gentle affection in the person of Ralph Touchett. To return to the Radcliffean banality—Mason "had thus the great satisfaction of discussing with the woman on whom of all others his selfish and personal happiness was most dependent those great themes in whose expansive magnitude persons and pleasures and passions are absorbed and extinguished, and in whose austere effulgence the brightest divinities of earth remit their shining."

Appreciation manifested itself most fully, of course, in silent communication between two characters. James was to use silent communion even to the degree of obscurity before he quit. The practice began early. It was in part a technical device, sometimes as clumsy as what it replaced, by which, instead of frankly going behind a second character to tell what he thought, James could attempt to imply his thoughts. Thus, in our present story, in which we are generally behind Mason, James wanted to give both Mason's unexpressed feelings toward Caroline and her interpretation of them; and so he resorted to speculation as to Caroline's own inferences: "It is a delicate question whether Miss Hofmann now ceased to be perplexed; whether she discerned in the young man's accents—it was his tone, his attitude, his eyes that were fully significant, rather than his words—an intimation of that sublime and simple truth in the presence of which a wise woman puts off coquetry and prudery, and stands invested with perfect charity." James fumbled a great deal in his search for a technique to preserve a limited point of view; indeed, a long catalog could be given of his self-conscious attempts, particularly from works of the early years, though not without late examples, too. Sometimes he would apologetically explain that the reader was entitled to know some background fact about a second character, or that, if he were telling the story in a different way, he could divulge in detail what he could now only suggest. But more and more he came to let one character do the speculating for him through the reading of gestures or accents. To the extent that the method was successful it was essentially a refinement of what he did with Caroline, and to that extent also it represented the fusion of subject and technique.

Much more experimental was *Watch and Ward*, 1871, in which James tried to develop the two principal characters, Roger Lawrence and his young ward Nora, from unformed, inexperienced persons into mature, poised beings ready for a sober marriage and a life of mutual understanding. In the waste of action which occurs neither character really evolves, though both change substantially with the shifting of scenes. We are to assume that, with her wretched, even sordid, childhood, Nora suddenly finds herself lost in the new world to which Roger introduces her, and that it is because of this fact that she wanders about inconsistently, unsure of her own mind and half in love with, half hostile to Roger. The portrait is unsuccessful, as Nora is pulled about as by strings without our ever getting more than a superficial glimpse of her mind. With her, too, however, we see a blurred image of both a theme and characters to come. Particularly are we reminded of Maisie and her search for her identity in a strange universe. As for Roger, he has powerful emotions, rugged character, and a mind reportedly stocked with culture. He once thinks that he should treat Nora "as Rochester treats Jane Eyre." Again he is reminded of Lady Castlewood in *Henry Esmond*.

These stories are all laid in America. There is a definite attempt, only in part revealed in the quotations given above, to unite the firm integrity of American life with the tradition of sensibility from abroad. Roger is a good sensitive man who prospers; Severn, Bingham, and Mason are sensitive men who die. The rough manner of Roger varies the portrait, but only as a splash of contrasting color would enliven a painting otherwise monotonously mauve. It was the sensibility of each that interested James. When he later came to the depiction of Casper Goodwood, who reminds one of Roger as doer, there was not much he could say. It was Ralph Touchett upon whom he lavished his affection and care.

James found "A Passionate Pilgrim," also of 1871, worthy of being salvaged, and he retouched it in later editions. He had already experimented briefly with romantic tales laid in Europe, and now he chose to take an American of sensibility to England, where he could meet old-world persons of similar emotional attunement and could feast discriminately upon the picturesque. The American is mortally ill; James seems to have felt from the beginning, not only that the imminence of death made the love of life more poignant, but that, through forcing its victim to live a quiet life, a lingering illness freed him for contemplation. The novelist had also already become impressed with the fact that Americans with imagination could possess a rare feeling for things of beauty at the same time that they had had little to foster it. To try to account for the paradox, the narrator of the story interprets Searle as a mixture: "I foresaw that I should find him a true American, full of that perplexing interfusion of refinement and crudity which marks the American mind. His perceptions, I divined, were delicate; his opinions, possibly, gross." [1] The fact is, however, that neither Searle, nor Caroline Spencer, nor Isabel Archer, nor Milly Theale, nor William Wetmore Story fits such a description of an American. There is nothing crude in any of them; they are not Miranda Hopes. And though they are capable of idealistic illusions about Europe, their opinions are hardly gross.

That is, unless in "A Passionate Pilgrim" James's own sentimental approach to English life be considered gross. For through Searle the author was presenting a sentimental journey and sometimes he forced the emotions. He was trying to distinguish between the atmosphere of England and that of America; and since he could not significantly individualize the picturesque, he contented himself with letting his narrator assert its charm. So we have commonplace summaries of how the narrator feels—really of how James believed one ought to feel. Thus we are told, "There are few sensations so exquisite in life as to stand with a companion in a foreign land and inhale to the depths of your consciousness the alien burden of the air and the tonic picturesqueness of things. This common perception of a local mystery solders friend to friend with a closeness unfelt at home." After a vaguely concrete reference to a vista of horse-chestnuts, the assertion continues, "There is a rare emotion, familiar to every intelligent traveller, in which the mind, with a great passionate throb, asserts a magical synthesis of its impressions." An English girl comes "cantering down the shallow

---

[1] From biographical considerations I have quoted from the first version. Not all the quoted passages were revised, but the general effect of the revisions was toward simplicity of style and greater concreteness. See Albert F. Gegenheimer, "Early and Late Revisions in Henry James's 'A Passionate Pilgrim'" (bibliography, "A Passionate Pilgrim").

glade of the avenue . . . on a fine black horse,—one of those lovely budding gentlewomen, perfectly mounted and equipped, who form to American eyes the sweetest incident of English scenery." A "rosy English lad" coming forth from an "old foundation school" causes Searle and the narrator to stand "musing together on the effect on one's mind of having in one's boyhood haunted such cathedral shades as a King's scholar, and yet kept ruddy with much cricket in misty meadows by the Severn." A housekeeper is "an exquisite specimen of refined and venerable servility." Then, as if out of the past, enters Searle's relative, whose mind we do not really enter, despite the narrator's commentary: "Of all the old things I had seen in England, this mind of Miss Searle's seemed to me the oldest, the quaintest, the most ripely verdant; so fenced and protected by convention and precedent and usage; so passive and mild and docile. I felt as if I were talking with a potential heroine of Miss Burney." Searle falls in love with her for her tone of time: "Let me fancy you the soul of all the dead women who have trod these terrace-flags . . . ." Finally, though still in vague, abstract terms, comes a new kind of idea, which was to be worked on afresh in *The Sense of the Past* and left unfinished at James's death: "He [Searle] had already taken a fancy to confound his identity with that of the earlier Clement Searle; he now [seriously ill] began to speak almost wholly as from the imagined consciousness of his old-time kinsman."

These passages—and there are more like them—sound quite bad; yet the total effect of the story is better. Through the persistent reiteration of its theme and enough concrete or semiconcrete details to guide the imagination, even in the original version, from which our quotations have come, the story manages to create a mood and to impress upon one the charm and grace of a way of seeing life. One has to start with the type of consciousness and the longings of a Searle if one is to appreciate the scenes James has presented. What, then, is the difference between Searle's or the narrator's view of life and that of Milly Theale or Strether, or of Searle's reported living in the past and that of Ralph Pendrel? The difference is, of course, that in "A Passionate Pilgrim," though there are a few harsh notes, the tone of pleasant melancholy is imposed by the author's determination, and life is stopped

117

to be viewed in vistas of one quiet pastoral or village scene after another. To appreciate was to do little more than let the mind evoke pensive associations in the midst of a gallery of pictures. What happened between 1871 and 1900 was that James came increasingly to see life as a dramatic and creative affair. Searle's mind may not be passive, but we do not see its activity. It seems merely to drink in the surrounding atmosphere in an essentially effortless manner; and presumably it undergoes almost no struggle in slipping back into the past. In contrast, when Strether takes his journey and sees the countryside as in a picture by Lambinet, we enter into all the difficulty, all the excitement, that is seething in his mind in his determined, yet finally unsuccessful effort to conform the occasion to his will. And when Ralph Pendrel tries to go back to an earlier time, he has to struggle desperately even to understand it, and he never shapes it to his wish.

In the later works we can still stop the action and see a picture, and after the reading is finished we may remember tableaux—Strether, for example, before a shop window or looking up at a balcony. We even retain a memory of Milly in a scene which we have had to imagine, as it is never actually presented. But we have suddenly arrested an action that has been unfolding before us in concrete images that possess individuality and are rich in suggestion. We have worked our way with James toward the picture; appreciation has become a strenuously active process. A comparison of the first version of "A Passionate Pilgrim" and the final revision shows some, though admittedly limited, attempt by James to give his story something of his later insight. Passages were stricken, and here and there the imagery was made sharper and more precise. Coming back to his narrative, James did not question the general nature of the impressions. What made the difference was that he was better able to analyze the way in which one would reach them. It was the process of arrival that really constituted the appreciation.

To live most richly one must escape from the narrow confines of self-concern into a world outside, a world which directly or by implication was a social one. A feeling for the picturesque or the past, as revealed in "A Passionate Pilgrim," was basically an appreciation of what had been achieved by one's fellows, living or dead; hence it represented an adventure in the affinity of minds. James admitted his own addiction to the picturesque. In "The Pension Beaurepas," 1879, the narrator confesses to his naïveté in finding the pension "picturesque," and he goes on to admit that "this, with me, at that time was a great word." It had been a great word with James himself, but the author came in time to see that external picturesqueness was not enough; a scene must suggest a reflective, appreciative attitude toward life. When, in 1883–1884, he wrote his sketches which became *A Little Tour in France,* he tried to pick out concrete details of French life which gave him a feeling for the past or revealed a leisurely, gracious present. Evidently thinking of the French connotation of the adjective, he admitted that he was a "sentimental tourist" ("Macon"). Thus he found the eggs at an inn in Bourg "so good that I am ashamed to say how many of them I consumed. . . . It was the poetry of butter, and I ate a pound or two of it; after which I came away with a strange mixture of impressions of late gothic sculpture and thick *tartines*" ("The Church of Brou"). James the tourist determined to enjoy his eggs and butter with a special relish because they were French is mildly amusing. But twenty years later James the novelist achieved one of his most brilliant characterizations when, in taking Strether on a similar journey, he provided just the right degree of concreteness and vagueness to convey his half-fearful romantic anticipation. On his trip to the country Strether hopes to find at an inn "something fried and felicitous." What Strether wants is exactly what James himself sought—food not as mere sensation for the tongue, but as a clue to a strange, charming way of life. Such was the invitation of the picturesque.

As to a sense of the past—there are a great number of others besides Searle who appreciate or themselves embody the best from an earlier time. As hinted above, the best examples can usually be found in the late stories. One of the most delightful of James's sentimental tourists is Mrs. Gracedew, who appears in the three different versions of the same story—"Covering End," 1898, *Summersoft,* and *The High Bid.* Mrs. Gracedew is as clever as the French heroines of light comedy with whom James was familiar; she has a fresh, naïve sense of wonder; and she is a dominating American woman who, with the fairy wand of her money, gets what she wants—both a fine old English home and a

119

new husband. The husband is at first not quite to her liking because of certain radical views, but she quickly converts him to his ancestral traditions. Hailing from "Missoura Top," which, for James, was even more remote from the founts of culture than Bangor or Utica, Mrs. Gracedew says quite unashamedly, "We're making a Past at Missoura Top as fast as ever we *can*" (*The High Bid*). Accordingly, she would like to buy up English art to take home. To the young would-be radical Yule she remarks, "What on earth is more precious than what the Ages have slowly *wrought?* . . . They've trusted us—the brave centuries!—to *keep* it; to do something, in our turn, for them (*The High Bid*). Again, she asks him not to profane the "Temple," that is, his cultural heritage. She would like to carry Chivers, the butler, home with her. As she explains, "I try, . . . but you do nothing: here you simply *are*—you can't help it!" ("Covering End"). But Mrs. Gracedew has too much sensibility to remain a vandal. She came to buy and take home; she does buy, but she herself stays to become immersed in the old-world atmosphere. Though she has been in the house only part of one day, in an overflow of gaiety she poses as a guide for the customary flock of tourists, giving them the palaver which they expect to hear, but inserting some words dear to her author's heart: ". . . one of the most interesting old houses, of its type, in England; for which the ages have been tender and the generations wise: letting it change so slowly that there's always more left than taken—living their lives in it, but letting it shape their lives!" ("Covering End").

When Mr. Longdon first appears before us in *The Awkward Age,* he is a rebel against the present as represented by Mrs. Brookenham's circle. Having been in love with Mrs. Brook's mother, Lady Julia, he is attracted to young Nanda because she is associated for him with an earlier time. Van calls Nanda's face a Lawrence, and Mr. Longdon replies with spirit, "It's a face of Gainsborough!" Elsewhere, as in "The Author of Beltraffio," James was not kind to Gainsborough women, identifying them with Philistinism, but here, though Mr. Longdon's judgment is soon proved to be inaccurate, his intent is complimentary. Later we are told concerning his own home, "Mr. Longdon had not made his house, he had simply lived in it, and the 'taste' of the place . . . was just nothing more than the beauty of his life." The reversal that takes place for the elderly man is in his changed concept of Nanda. He has begun by being reminded of her grandmother, of whom he likes to talk with her, and he ends by being interested in Nanda for herself, a modern girl, very different really from Lady Julia, but, like her, sensitive and timeless. He has appreciated Nanda as others cannot because he has brought to his interpretation of the present his feeling for the past.

When James first wrote of the historical associations of places he had difficulty in giving vividness to his accounts. The past was something glimpsed dimly as through a mist. But he came to see that, though inevitably the past would extend into the regions of half-light and would finally recede into the darkness, the feeling for it might have a very different, a much more vivid, quality. Thus in "Flicker-bridge," 1902, the narrator, a portrait painter, sees the old mansion and the life of its mistress, Miss Wenham, as a means of escape from the blurred confusion of a busy life into a world where all is remarkably distinct and fresh: "He had been floated by the strangest of chances out of the rushing stream into a clear, still backwater—a deep and quiet pool in which objects were sharply mirrored. He had hitherto in life known nothing that was old except a few statues and pictures; but here everything was old, was immemorial, and nothing so much so as the very freshness itself." Miss Wenham permits cigarette smoking and is in no way shocked by modernism. She has simply kept the clarity of vision which the world of affairs has never known. The artist, we are told, "lost himself in the things about him, in the type of the room, the last century with not a chair moved, not a point stretched."

In "Crapy Cornelia," 1909, White-Mason has managed to persuade himself that he is in love with a Mrs. Worthingham, who is pretty and lively, but belongs to a younger generation than his and is without cultural antecedents. Her home affects him as if he had come "from a shelter to a blinding light." James continues to characterize White-Mason by describing his feeling for the past: "The high pitch of interest, to his taste, was the pitch of history, the pitch of acquired and earned suggestions, the pitch of association, in a word; so that he lived by preference, incontestably, if not in a rich gloom, which would have

121

been beyond his means and spirits, at least amid objects and images that confessed to the tone of time." Continuing the metaphor, James adds that the "maturer tone was after all most appreciable and most consoling when one staggered back to it, wounded, bleeding, blinded, from the riot of the raw—or, to put the whole experience more prettily, no doubt, from excesses of light." It is the maturer tone which he finds in Cornelia. The two are "conscious, ironic pathetic survivors together of a dead and buried society."

Finally, in one of his several works which can best be examined in terms of a man's search for reality, James sent Ralph Pendrel back to exchange places with a person who had long been dead, but whose ghost an ancestral home helped Ralph bring back to life.

The picturesque might change with increase of one's knowledge, and the past, as Pendrel came to perceive, could not be kept static at one's will. The imagination could consequently find unending exercise in its preoccupation with either. Perhaps yet more challenging, however, was the attempt to see imaginatively into the mind of another person. James does not cite Browning's "Two in the Campagna," but many of his own works are concerned with the same fascinating theme as the poem. The early stories which we have reviewed contribute little to the illumination of the affinity of minds. The middle and later works explore its implications searchingly. James recognized the impossibility of a full vision of another mind; indeed, his characters are frequently in error in their efforts to understand others. The imaginative projection achieved, however, in the attempt represents for them an increase in their own awareness of life.

Imaginative understanding in James's fiction ranges from the usual to the esoteric, and it can lead to romance of adventure or to heartbreak. It is indispensable for the common affairs of life. Sometimes it takes the form of simple compassion, as in Mrs. Meldrum's humoring of Flora, in "Glasses," and Mrs. Wix's kindness to Maisie. It may represent a kindred attitude, as in the military coach Doyle's support of Owen Wingrave's antimilitarism or the insight of the Hayeses into Gedge's predicament, in "The Birthplace." Sometimes it expresses itself as sensitive restraint, as in Severn and other early lovers. Thus Rowland Mallet is the philosophical friend of Roderick and the undeclared lover of Mary Garland. Ralph Touchett, too, is akin to but subtler than the earlier young men who died for love. He seriously misjudges Isabel's nature and does not foresee that his munificence will bring sorrow, but he does live the more intensely during the short remainder of his life as he imagines a career of freedom and adventure for Isabel. A spirit of chivalry rules Adrian, in "The Impressions of a Cousin," and Dawling, who, at whatever cost to himself, will protect Flora's pathetic vanity. Equally noble is the quiet virtue of Wilmerding, who pays to redress a wrong of which he was really innocent, or the unquestioning love of Dashwood for Miriam in *The Tragic Muse.*

An ingenious variation of the sensitive lover appears in "Sir Edmund Orme," 1891. Wronged by a woman, Sir Edmund kills himself, and, years later, after her husband's death, he returns to haunt her. The narrator, afterward her daughter's husband, sees the ghost, and he concludes that if Charlotte herself is ever guilty of "some breach of faith or some heartless act," she, too, will see him. Sir Edmund is "young pale handsome clean-shaven decorous, with extraordinary light blue eyes and something old-fashioned, like a portrait of years ago, in his head and in his manner of wearing his hair." Though, of course, Sir Edmund has symbolic meaning, it is simplest to accept him as an actual ghost; for the narrator is not neurotic and he has no guilt to become objectified. The question is only whether Charlotte sees him. As her mother lies dying, Sir Edmund appears, and the narrator feels certain that Charlotte "dreadfully saw." If she did see, the ghost has convicted her of coquetry and so shocked her into penitence that she is never guilty of it again. But she never confesses, and her future husband never asks her. Though performing an unpleasant duty, Sir Edmund has always been impeccably courteous, and the young lover obviously imitates his restraint. Viewed from one perspective, the story is really a study of the narrator's appreciation of the sorrows of Mrs. Marden and Sir Edmund and of the temptation threatening Charlotte. For Mrs. Marden he has compassion, for Sir Edmund both pity and respect; and he so loves Charlotte that he would first protect her from knowledge of sin and will later accept her without inquiring as to her possible guilt.

Perhaps the most chivalric of all James's lovers is Chilver, of "The

Great Condition," 1899. In love with a woman who has a suspicious past, which she will divulge only after six months of marriage, he changes the time to a year and then declines ever to ask. There really is no unpleasant secret; but his wife will not admit the fact, because, as she explains, Chilver may still suspect that there is, and it is his sacrifice not to ask. There is a neat twist to the story in the wife's own generous protection of her husband's right to chivalry.

In Mrs. Capadose, of "The Liar," James deliberately created an enigma, and yet in Lyon's distorted interpretation of her we do have some clues. Lyon remembers her as having been "simple, kind and good; inexpressive but not inhuman or stupid." She was not proud, but told him that for the sake of her family she must marry well. Yet she has married a man who is poor; she admits frankly that they sold Lyon's earlier portrait of her because they needed money. She now says, too, that she knew that Lyon would become successful. Upon seeing her again he is instantly convinced that she loves her husband; the fact is immediately repeated. Sir David tells him that he has seen her come to the support of the colonel when he has told a fantastic fabrication in her presence, and she herself assures Lyon that her husband "hasn't a fault." Upon seeing the treacherous portrait she shrieks and bursts into violent sobs, but at the last meeting she is at least outwardly calm as she again lies to protect the man she has married.

Though she has certainly never been "clear as a bell," as Lyon wants to believe, Mrs. Capadose may still have been simple, and she may be entirely so at the end. She may have meant what she said when she told Lyon she must marry well, or she may merely have been sparing the feelings of the egoist. Except when protecting the colonel she seems to be utterly frank. It is not impossible that her lying is really an expression of simplicity; Dawling participates in Flora's fiction to preserve her illusion and he is yet a very simple man. All the evidence suggests that Mrs. Capadose *is* in love with her husband; and, if so, it would appear that she loves him because he loves her; his slashing the portrait is for her sake. We are left to imagine what goes on in her mind, but the implication of her actions is that, though the colonel's stories cause her pain, she lives primarily in her appreciation of his excellence. At the end Lyon complains cynically that "she was still in love with the man of her choice, and since she couldn't redeem him she would adopt and protect him. So he had trained her." Put in more sympathetic language the last phrase may have ironic truth. The colonel has helped to make her what she is by earning her love. Together the two live in a precarious Eden, but one which the machinations of Lyon have been unable to destroy.[2]

One of the most curious of James's studies of the ways of the imagination is "Maud-Evelyn," 1900, in which the parents of a dead girl persuade young Marmaduke to become her husband in order to give her posthumously the romance she never had. It has been suggested that Marmaduke's participation in the make-believe existence represents a withdrawal from life, but the evidence is at variance with such an interpretation.

Before he fell in love with the dead Maud-Evelyn, Marmaduke really had almost no life. He was "taking," and Lavinia loved him, but his existence was devoid of individuality. He never becomes a dashing lover, but his imaginary experience as husband and then widower raises him out of a colorless realm into something more interesting. We must, of course, with Lady Emma, the narrator, suspend any disbelief. At first she was skeptical as to the sanity of the affair, but she ends by accepting it because it is "saved somehow from grotesquesness." Marmaduke acquires a "vivid bloom. He had grown fat—or almost, but not with grossness—and might perfectly have passed for the handsome, happy, full-blown son of doting parents . . . ." We must recall that Bingham grew stout as a contented philosopher. When Lavinia is asked whether Marmaduke is "decidedly mad," she replies, "Oh no, it's too beautiful!" And though Lady Emma admits, "It's the oddest thing I ever heard of," she adds, "but it is, in its way, a reality." Marmaduke is not a deep thinker, but he does create for himself a new personality: "He had grown like a person with a position and a history." He is no Dante, but he lives in his devotion. After he has chosen to imagine himself a widower, he is "positively gay in his black

---

[2] A similar loyalty of husband and wife is portrayed in "The Real Thing," 1892. See Walter F. Wright, "The Real Thing," *Research Studies of the State College of Washington*, XXV (1957), 85–90, abridged in Edward Stone, *Henry James: Seven Stories and Studies* (bibliography, "The Real Thing").

suit, his black gloves, his high hatband," and he tells Lady Emma that "the more we live in the past, the more things we find in it." He is "a gentleman to the end," and leaves behind him "relics" inherited from Maud-Evelyn's parents which are "really marvels, it appears, treasures extraordinary." Lavinia has not lost Marmaduke; on the contrary, by accepting his actions she, too, has found imaginative excitement.

We expect a lover to cherish the memory of his beloved, and we grant an author the right to create imaginary characters who then become real to him. James has merely given an additional turn to the screw. Lady Emma is his spokesman in calling Marmaduke's strange sense of affinity a "reality," and, in its humorous way, the story attests to James's belief that true reality is of the imagination.

II. THE ROMANCE OF ADVENTURE

JAMES'S FIRST REQUISITE for an artist, as we have noted, was an "active sense of life." It was, in fact, the requisite for all worthwhile experience. Given such a sense, one was equipped for adventure.

The simplest form of adventure, for James, was the traditional love romance, involving escape from some form of tyranny or conventionality to freedom for self-expression. James made only minor variations on the traditional theme in "Gabrielle de Bergerac," 1869, to which he gave some historical coloring by placing the action in pre-Revolutionary France; in "At Isella," 1871, narrating a woman's escape from a husband to a lover; in "Adina," 1874, in which the heroine chooses a dashing peasant in preference to a lover of higher rank; and in "The Sweetheart of M. Briseux," 1873, where admiration for a bohemian painter triumphs over stuffy security: "Poor little Briseux, ugly, shabby, disreputable, seemed to me some appealing messenger from the mysterious immensity of life; and Harold, beside him, comely, elegant, imposing, justly indignant, seemed to me simply his narrow, personal, ineffectual self."

In "Eugene Pickering," 1874, James was trying to work his way through some elementary theories about the romance of adventure and at the same time to secure novelty of plot. Eugene, at a casino in Germany, is annoyed because his now dead father has held him to a restricted life and even arranged betrothal to a girl with whom he is not in love. He insists that, before sacrificing himself, he wants "to *live* first." To this the young narrator replies, for James, "My dear fellow, you're living now. All this passionate consciousness of your situation is a very ardent life." After a disillusioning engagement with a widow and a letter from the girl releasing him, he suddenly finds himself in love with her and will hurry to Smyrna to meet her. The story lacks depth, but the narrator's pronouncement is significant, for it became a major tenet in James's thinking.

Generally in James's later stories the concept of love as a romance of adventure became united with other themes, pursued in the chapters to follow. From time to time, however, he did give a simple picture in the early manner, except with greater implication and subtlety. One such example shows what experience in the practice of fiction writing had done for him. "The Story in It," 1902, is a *tour de force*, but written by the author of *The Awkward Age*. Colonel Voyt, who is having an improper love affair with Mrs. Dyott, maintains that, whereas stories can be written about the intrigues of wicked persons, it is impossible to make one about the love of a good woman. Maud Blessingbourne, a young widow, disagrees. She has read such tales as Voyt describes, for she reads extensively in French novels, and the one she is currently reading she finds "timid and tame." She herself, as Mrs. Dyott discovers, is having a romance of her own, for she is secretly in love with Voyt. With pointed irony on the author's part, the sophisticated Voyt and Mrs. Dyott conclude that Maud's "consciousness . . . *was*, in the last analysis, a kind of shy romance. Not a romance like their own . . . . Who but a duffer—he stuck to his contention—would see the shadow of a 'story' in it?"

James's supreme achievement in the portrayal of love as a romance of adventure was, of course, to be the complex drama of *The Golden Bowl*.

The kind of adventure story in which man struggles against the world of nature held no interest for James. There is little evidence in his writing of a sense of wonder about the physical universe; his most common expressions of admiration are for gardens or countrysides which bear the mark of civilization. After the early years there is very little, too, of simple conflict of good persons with bad. It was the psychological adventure that mattered.

That adventure could have all the drama and suspense óf an ingenious detective story, because it involved the unfolding of the strange ways of the mind and wonder at the eternal mystery of life. Sometimes it took the form of a guessing game in which the characters sought to penetrate the inner nature of their fellows, at times with comic results, but always with lively excitement. In "A Bundle of Letters," 1879, for example, the fun is in the errors that the characters make. The guessing goes on in story after story. In *The Awkward Age* nearly everyone considers himself an expert as to the motives of nearly everyone else. In *The Golden Bowl* the Assinghams perform at one level, Maggie with a higher awareness. The girl in *In the Cage*, 1898, has almost no real existence apart from her guessing. In "The Figure in the Carpet," 1896, the subject for detective work is the secret to Hugh Vereker's novels, hence in James's scheme of things to Vereker himself. The secret is never found, but the search is of absorbing interest. As the narrator sums it up, "For the few persons, at any rate, abnormal or not, with whom my anecdote is concerned, literature was a game of skill, and skill meant courage, and courage meant honour, and honour meant passion, meant life."

Perhaps the most explicit statement of the fascination of guessing is in the humorous story "Mora Montravers," 1909. Traffle, who is really the center of interest, the person we go behind, is in a comic predicament, playing his game sometimes with, sometimes against, his wife, Jane, whose niece, Mora, is the subject for speculation. The somewhat puritanical Jane, wanting to regularize Mora's love affair with the presumably bohemian artist, Puddick, pledges £450 if they will marry. They do because, according to Mora, she likes Puddick and wants him to have the money. But she is soon discovered awaiting an assignation with one Sir Bruce, and scandal threatens all over again. We know that Puddick is really an admirable man and that he idealizes Mora. She, on the other hand, is an enigma. While awaiting Sir Bruce she tells Traffle that she has been a "good girl," and she appears to be sincere in saying, "I want to be free. . . . But I don't want him [Puddick] you see, to suffer." Traffle is both a troubled mortal, caught up in the action because he is somewhat responsible for Mora and his reputation is affected by her conduct, and yet a fascinated spectator. As he tells Jane early in the story, "If we're having the strain and the pain of it let us also have the relief and the fun." Traffle is neither a philosopher nor a novelist, but his wry comment speaks absolutely for James. The poor man, though less puritan than Jane, cannot escape being an Hebraist; yet he yearns for Olympian detachment, for the free play of imagination.

At one moment he feels exalted because Mora has confided a secret to him and so given him an advantage over Jane, of whom he can think patronizingly as a "goose." Later, when Jane comes to Puddick's support, Traffle finds himself on the outside, reduced to comparative unimportance. He has a wholesome, naïve admiration for Puddick, but it makes him conscious of his own inferiority. He wonders "if it was quite inevitable one should come back to feeling, as the result of every sort of brush with people who were really living, like so very small a boy." During the lull before the new threat Traffle confides to Jane, "I, for one, confess I miss the fun—put it only at the fun of our having had to wriggle so with shame, . . . to live so under arms . . . ." He fears that life will be "tame again—as tame as it was before ever Mora came into it so immensely to enrich and agitate it," and he recalls fondly the wonderful times "when everything was nice and dreadful."

When the new blow strikes, Traffle begins to live again: "Even while he had looked askance in the greyness at the importunate fiend of fancy it was riding him again as the very genius of twilight . . . . He wondered about Sir Bruce, recalling his face and his type and his effect— his effect so immediate, on Mora; wondered how he had proceeded, how he would still proceed, how far perhaps even they had got by that time. Lord, the fun some people did have! Even Jane, with her conscientious new care [Puddick]—even Jane, unmistakably, was in for such a lot."

In such a story as "Mora Montravers" James leaves out what some readers most want and gives his attention to a matter quite different. What were Mora's emotions? How could she marry an excellent man to get him a dowry while plotting infidelity? Zola would have told us, or at least have pretended to tell. George Eliot would have struggled with the psychological probabilities of her conduct without needing any help from Traffle. It is precisely the predicament of Traffle, however, that is dear to James. It is the stuff of our daily lives as social beings, and more important here, it is fundamental in James's philosophy of the art of fiction. Traffle does not live in a world where everything can be known and labeled. On the contrary, he is surrounded by a wilderness of mystery. At times his attempts to penetrate it end in ludicrous error, yet he has no choice but to continue the search. His is an intellectual exercise, a game of testing his speculative ingenuity. As to the emotion involved—for James it was the inexhaustible passion of curiosity. One might live for brief moments on the high peaks of tragic emotion; but the writer of fiction, above all, knew that he must spend day after day in the realm of artistic speculation, wandering where his curiosity might lead and finding excitement in the unending romance of the adventure. Indeed, as we shall see in Chapter Four, it might lead him into the philosophic quest for reality, in which emotion, imagination, and deductive reason would all work together for his advantage.

Artistic creation, as we have noted, was, for James, the very highest of all adventures. Besides theorizing on art in his critical essays and his autobiography, he worked out his beliefs in concrete form in the thoughts and actions of numerous writers and other artists in his fiction. Thus we have a double adventure—that of the artist-character and that of James as his creator—for each of James's artist spokesmen or registers begins with a sense of wonder at the scene before him and then becomes immersed in its interpretation, in giving it a logic of its own.

As early as 1868, in "The Story of a Masterpiece," James emphasized the special mission of the artist and the relation of art to life. The portraitist Baxter is disillusioned about the apparently fickle Marian Everett and paints a portrait intended to reveal her shallowness. In a scene which anticipates "The Liar," her present fiancé, Lennox, admits the truthfulness of the picture and then slashes it to pieces; a romantic realist, he will accept Marian both as she is and as he believes she wishes to be. Lennox is, of course, the nobler of the two; but, despite his limitations, Baxter is nonetheless a Jamesian register, and the author's interpretaton of his artistic perspective, though slightly sentimental, is significant. Although he created a cruelly honest picture of Marian as he saw her, Baxter proceeded "without effort and without malice. The artistic half of Baxter's nature exerted a lusty dominion over the human half—fed upon its disappointments and grew fat upon its joys and tribulations. This, indeed, is simply saying that the young man was a true artist. Deep, then, in the unfathomed recesses of his strong and sensitive nature, his genius had held communion with his heart and had transferred to canvas the burden of its disenchantment and its resignation."

One is reminded of James's later comment on Musset, that it took a "great deal of life" to create his art, for there is an immediate auto-biographic origin of the portrait which Baxter paints. What is more interesting is the concept of the relationship of the two halves of his nature. It is essentially the relation which poor Traffle was to sense, for even though he lacked the artist's technique, Traffle shared his basic awareness. It was the artistic half that enabled one to transcend ordinary mortal frustrations and to live in a new, creative adventure, an adventure which might derive its subject matter from the very frustrations themselves. Where Baxter falls short is in philosophic understanding; he does not grasp the fact that what Marian wishes to be is part of what she is. James goes a step beyond Baxter's art in that he encompasses a more inclusive theme in his portrait of Lennox. Thus was established, though somewhat crudely, what was to become a successful Jamesian method. The artist registers were to live intense creative adventures of their own, and their creator was to fit these into a still larger adventure, his own artistic creation.

Some sixteen years later, in "The Author of Beltraffio," James put in different terms much the same concept of the relation of art to life as that which animated Baxter. The narrator remarks that he found himself "on Mark Ambient's 'side.' This was the taken stand of the artist to whom every manifestation of human energy was a thrilling spectacle, and who felt for ever the desire to resolve his experience of life into a literary form." Later, speaking for himself, Ambient contrasts his own "Pagan" view with that of his "Christian" wife: "It's the difference between making the most of life and making the least, so that you'll get another better one in some other time and place." For Ambient, making the most was synonymous with artistic creation. James could subscribe to Ambient's philosophy, though, of course, with an Hebraic bent.

In "Glasses," James entered into the excitement involved in the technical mastery of a subject. His narrator, a portraitist by profession, recognizes his problem as a storyteller. The facts are all before him as he begins to narrate. He has painted Flora's picture, heard of the incidents in her pathetic life, and seen her at the opera, where, though blind, she used opera glasses and smiled in the direction of imaginary friends. The facts are there, but the truth is still to be found. As the narrator explains, "the thread, as I call it, is a row of coloured beads on a string. None of the beads are missing—at least I think they're not: that's exactly what I shall amuse myself with finding out." The adjective *coloured* is, of course, ironically modest. The term appears intended to suggest Flora's vanity and the sensational nature of the action. The beads are nonetheless worthy of being strung with the greatest of care. They will complete a strand if they are arranged in the proper order, which is by no means a matter of simple chronology. The metaphor is repeated after the general pattern of the action has been established: "I have spoken of these reminiscences as of a row of coloured beads, and I confess that as I continue to straighten out my chaplet I am rather proud of the comparison." Speaking of his earlier sketching of Dawling, who is to become the guardian of Flora's illusion, the painter remarks on the man's "want of modelling," then adds, "I was really digging in that sandy desert for the buried treasure of his soul." In its context the painter's comment that he will *amuse* himself seems casual enough, but it is simply part of his understatement of his task. From his tenseness in pursuit of his subject we soon come to perceive the high seriousness with which he searches for the truth and carries on his art. He has been blessed with the gift of the beads and offered the priceless adventure of stringing them. From the seemingly trivial, whimsical, and fantastically sensational he must fashion what, if he is successful, he feels will prove beautiful and universal.

If one seeks in the short story "The Middle Years," 1893, for overt autobiography, he will find only casual and superficial resemblances to James's own history. Dencombe is a novelist, but there the outer resemblance comes to an end. Yet in everything that matters the story is the essence of spiritual autobiography. The novelist drew upon his own sensations to create Dencombe's, and the imaginary novelist speaks James's own thoughts and follows his own methods. Characteristic is a passage which might go unnoticed if one did not bring to it memory of other comments by James, both before and after 1893. Upon seeing three persons—a middle-aged woman, a younger woman, and a young man—in the distance, Dencombe at once begins to speculate on their relationship: "Where moreover was the virtue of an approved novelist if one couldn't establish a relation between such figures? the clever theory for instance that the young man was the son of the opulent matron and that the humble dependent, the daughter of a clergyman or an officer, nourished a secret passion for him." The novelist is, of course, wrong as to details, and there is, in his grouping, evidence of a conventional literary concept. When we read the notebooks, we notice that James himself likewise fitted données into conventional moulds. But there is, in Dencombe's fancied relationship, an initial validity, even as usually in the notebooks. Details will need revision and meaning must be established. Before he is finished Dencombe will be able to add more pertinent adjectives than *opulent* and *humble* without rejecting these, and for the mother-son connection he will retain the spiritual, though not the legal, image and give it a sinister meaning.

For Dencombe the search for mastery of his art has been the one great adventure. In the process of his learning he has used up life itself; but he finds himself revising his latest published novel because even now he sees, perhaps more than ever, that there is no end to the possibilities for artistic aptness, for the tapping on golden nails. He has come to an awareness of the wonderful, indeed magical, nature of his craft. Though quoted earlier, his words bear repeating: "We work in the dark—we do what we can—we give what we have. Our doubt is our passion and our passion is our task. The rest is the madness of art." When he modestly tells Dr. Hugh, "We've done something or other," the young man replies, "Something or other is everything. It's the feasible. It's *you!*"

The words of both men accord with those on Baxter twenty-five years before. But whereas James's summary of Baxter's thoughts was slightly forced, here the cadences are tense with emotion held in restraint. Twenty-five years had not changed the author's basic views, but they had imbued them with the hard-won magic of art.

The theme of Dr. Hugh's last sentence is picked up again the next year in "The Death of the Lion." The narrator, a journalist with a feeling for human privacy and an understanding of art, is rebuking a fellow journalist, who has just remarked, "There's a great interest always felt in the scene of an author's labours." The narrator's reply speaks for James himself: "The artist's life's his work, and this is the place to observe him. What he tells us he tells us with *this* perfection. My dear sir, the best interviewer's the best reader." The story pointedly indicates that, apart from his work, Neil Paraday is of little consequence. It is the adventures of his sensitive imagination that give him life.

In "The Next Time," as we have noted, James remembered his own feelings toward the New York *Tribune* in remarking, apropos of Ralph Limbert's attempt to write a popular novel, that "you can't make a sow's ear of a silk purse!" With caustic irony Limbert says to the narrator, "We've sat prating here of 'success,' heaven help us, like chanting monks in a cloister, hugging the sweet delusion that it lies somewhere in the work itself, in the expression, as you said, of one's subject or the intensification, as somebody else somewhere says, of one's note." At the time Limbert is confused as to his own purposes and is trying to write below his standard. But he believes what he implies, and before his death he becomes clear-eyed again, to leave behind him "a splendid fragment": "What had happened, I was afterwards satisfied, was that he had quite forgotten whether he generally sold or not. He had merely waked up one morning again in the country of the blue and had stayed there with a good conscience and a great idea." Whereas Dencombe suffered only the throes of uncertainty as to the mastery of his art, Limbert has gone through a tumult that has led him to apostasy and self-revulsion before he has regained his initial state of grace.

134

When we turn from the ringing phrases we have been quoting to the more subdued language with which James discoursed on the selection of subject matter or on technique, we must not be deceived. In "The Beldonald Holbein," 1901, for example, the artist-narrator wishes to appear calmly intellectual; but though he plays with his topic as if it were amusing entertainment, we recognize his—and even more, James's—total absorption in his task.

As seen by the artist, there are two actions in the story, the one completed, the other only outlined as a technical problem for the future. The first concerns Lady Beldonald's companion, the homely Mrs. Brash, whose character as revealed in her features brings her recognition in London as a "Holbein" and then exile when her envious hostess returns her to America. Speaking of Mrs. Brash's brief career, the artist states his own bias: "It was at all events for myself the most attaching; it's not my fault if I am so put together as often to find more life in situations obscure and subject to interpretation than in the gross rattle of the foreground."

The second action is introduced by the narrator as if it were hardly more than a frame for the first. It is this action, however, which has the greater technical interest. Lady Beldonald has wanted her own portrait painted. She is beautiful and vain and has been kept "safe and sound" by her vanity, as if in a "plate-glass case." The artist remarks that she "looks *naturally* new, as if she took out every night her large, lovely, varnished eyes and put them in water." Then he adds significantly, "The thing was to paint her, I perceived, *in* the glass case —a most tempting, attaching feat; render to the full the shining, interposing plate and the general show-window effect." At the end, after Mrs. Brash's banishment, Lady Beldonald again wants her portrait painted, and the artist concludes the story, "Let me settle it then at last. Since she *will* have the real thing—well, hang it, she shall!" The technical neatness of the story is, of course, in the fact that it has already given Lady Beldonald the real thing. For we have always seen her inside the glass case of illusion in which her vanity has preserved her. The case is inseparable from her; it is a part of her personality. Her defects can be enumerated, but even they have their own peculiar quality seen in the context of the case. She is universal in her generic faults, and yet she is, as the artist has called her, "sole of her kind."

The portrait of Mrs. Brash is not difficult to paint, at least not in words. Insight is needed to detect the inner beauty, and there must be an objective representation of it. But the technical problem with Lady Beldonald is subtler. The danger was of taking her out of her illusion and saying, "Here she stands, stripped of all ornaments and revealed as she really is." To paint her as she truly was required the oblique method which James used, a technique which disguises from the narrator himself the fact that his portrait is already done. Even while the narrator has been trying to see his artistic problem in its larger aspects, James has been carefully checking the intricacy of the pattern and tapping the golden nails. In this task, so subdued and unobtrusive in tone, lay his own romance of creative adventure.

III. THE POIGNANT FACE OF THE MEDAL

"No THEMES ARE SO HUMAN as those that reflect for us, out of the confusion of life, the close connection of bliss and bale, of the things that help with the things that hurt, so dangling before us for ever that bright hard medal, of so strange an alloy, one face of which is somebody's right and ease and the other somebody's pain and wrong" (Preface to *What Maisie Knew*).

James remarked, as we have noted, that we should have no stories if we were not sometimes bewildered, and he also spoke of certain of his characters as "intense perceivers" of their own "predicaments." Every one of his victims of bale is in some respect bewildered and at the same time has an awareness of his pathetic, in some instances tragic, condition. This is not to say that each can state articulately in rational form just what is awry. His recognition may, on the contrary, express itself as a cry or act of utter despair. Of the characters who recover to live in a world of partial or complete illusion or to become resigned to their destinies, all have still had first to undergo the shock of recognition.

In the earliest stories the pathos or tragedy is of a sensational nature. In the bizarre narrative "A Problem," 1868, fortunetelling and jealousy are mixed with the pathos of the death of a little girl before the tale reaches a happy ending in the remarriage of the girl's separated parents. "De Grey," also of 1868, is concerned with an evil curse, which leads, as a by-product, to the insanity of the dying hero's mother. Becoming interested briefly in the importance of suffering as an initiation into life, James remarked of Mrs. De Grey, who has never previously experienced sorrow, "She had the very best taste; but, morally, one may say that she had had no history." The history that she acquires is of little philosophic value, as it is first anxiety and then the mind-unsettling shock. In "Guest's Confession," 1872, a proud man is degraded by the narrator's vengeful stepbrother into kneeling and signing a confession. The humiliation so shames the narrator that he brings about what is purportedly a happy ending.

There is no merit in the three stories; but there is some attempt to deal with the theme of spiritual isolation. In the short stories and novels which followed, human loneliness was to become of increasing interest to James. Sometimes it is imposed by external circumstances, sometimes it is inevitable because of deep human longing, and it may stem from repentance. Those who are simple pathetic victims are most commonly women. In *Roderick Hudson*, Christina Light is a bad influence on Roderick, but she herself is helplessly subjected to the machinations of her unscrupulous mother. As James later admitted, he slighted her portrait, and so he brought her back in *The Princess Casamassima*; but he had managed to give a short, somewhat casual sketch of a girl whose very whimsicality and apparent heartlessness are only expressions of her blind rebellion amid conditions of moral chaos.

The pathos of Daisy Miller stems from her rebuffs in an alien world, but most of all from her rejection by the tradition-bound Winterbourne. In her shy way, despite her noisy manner, she has virtually declared her love for him, only to be misunderstood. A variant which never reaches the intensity of Daisy's humiliation is provided in Blanche Evers, of *Confidence*, 1879, in which a happy ending is contrived. Blanche, even more than Daisy, appears to be a flirt, and it is only at the end that she is revealed to be desperately in love with her husband. Lacking the quality of intellect to live with dignity and self-assurance, she has played the only game she knows in her gamble to win some kind of expression of her husband's concern. James's concept of Blanche's prob-

137

lem was valid, though the representation was slight and sentimental.

In the portrayal of Catherine Sloper, in *Washington Square*, the pathos is emphasized to a point of painfulness. James did not stop with an indication that Catherine was estranged from her father; he gave repeated examples of Dr. Sloper's sadistic treatment of her. Since Catherine offers no overt resistance—her one attempt to escape is not open rebellion—she is helplessly pathetic. She has even told her supposed lover that she is "ugly and stupid," thus accepting her father's oft-repeated verdict. She goes so far as to beg Townsend for affection, and when he rejects her, she is doubly humiliated. That Townsend should return years later and unsuccessfully ask her to marry him permits an ironic ending, but it also refreshes bitter memories. Catherine has not sacrificed her love through any noble feeling of resignation; she has simply absorbed all the cruelty that has been meted out to her. In the last scene, as she picks up her "fancy work" and seats herself again "for life as it were," she has a dignity of manner which she lacked before, but her outward poise cannot disguise the fact that she is eternally alone.

The subject of rejection of a woman's love or trust continued to interest James. In "The Solution," Veronica is an innocent victim. In "The Visits," 1892, the young heroine dies of shame for having impulsively and uninvitedly revealed her love for a young man. "The Wheel of Time," 1892, is twice concerned with the pathos of rejection. The tall, ugly Fanny survives the flight of Maurice and becomes a beautiful woman. When her son, however, similarly flees to avoid an engagement to Maurice's unattractive daughter, the girl soon dies. Public humiliation provides the pathos in "The Two Faces," 1900, in which the jilted Mrs. Grantham gets her revenge on Lord Gwyther by tricking his ingenuous wife into wearing outlandish attire for her social debut. One must accept the fact that the young wife will be "lost." The anecdote then justifies the choral pronouncement that it is "Exquisite. . . . For unimaginable pathos."

One of the most poignant of James's short stories is the ingenious and ironic "The Velvet Glove," 1909. The heroine, a young and beautiful princess, is living in the midst of what is commonly called romance. Indeed, the novelist whose help she seeks tells her, "You *are* Romance."

He would like to think of her as a goddess; but she is also, alas, the woman who, as Amy Evans, writes trite, sentimental, pseudoromantic stories, and who, after trying a princess' flattery, kisses his hand and begs him for a favorable review of her—that is, Amy's—latest book. Her abject, unscrupulous conduct is "disconcerting, deplorable, dreadful," and he confesses his shock: "Princess, I adore you. But I'm ashamed for you." When the woman complains that she does not understand his calling her Romance, he tries to explain to her that she does not need to: "Don't attempt such base things. Leave those to us. Only live. Only be. We'll do the rest." Repeating that she is Romance, he kisses her emphatically and walks away. But the kiss has not achieved its intent. It has not banished Amy and left only the princess: ". . . he had no further sound from her than if, all divinely indulgent but all humanly defeated, she had given up, falling back to infinite wonder." We, too, are left with wonder. The divine princess is deficient in understanding, and so, though she uses her rank and beauty in the cause of Amy Evans, she cannot see the romance in her position. What makes the woman truly romantic is really not her position as princess, but her pathetic illusion as Amy. Amy is naïve and mawkish, but she can suffer, and the measure of her suffering is the abject sacrifice made for her by the princess-goddess.

There are certain Jamesian characters whose careers might be described as exile from bliss. We have spoken of Mrs. Brash, who, after her short Indian summer of fame, is sent back to oblivion. Brooksmith, the butler, is perhaps the best known of the exiles. His spiritual descent is symbolized by his literal one upon the death of Mr. Offord. Like the women we have been studying, Brooksmith is not self-sufficient; he must find inspiration from another, and when the source is gone, he can only lament "the loss of something that was everything": "I go back to my place . . . . I just go downstairs, sir, again, and I stay there." It is the contrast that hurts; he has "seen the fireworks" of conversation. That he endures for three years does not mean that he is resigned, for finally despair triumphs in his suicide. Each of the other stories has universal implications, and "Brooksmith" unmistakably shows the fragile hold on bliss of the imaginative person in a world in general hostile to the imagination.

139

The hero of "The Bench of Desolation," 1909, does live to receive compassion, but with a sense that much of his life has been wasted. The singular plot is not wholly convincing. Kate Cookham has sued Herbert Dodd for breach of promise because she thought she could manage his money better than he. Now that his wife and child are dead, after a frugal life, and after he has given up his bookstore, Kate returns to assure him of her love and to bestow money upon him. She seems like another person now, and there is a wistful gratitude mingled with Herbert's sorrow. Kate has suffered for him, and as they sit on the bench together, he realizes that "this unextinguished and apparently inextinguishable charm by which he had held her was a fact incredibly romantic . . . ." If we accept the oddity of Kate's motivation, we have, at the end, affinity in sadness. But it is not ordinary sadness; it is desolation. Herbert does not blame Kate, but there is the dreary desert of a past that cannot now be replaced.

In 1910 James made a startling excursion into the moral isolation that springs from guilt. Newton Winch, of "A Round of Visits," has been responsible for the loss of money entrusted to him; and, though the nature of his mismanagement is not stated, he has recognized and lived with a sense of his wrongdoing. When his visitor reveals that he is the victim of embezzlement and that he pities his betrayer, Winch admits his own misconduct, but adds that he has not fled. Winch, who was once coarse and unpolished, has become refined and distinguished looking; we are to conclude that his reflections upon his actions have improved him. How intense his suffering has been is indicated by the fact that he has a revolver at hand and, after hearing how a victim has responded to betrayal and learning that a bailiff is at the door, kills himself.

The short stories we have been reviewing are rather more anecdotes than pictures, and some of them are melodramatic. James's most significant venture into simple pathos unsustained by resignation was *The Princess Casamassima*, 1885.

The novel covers a large canvas and catches the atmosphere of a torn civilization at war with itself. It does this, however, not by showing social forces in mass actions, but through the study of individuals. The story is primarily of Hyacinth Robinson as a single, spiritually isolated man and, to a somewhat less degree, of Christina Light, now the Princess Casamassima, as an equally lonely woman. There are other isolated characters, too. There is Lady Aurora, who works as a visionary benefactress because she has no true occupation in her own social rank; and there is Mr. Vetch, "a lonely, disappointed, embittered, cynical little man, . . . who had the nerves and sensibilities of a gentleman, yet whose fate had condemned him for the last ten years to play a fiddle at a second-rate establishment for a few shillings a week." The novel brings the various characters together in ways which reveal how far they are really apart. They cannot share their fears with one another or be sincere when trying to work together. Even the somewhat vulgar Millicent is pitiable as she tries to improve her wretched lot and to find honest friendship. She, too, has her secrets, her defensive hypocrisy, and a bewilderment that makes her impulsively kind or cruel. The beginning of the action takes us to a prison where a dying murderess yearns vainly for affection.

Sprung, as James says, from the London pavements, Hyacinth must try to work out a destiny in the strange wilderness about him. He is specially isolated from the others, no matter how compassionate Mr. Vetch, his foster-mother, Miss Pynsent, or, upon occasion, Millicent or the princess may be to him. His father, an English nobleman, was killed by Hyacinth's mother, a French prostitute, whose father had fallen on a French barricade. Hyacinth cannot escape from his heritage. By environment he is immersed in the hardships and penury of the life known by his mother, and by imagination and temperament he is attuned to appreciation of the world of culture symbolized by his father. As the gruff Mr. Vetch describes him, he is "a thin-skinned, morbid, mooning, introspective little beggar, with a good deal of imagination and not much perseverance, who'll expect a good deal more of life than he'll find in it. That's why he won't be happy." Mr Vetch's adjectives are too severe, but James wanted to emphasize the fragile, wistful, and melancholy nature of Hyacinth.

In time, Hyacinth is able to formulate his feelings toward the father whom he never knew and to regard himself "immutably as the son of the recreant and sacrificed Lord Frederick." His home life and associates, however, draw him toward sympathy with the concept of revolution, though he is no political theorist, and to eventual involvement in conspiracy. It is his heart that leads him to trust even unknown conspirators, for somehow he must do right by his mother's memory and fight against the squalor and frustration which he sees enveloping the lives of sensitive persons around him. A visit, however, at the home of the princess brings before him concretely what he imagines to have been the world of his father. There is beauty and grace in it, and, above all, a romantic strangeness. The princess states his case to him succinctly: "Fancy the strange, the bitter fate: to be constituted as you're constituted, to be conscious of the capacity you must feel, and yet to look at the good things of life only through the glass of the pastry-cook's window!" Returning home, he finds the familiar scene, formerly "hideous and sordid," is now "pitiful to the verge of the sickening." A visit to Paris and Venice gives him an awareness of the cultural traditions preserved by the aristocracy. He admits that civilization may be based on "the despotisms, the cruelties, the exclusions, the monopolies and the rapacities of the past," but he values what the revolutionaries slight —"things with which the yearnings and tears of generations have been mixed."

Meanwhile the reflections of the cynical yet kindly Mr. Vetch have provided a choral commentary on life: "The figures on the chessboard were still the passions and jealousies and superstitions and stupidities of men, and their position with regard to each other at any given moment could be of interest only to the grim invisible fates who played the game—who sat, through the ages, bow-backed over the table." Mr. Vetch's view does not express James's own metaphysics, but it does warn us that the struggling Hyacinth, who hopes somehow to conquer his destiny, has his place on the chessboard of fate. When the conflict returns to Hyacinth's mind we are told, "There was no peace for him between the two currents that flowed in his nature, the blood of his passionate plebeian mother and that of his long-descended supercivilised sire." As his involvement in the conspiracy deepens, he is engulfed in loneliness: "The darkness had become a haunted element; it had visions for him that passed even before his closed eyes—sharp doubts and fears and suspicions, suggestions of evil, revelations of pain."

Under command from the conspirators to commit an assassination,

142

he believes mistakenly that the princess is "done with him for ever," and he sees Millicent's back turned toward him as she talks to a rival. His suicide, which replaces the planned murder, is not a reasoned, philosophic act. There is no profound, sacrificial renunciation. Hyacinth's problem has been insoluble from the beginning. Moreover, the very qualities which have made him appreciate the excellence of life have doomed him to a tragic awareness of its horror. The paradox, of course, is that from the portrait of his melancholy and even his anguish there emerges a wistful beauty—reminiscent of that of a lad's face as he looks through the pastry-cook's window.

The Christina of *The Princess Casamassima* can be interpreted without reference to *Roderick Hudson;* but since the portrait is consistent with that of Christina Light, one recalls the sordid humiliations which led to the girl's marrying a proud but fatuous prince and to her inner rebellion against her fate. Now separated from her husband, she is trying, in desperation, to be a fairy queen, whose magical wand will somehow win for her respect and perhaps love. She is seeking for her identity in a world which she cannot understand. Unable to enjoy her riches, she tries to live as if she were poor; but she has sensibilities which only wealth will satisfy. As her companion, Madame Grandoni, tells the prince, Christina "must try everything; at present she's trying democracy, she's going all lengths in radicalism." She reminds him that Christina "considers that in the darkest hour of her life she sold herself for a title and a fortune. She regards her doing so as such a horrible piece of frivolity that she can't for the rest of her days be serious enough to make up for it." When Hyacinth escorts the princess to the slums, where she gives largesse, he sees that "her behaviour, after all, was more addressed to relieving herself than to relieving others," and he perceives the futility of her efforts in the midst of the "brutal insensibility."

Toward Hyacinth, Christina's manner seems capricious; and, having endured torment from doubt of her love, he gives up, as we have seen, in despair. But it eventually becomes clear that Christina's apparent whimsicality is only the measure of her fears and sense of isolation. Hyacinth appeals to her at first solely because his poverty and sensibility seem to give her a chance to win his affection. As she discusses serious matters with him—and she does know something about political and social theory, despite her ingenuous illusions as to a panacea—she feels herself important as an individual rather than as a princess; but she still has had no opportunity to share with him what lies deepest in her heart. She simply does not know whether he loves her or even whether her own love for him is not an illusion. But when he is dead she needs no longer to conceal her feelings; she "flung herself, beside the bed, upon her knees."

Theirs has been a strange love affair, if one thinks of the specific nature of the events. Yet the impelling forces are not greatly different from those in "The Altar of the Dead," *The Golden Bowl,* or other Jamesian love stories both before and after 1885. Each of the two has made shy and tremulous attempts to tell the other secrets which he himself does not quite understand, and each has watched anxiously for a hint of sympathy. Circumstantial evidence has led to doubts, even jealousy; and rebuffs, real or fancied, have been magnified into major affronts. In his gravest hour Hyacinth has succumbed to apostasy and consequent despair. Yet between these two who have been wandering in search of a world which they can call home, there has been an exceptional affinity of spirit. They have known the bale of life; but, despite all the forces of disintegration at work upon and within them, they have had moments of fragile beauty, intimations of a strange, hidden sweetness in the midst of the chaos and night.

For most people life does go on after crises, and James was interested in the moral and psychological aspects of the acceptance of one's fate. Some characters, notably Maggie Verver, survive the shock of disillusionment to pursue triumphantly their search for an ideal happiness. With others a semblance of the ideal is preserved only as an illusion wilfully maintained. For most the shock leads to poignant resignation.

Of a search for refuge in illusion the two most striking examples are in "Four Meetings," 1877, and "Glasses," 1896. For Caroline Spencer, Europe symbolizes romance; though we may find Caroline herself intensely romantic, she lives in the dream of her ideal. If Le Havre will not provide it—if the France which she has wanted to visit really has

144

no existence outside her mind—she will still not yield. James indicates in his initial characterization that though her eyes are "too inveterately surprised," yet her lips have "a certain mild decision." At the end, her eyes can no longer be surprised, for they have seen the truth; instead they must be closed tightly to the manners of Caroline's French guest. To send the woman packing would be to admit defeat, and so, even against the most glaring evidence, the illusion still prevails. In "Glasses," Flora would be lost if she had not the precarious comfort of her illusion. As she visualizes herself, she has no charm apart from the remarkable beauty of her face, and she cannot give up her one distinction by wearing hideous glasses. When she tries to make the sacrifice, the humiliation is too great. Only when she has become blind is she free of conflict. She knows that she is beautiful as she sits in her box gracefully holding her opera glasses to her eyes. With both Caroline and Flora we must accept their own visions of their lives. Their choice is not between self-deception and sensible recognition of reality; it is between an ordered existence, which they manage to preserve, and despair.

The shadow line between illusion and resignation is not to be precisely defined. The puritan Caroline has a sense of right conduct, which helps her through the shock of recognition and makes the illusion possible. So, too, have those who find no escape from reality. Sometimes their concept is consciously ethical; sometimes it is an ideal image of themselves acting with self-respect in adversity.

The young puritan American who marries a French philanderer in *Madame de Mauves,* 1874, is somewhat priggishly moral; at one time she tells her American admirer that she has "nothing but a dogged obstinate clinging conscience." But she also has a firm concept of herself as a lady. She has wished for marriage into the nobility because she has expected to find there "an ideal delicacy of feeling." After she has experienced disillusionment, she is still determined to avoid unpleasantness: "I hate tragedy . . . I'm a dreadful coward about having to suffer or to bleed. I've always tried to believe that—without base concessions—such extremities may always somehow be dodged or indefinitely postponed."

Unpleasantnesses cannot be wholly avoided; but understanding can accept them. When Longmore later reminds her of her "loneliness," [3] she replies that she has been introduced to "people and things which seemed to me at first very strange and then very horrible, and then, to tell the truth, of very little importance." Because, after her wayward husband falls in love with her, "she was stone, she was ice, she was outraged virtue," poor Madame de Mauves has been accused of being a wicked, unforgiving absolutist. Longmore, however, who serves as a chorus, is less severe. He remembers her with "ardent tenderness," with which is mingled, to be sure, "a feeling of wonder, of uncertainty, of awe." Madame de Mauves is not an Isabel Archer, but in her acceptance of disillusionment she anticipates her.

The portrait of Madame de Cintré, in *The American*, is presented too much from without for more than commonplace speculation as to her feelings as she carries out her pledge of obedience by entering the convent. The resignation which comes to Newman and causes him to give up his desire for revenge is somewhat more concretely represented, though it is mainly a subconscious transformation. Although James started his novel with the question of what Newman would do, he drew only a brief and general picture of his mental crisis and its resolution. Newman finds comfort by gazing at the convent walls and then resting in Notre Dame: "He thought of the Bellegardes; he had almost forgotten them. . . . the bottom suddenly had fallen out of his revenge. Whether it was Christian charity or mere human weakness of will— what it was, in the background of his spirit—I don't pretend to say; but Newman's last thought was that of course he would let the Bellegardes go." Because we feel that, for the emotional resolution of the story, Newman must renounce vengeance, we accept James's scanting of the mental process itself. Similarly, we accept what follows. Newman leaves the church "not with the elastic step of a man who has won a victory or taken a resolve—rather to the quiet measure of a discreet escape, of a retreat with appearances preserved." James appears to be saying that he sees his proper role as that of a gentleman quietly resigned in manner. He has come dangerously near to destroying the image, but the concept itself has rescued him.

Resignation culminates the destinies of a great many Jamesian char-

[3] The first version reads "moral isolation."

acters. Perhaps the most distinctive examples are in *The Portrait of a Lady, The Spoils of Poynton,* and *The Awkward Age.*[4]

Isabel Archer is not without precursors in James's fiction. Miss Blunt, as we have noted, was reserved and proud and, of course, intelligent; and in summing up her qualities James used the exact words of his later title. Like the other American girls in James's works, Isabel is determined to maintain her liberty. Like them, she has a romantic idealization of Europe, and like some of them, she is a reader of literature. What we find in her portrait that gives it special significance is the patient care in the delineation of each feature. In *The Portrait of a Lady* there are a few awkward touches—an occasional self-conscious device in narration, resort two or three times to forced descriptions of Isabel's feelings, and a woodenness in some characterizations. But the reader, nevertheless, comes to feel that he has entered Isabel's mind and that he can appreciate her conflict and its resolution.

Isabel has lived much in her imagination, shaping her image of the world from her reading; she has even preferred to keep a door closed in order to imagine what lies beyond, and Henrietta Stackpole warns her that she lives "too much in the world of your own dreams." Isabel's life has been free of sorrow and unpleasantness. Indeed, she tells Ralph Touchett that "It's not absolutely necessary to suffer; we were not made for that." By her sensibility and her reading she is inclined toward a love of the past and a gentle, pensive appreciation of sadness removed from the immediate present. But she also possesses a wilful illusion that life should be recklessly daring. When asked by Henrietta whether she knows where she is "drifting," she replies, "No, I haven't the least idea, and I find it very pleasant not to know. A swift carriage, of a dark night, rattling with four horses over roads that one can't see— that's my idea of happiness."

It is Isabel's own choices that introduce her unwittingly to sorrow and curtail the range in which choices can thereafter be made. Her decision to marry Osmond, she perceives, has brought sadness for Ralph, and her thoughts anticipate James's comment on the bliss and the bale: "It was the tragic part of happiness; one's right was always made of the wrong of some one else." From this time onward her

[4] *Julia Bride,* 1908, provides a variant of the motif in the story of Nanda Brookenham.

experience in suffering widens rapidly; and though she has erred through ignorance, she insists on enduring the consequences. All sorts of choices have now been closed to her, but she holds to her freedom to choose. As she tells Henrietta, "one must accept one's deeds. . . . I was perfectly free [to marry or not marry Osmond]." She adds what has been implicit in her conduct: "It's not of him that I'm considerate—it's of myself!" Even after she has suffered humiliation and disillusionment she is still determined to seek no escape from responsibility; and though she cannot believe that it will be her fate to experience only suffering, she is resigned. That the price she pays is heavy is revealed in the last scenes. She must admit her love for the dying Ralph, and the admission reveals the bleak contrast between his world and her present married life. When kissed by the still-faithful Goodwood, she seems for a moment to float "in fathomless waters" before she regains mastery of herself and flees.

James remarks that she is "not a daughter of the Puritans." But in describing her independence in adversity, he writes, "The old Protestant tradition had never faded from Isabel's imagination . . . ." In her zest for a full, even perilous adventure, Isabel is indeed not puritan, and though she has not found much cultural nourishment in Europe, she has avidly learned what she could of the Hellenic aspect of life. Her conduct springs, not from reasoning about moral questions, but from her concept of herself as a lady. In telling Henrietta that she is thinking of herself rather than of Osmond she is stating the principle of her very being. Her concept owes something to the Protestant, perhaps even to the Puritan, tradition; and yet Isabel is a romantic, and the portrait of herself which she keeps before her is a romantic ideal. Her final choice—to return to Osmond and to Pansy, who needs her— is a free one. Yet the alternative is not really a life of comparative happiness with Goodwood, but the smashing of her ideal portrait of herself.

The characters in *The Spoils of Poynton* represent the gamut from exquisite sensitivity and feeling for others, in Fleda Vetch, to a virtual absence of sensibility in Mona Brigstock and her mother. Mrs. Gereth, Fleda's friend, who wants her for a daughter-in-law, is appreciative to the extent that she loves the spoils, that is, the furniture, for their beauty and associations. As for Owen Gereth, who is partly an actor in the conflict, partly akin to the spoils—he is good-humored, and he does not want to hurt anyone. He is also unimaginative, carelessly cruel, irresponsible, and even cowardly. Engaged to Mona, he begs Fleda for admission of her love, and he naïvely tells her how he has defended her against Mona's harsh charges. He cannot take responsibility for his actions and so puts his burdens on Fleda.

That Fleda should nonetheless love Owen—as Mary loves Roderick Hudson and Madame de Vionnet is to love the irresponsible Chad Newsome—may be unwise, but it makes her love the more bountiful. When he is weak, she is strong; when he drifts, she manages by desperate effort to be steadfast; when he suffers dumbly from frustration, she suffers for him. In her idealism she reminds one of Juliet. Her case is the more difficult in that she feels a duty both to Mrs. Gereth and to Owen during their quarrel over the spoils, and knowing Mona for what she is, she must still defend the stolid girl's rights when Owen forgets them. Mainly she speaks the factual truth, but she plays an intricate game with white lies when only they will serve. For Fleda sees things in context, and in her imagination she lives so intensively the lives which she attributes to the others that she is always concerned with what her words will do to preserve or shatter those lives. That she is much too generous in her reading of motives is irrelevant. She lives in a world of high, chivalric adventure because she makes it so.

When she recognizes a limitation of the actual Owen, Fleda turns it into something charming. At the beginning she pictures him as "absolutely beautiful and delightfully dense." When he has stupidly entrapped himself and cannot see the consequences, she blames circumstances: "She could easily see how wrong everything must be when a man so made to be manly was wanting in courage." She tries to put upon herself the responsibility for insuring his acting with honor toward Mona: "She couldn't in short do anything at all unless she could do it with a degree of pride, and there would be nothing to be proud of in having arranged for poor Owen to get off easily." Torn by her love for him, which has tempted her to let Mona be defeated, she is in need of moral support, and she makes Owen into a model and an inspiration: "Owen had grown larger to her: he would do, like a man, whatever he should have to do. He wouldn't be weak—not as she was: she herself was weak exceedingly." When he kisses her she has "not a shred of a secret left; it was as if a whirlwind had come and gone, laying low the great false front she had built up stone by stone." The kiss is an unpardonable theft, as it robs Fleda of her secret and offers nothing in return. Soon again, however, she turns Owen's deficiency into a claim upon her: "The very vision of him as he thus morally clung to her was the vision of a weakness somewhere at the core of his bloom, a blessed manly weakness which, had she only the valid right, it would be all easy and sweet to take care of." Having regained self-control, she has to remind Owen that he is not free and that he must "keep faith." Later she tries to praise him to Mrs. Gereth: "He's ever so much cleverer than he makes any show of . . . ." Again she remarks, "It's because he's weak that he needs me." When news comes of his marriage to Mona, she joins Mrs. Gereth in weeping.

Fleda's life has been an alternation of romantic idealization and resignation. At times she has managed to forget the certainty of her own loss when most active in bringing it about; but having made her relation with Owen the one absorbing adventure of her life, she now has nothing left. When she seems about to find sorrowful comfort by visiting Poynton, where the spoils are and where she can at least revive memories of a time now vanished, she arrives at the station only to see the house disappear in flames. A short time before, she has felt a kinship with a woman now dead, and she has wondered whether the dead woman perhaps suffered "a great accepted pain." As she turns away after her new shock, "mixed with the horror [of the fire], with the kindness of the station-master, with the smell of cinders and the riot of sound was the raw bitterness of a hope that she might never again in life have to give up so much at such short notice." Her farewell reflection is the resignation, not of a person easily comforted, but of a woman whose genius of imagination has made her especially susceptible to suffering, and who sees the world she has tried to hold together reduced, like the house itself, to cinders. Hers is, indeed, a great accepted pain.

From one perspective *The Awkward Age* might be called "What Nanda Knew," for it is concerned with Nanda Brookenham's initiation into self-knowledge. The conversation in Mrs. Brookenham's drawing room is considered by the participants to be unsuitable for a girl's ears; it consists mainly of gossip about intrigue and adultery. French novels are also regarded as inappropriate reading for a young unmarried woman. Nanda does not take an active part in the scandalmongering; instead, she becomes acquainted at first hand with a young married woman who is one of its subjects. And she not only reads French novels, but decides whether one of them is appropriate for her married friend. She also smokes, and she visits a young man's rooms. Knowing these facts about Nanda, we are not permitted to declare her innocent, however broad our tolerance. What matters is, not what we think of her conduct, but how she herself judges it; and when her initiation is complete, she suffers penitence.

For the impatient reader *The Awkward Age* may well seem one of the most "precious" of James's novels, being outranked in this respect perhaps only by *The Sacred Fount*. There is much speculative talk as characters engage in a guessing game concerning the relationships of others; and particularly there is talk about the position of Nanda in relation to Vanderbank, whom she loves, the elderly Mr. Longdon, who loves her, and her mother, who is her rival. Moreover, the discussions are oblique and at times obscure, for the speakers are guarded, having their own motives which they are loath to disclose. Eventually, however, we can establish certain impressions, all pertinent to our understanding of Nanda. Mrs. Brookenham is pretty and clever; and young men, including Vanderbank, admire her. There is a seamy side to Brookenham life, because money is scarce and Mrs. Brook has to make the best she can of her son's borrowing from friends. She has also to gamble on her own cleverness, sometimes lying, sometimes imposing on the sportsmanship of others. Wanting financial security for Nanda, she convinces Mr. Longdon by her own shocking conduct that he must rescue the girl from her influence; and wanting Vanderbank for herself she lies to him about Nanda.

Animating the conversation in the Brookenham circle is an unadmitted cynicism, at times a tawdry egoism. In this milieu Vanderbank plays an inconsistent role. He has refinement of taste and is an attractive person. But if he finds the drawing room an unsatisfactory place for Nanda, he has helped to make it unfit; if Nanda is not sufficiently

151

inexperienced to become his wife, he himself is to blame. It is only the old-fashioned Mr. Longdon, who once loved Nanda's grandmother, who is willing to accept this very modern girl, and even he regrets her education.

In commenting on the novel James stressed the fact that its subject matter was the relationship of each of the characters to all the others. In respect to Nanda this relationship is not at all simple. In part she sees the others as they are, but she is too generous in judging them. She herself wants to be independent, yet eventually she looks at herself through the eyes of others, particularly of an idealized Vanderbank. Her words must be taken in context, and even then they are sometimes ambiguous. The reader has to fall back on his over-all impression of Nanda for their meaning.

Early in the story the girl begins to sense danger in the part she is playing, a part for which she is little responsible. To the agreeable but boyish Mitchett she remarks, "Don't 'adore' a girl, Mr. Mitchy—just help her," and she adds, though without bitterness, that her mother is "throwing" her "into the world." The chasm between her and Vanderbank is revealed by the latter's comment to Mr. Longdon that Nanda's face is that of a Lawrence, even of a Raphael, and that she should be "a reader of Mrs. Radcliffe." Trying to discuss the modern girl with Van, Nanda explains, "Girls understand now." Her perception of the futility of her attempt amounts to a "strange grave calm consciousness of their common doom and of what in especial in it would be worst for herself." Her self-revulsion has already begun. She has previously called the sheltered Aggie "the real thing"; and now, after commenting to Mitchett that Aggie "knows nothing," she continues, "Ah, say what you will—it *is* the way we ought to be!" The fact that upon marriage Aggie will ignorantly blossom into a silly flirt is irrelevant; Nanda is now thoroughly unhappy about her own life. To her willing listener she confesses, ". . . but my situation, my exposure—all the results of them I show. Doesn't one become a sort of a little drain-pipe with everything flowing through?" In answer to a question from Mitchett she admits that she can love only someone who disapproves of her.

Having condemned herself, Nanda determinedly carries out the role of a lady by disguising from Van her own tragic feelings. She pretends to be only a good friend and urges him not to desert her mother, of whom she speaks with an air of assumed maturity: "When I think of her downstairs there so often nowadays practically alone I feel as if I could scarcely bear it. She's so fearfully young." But alone with Mr. Longdon, she confesses that when one "wants to take the most" from things "I suppose one must rather grovel." After attempting to lie to him that she does not love Van, she breaks into weeping and blames herself for being what Van thinks she is. With praise rather than complaint she adds that Van is "more old-fashioned" than Mr. Longdon. She will now go to live with the latter because she has no one else to whom to turn. Having acknowledged her sin, she is resigned to the consequence.

James called his story *The Awkward Age* because, though precocious in her understanding of some things, Nanda is still a girl, not a strong, independent soul who can go her way confident of her ethical purity. She has erred from her own concept of a young lady's behavior, and she has accepted Van's judgment upon her; indeed, she has magnified its severity. Being at the awkward age, she is dependent upon the opinions of others, and above all of the man she has idealized. That she is, of course, far more wonderful than the maiden from Raphael who should read Mrs. Radcliffe surpasses the actual Van's capacity for understanding; for, honorable as he is, and sensitive as he may be in some matters of taste, he is not among the emancipated. He will not greatly suffer. In contrast, it is the genius of her imagination that has made Nanda intensely romantic and, in her ultimate resignation, worthy of compassion.

CHAPTER FOUR

THE ULTIMATE THEME:
THE QUEST FOR REALITY

THE REALITY which interested James was the mystery of human thought and of human passion. In the quest for intimations of that reality the imaginative impression was, for him, the beginning and end. In the letters, the notebooks, and even the most subtly artistic of his fiction, he of course used conventional tools of logical thought. But these were for him only the guide marks. To talk abstractly about strangeness, about mystery, was not necessarily to experience it; indeed, it might be to deny it by treating it as something familiar and definable. To invent a plot intended to demonstrate that life was unpredictable, even unfathomable, might be only to give a thin, allegorical veil for the all-too-obvious concept. This James did in some of his notebook jottings, and at times he went only uncertainly beyond it in the fiction, especially of the early years. But the world of the imagination is not an abstraction, and the figures that move about within it, even when most shadowy, have a concrete fullness which words can merely suggest. It was that world which James explored and of which he tried to give his impressions.

The "overtreatment" to which James submitted his subjects during the later years was his means of trying to apprehend them in their complete natures. Their mystery must be felt, not asserted, and, for James, the sensation of it was rarely a sudden thing. If the conscious recognition, when it came, was swift, it sprang from one's immersion in a slowly developed imaginative experience. The difference between slight development and overtreatment in the search for intimations of reality is illustrated by the first and the last stories with which we shall now be concerned—"The Story of a Masterpiece," 1868, and "The Jolly Corner," 1908. It is not to be concluded that there is a uniform progression, but only one of our significant examples precedes 1890, and it is of 1888. It was particularly in the 1890's and 1900's that James was inquiring into the human mystery.

In the wide range of James's perspectives there are a few with which he was most preoccupied. They are not fully separable; indeed, the first we shall consider looks out upon an expanse visible from the others. But distinctions can be made among them as to emphasis and profundity.

I. THE STRANGENESS OF HUMAN HEARTS

MANY A JAMESIAN NOVEL ends in a revelation of a character's essential motives and feelings. The originality consists in the degree to which the portrait is individualized and intensified within the generic type. The revelation does not provide full identification, but it limits acutely the range of speculation. James was also interested, however, in a different kind of resolution, which, far from assuring the reader as to a character's identity, left him more than ever wondering. Not wondering aimlessly, of course; on the contrary, speculating on some essential aspect of life. The reader must believe that the paradoxes which are presented are not implausible psychologically. The interest, however, is not in the unfolding of a case history, but in the philosophic contemplation of human passions.

In "The Story of a Masterpiece," the focal question is: Who is Marian Everett? For the embittered painter, as we have noted, she is a coquette; for her fiancé she is an imperfect yet sincere woman, who will make a faithful wife. The motif of ambiguity was sound, but James was wanting in insight and technical skill. He reported that Marian appeared to be a coquette, yet he went "behind" her to give her qualities not compatible with coquetry. The resultant portrait is more inconsistent than intriguing.

Eleven years later, in "The Diary of a Man of Fifty," the novelist had a better understanding of his technical problem, though his story was thinly anecdotal. The diarist was once in love with the Countess Salvi, who considered her dead husband a brute and was accepting the attentions of the man who had killed him in a duel. She also welcomed the allegiance of the diarist, who, however, annoyed with her

apparent coquetry, quarreled with her; afterward she married the duel-
ist. Years later he sees her widowed daughter, whose conduct amazingly resembles that of her now dead mother, and he feels obliged to
warn her unsuspecting lover. The lover marries her regardless, is most
happy with her, and suggests that, since she is like her mother, the
latter must have been as good as she. The bewildered diarist is left
with the melancholy reflection, "If I marred her happiness, I certainly
didn't make my own. And I might have made it—eh? That's a charming
discovery for a man of my age!"

In "The Impressions of a Cousin," 1883, we are confronted with the
unanswered question: Why does Eunice love Mr. Caliph, who has mis-
managed her money, rather than his gallant half-brother, who has presumably provided the funds to pay her back? Eunice's cousin remarks
for James, "If the passions of men are strange, the passions of women
are stranger still! It was sweeter for her to suffer at Mr. Caliph's hands
than to receive her simple dues from them." As to why it was sweeter
we have to supply our own guesses about an apparently romantic
young woman.

As we have seen, in "Sir Edmund Orme," 1891, part of the interest
lies in whether Charlotte actually sees Orme's ghost, which she would
behold only if she were guilty of "some breach of faith or some heartless act." She does not do anything heartless, and the narrator, who
marries her, refrains from inquiring into her thoughts. Her cry of surprise and fright may or may not have been inspired by sight of the
ghost. In "The Private Life," 1892, the allegorical statement is explicit
—that one man has no existence except in the presence of others and
that another has a private creative spirit at work even while he is
engaged in commonplace conversation. There is, however, just enough
of a ghostly atmosphere—with the writer discovered working in a darkened room when he is unmistakably elsewhere—to suggest the uncanny
nature of the mind. "The Tone of Time," 1900, with its female rivalry
over a dead man, involves the strange association of love and hate.
Though Mary Tredick, working from memory, has painted the man's
portrait in hatred—"I shall make him supremely beautiful—and supremely base"—upon finding that the purchaser is a one-time rival, she
keeps it in "joy." Again there is something strange, something more

than ordinary jealousy would account for. And, as we have seen, in one of his latest works, "The Velvet Glove," James retained an aura of strangeness in the portrait of the romantic princess who shares the fate of the pathetic authoress of trashy romances.

The most illuminating exploration of the enigmatic nature of the human soul is in "Louisa Pallant," 1888, a story concerned exclusively with the mulling over of evidence in the search for certainty about human motives, a certainty which the narrator can never achieve. The story is an *amusette* of the most careful craftsmanship, in that every incident involving Louisa, her daughter Linda, and the narrator's nephew Archie is capable of two or more interpretations. If its tone is amusing, however, its overtones have philosophic implication. The narrator is given "authority," to use again James's remark about his governess of "The Turn of the Screw." That is to say, he is absolutely reliable in recording what he heard and saw. As to his attempts at interpretation, only his first sentence is incontrovertible, and, though introducing the story, it actually concludes it: "Never say you know the last word about any human heart!"

We do know that many years earlier Louisa jilted the narrator, and we now see her in action and hear her words. In an almost hysterical manner she protests her repentance, holds herself responsible for her daughter's being a heartless creature, says she is doing penance through the anguish Linda causes her, and insists that she must save Archie from her; indeed, she reports eventually that she has disclosed to Archie the monstrous nature of the girl. To quote typical remarks—"You make my reparation—my expiation—difficult! . . . She's ambitious, luxurious, determined to have what she wants . . . . My only child's my punishment, my only child's my stigma. . . . I'm horrified at my work. . . . I just pity her for what I've made of her." Louisa intimates that she is aware that when she speaks truth she will not be believed: "How can anyone *tell* . . . with people like us."

We know that Linda always appears obedient and gentle, that the words she uses seem naïvely genuine, and that she writes a modest, simple note to Archie. At the same time, the narrator has evidence that Louisa and Linda understand each other without the need for words, and Linda seems to him early—before he has had reason to be prejudiced—to be "a felicitous *final* product—after the fashion of some plant or some fruit, some waxen orchid or some perfect peach." She is accomplished in music, German, and French, and her manners connote studied refinement. In the light of Louisa's condemnation she may be, indeed, a waxen orchid, whose sweet, obedient deportment is but an ironic expression of implacable hatred for Louisa and cunning design toward Archie. It is also possible, however, that Linda later marries a rich Englishman only because she believes that Archie has deserted her, or because her mother has wanted her to. It is even possible that she is designedly obedient and charming—that her every action is egoistic— and yet that she is free of malice and eager to please.

As for Archie—his uncle believes that he is a specially naïve, unimaginative young man, and everything that Archie does could be done by such a simple person. But it could also be done by a subtle one. Archie appears to have no secrets from his uncle. Yet after Louisa's reported confession to him, the boy at first professes that nothing unusual happened and then he suddenly bolts. He may be telling the truth—if no confession occurred and Louisa lied to his uncle—though his sudden departure is more plausible if she did frighten him away. His remaining unmarried may accord with his being unimaginative, but it accords equally with his reflecting on things formerly outside his ken.

Central to everything is the role of the enigmatic Louisa. The narrator's sister, upon hearing the story, thoroughly condemns her, though the narrator does not spell out the grounds of condemnation.[1] He himself says that he is "convinced" that she was "sincere." He does not, however, speak for James; only the opening sentence does that. Louisa is demonstrably skilled in acting—she herself admits that she is naturally suspect—and she may have been acting a part, for Archie is not rich. Or she may have been utterly sincere and yet misguided, projecting into an innocent Linda her own guilt and sacrificing the girl as a substitute atonement; or, of course, she may have been correct. Finally, it is possible that her every act represents a mixture of deceit, deluded sincerity, and truth. Were Louisa not present it is possible that no

[1] Classroom experience reveals that numerous readers concur with the sister: others accept Louisa's words without question.

questions would arise about Linda and Archie. As it is, they become as enigmatic as she.

The story is atypical of life, perhaps, in its multiplicity of ambiguities; and yet its theme is fundamental. Try as we will, we cannot infallibly interpret the factual evidence abundantly before us. We have to content ourselves by reading into others what would be our own thoughts in the circumstances, and we work out inferences to make some kind of logical pattern, for we want the simplicity of a familiar design. James was not denying the importance of our customary search for order. He was merely exploring its complexity and trying to suggest how much might lie beyond its reach.

II. THE MYSTERY OF EVIL

IN CHAPTER Two we were concerned with the general nature of the forces of evil and their destructive power. Our interest here is in the quest for understanding in a world in which evil is always present. We could run through a long series of stories, for evil is ubiquitous in James's fictional world; but we can profitably confine our attention primarily to one—*What Maisie Knew,* 1897—for in that novel evil is so dominant that one may almost feel that nothing else exists.

For a touchstone two works are pertinent which preceded the novel. In "A London Life," 1888, James dealt with a young woman's initiation into evil. Upon coming to London to live with a married sister, the American Laura Wing, ingenuous and idealistic, has suddenly plunged into a world of corruption and adultery. Her brother-in-law, living in a beautiful home and supported by traditions of refinement, is nonetheless hollow and cynical; and his wife, who later elopes, is living frantically, yet aimlessly, in a moral void. It has taken more than a year for the evil to impress itself firmly upon Laura's understanding; and when, at the point where the action of the story begins, she recalls her year's schooling, she marvels at having "seen such sad, bad things in so short a time." Laura manages to escape back to America, but not without personal humiliation and a feeling of shame. We can easily identify the types of evil which have surrounded her, but the interest is in the impression they make upon her imagination, where they become overwhelming. The story is too sparely developed and it has structural defects, but it points the way toward *What Maisie Knew.*

We have already spoken of the world of the Moreens, in "The Pupil," 1891. As we noted, they are pathetically evil in their mad, opportunistic struggle for survival. It is not only the Moreens, however, who interest us; the story is really of Pemberton, the tutor. In the beginning Pemberton is merely a youngish American who, hired to instruct the sensitive, precocious Morgan, is in a position to observe with apparent detachment. Gradually, however, he finds himself preoccupied more and more with the life, not alone of Morgan, but of the entire family. When the possibility of a daughter's marriage threatens to disrupt the odd solidarity of the family, Pemberton is surprised into an awareness of his own identification with the Moreens: "And if the cohesion was to crumble, what would become of poor Pemberton? He felt quite enough bound up with them to figure to his alarm as a dislodged block in the edifice." It is not that Pemberton is any more likely than at first to participate in the contemptible vices which beset the Moreens, and he is in no great danger of having his sensibilities dulled by contact with their vulgar insensitivity. He has, nevertheless, been drawn, not alone to Morgan, but to the family; and he has no longer a simple escape through condemnation of their every action. He does still condemn, but only in a theoretical way. Even while deploring what he sees, he accepts it as his world.* Pemberton has an orderly, disciplined mind, which wants always to fit things into their places; his moral principles are firm, and his practical judgment is logical. Yet, when he has once broken free of the family, he ignores what his common sense tells him and returns. The fate of Morgan is a strong fascination, of course, but it is inseparable from the fate of the others. Though Pemberton loves Morgan, his return is not from any hope of protecting him from evil; for Pemberton has already come to feel that he himself is the pupil, that Morgan is his tutor in the exploration of evil.

As we see the Moreens proceeding of their own free will and yet in a pattern that seems almost prescribed by a malignant destiny, we feel repeatedly with Pemberton that their actions are cruel and stupid. In analyzing and labeling what they do, however, our reason manages only

161

a superficial paraphrase in which all is reduced to an ordered clarity. In our rational classification we have made things familiar and secure. The Moreens, however, are not to be put on cardboard with neat descriptions of genus and species. They are still haunting the imagination of Pemberton years later, when they live only in memory; and, like phantoms, they continue to haunt ours. They refuse to be exorcised. What we apprehend in their presence is a far greater evil than the well-known kinds with which reason is concerned; and this sense of evil that so possesses our imagination is, we are forced to believe, no illusion.

Laura and Pemberton have moral principles and mature habits of thought to help them. Maisie Farange, of *What Maisie Knew*, has only sensitivity. Though when her story begins she is a young girl, James denies her even the cloak of innate morality, the preference for good over evil, which we fondly associate with childhood. Maisie has merely a consciousness which is neither moral nor immoral, together with an unusual capacity for joy and pain. In fact, she seems at times more easily drawn toward what we know to be bad than toward the good. If we judge her conduct by ordinary standards, she is often ungrateful and she sometimes appears obtusely unshocked by what we recognize to be evil. We are not to be occupied, however, in pronouncing a moral judgment upon Maisie for what she does, even if we excuse her conduct, as we easily can, by blaming it upon the example of others. For the novel is not really on how not to rear children. It tells what Maisie did, but its primary subject, as the title indicates, is what she *knew*.

In our customary thinking about evil we are supported by our acquaintance with the traditional concepts of ethics. We use established terms and fit our knowledge into patterns. Thus as we read of Beale Farange, his first wife Ida, his new wife, and Sir Claude, Ida's second husband, we naturally affix to each of them the appropriate descriptions of their guilt. We are superior to them; they are very bad, but we do not fear them. Maisie, however, has no such points of reference. She is not looking on with detachment; she herself is being whirled about in their world, and she is part of what she must understand. She hears what they say about each other and about her, and she tries to find an interpretation which, if not pleasant, will at least be not too painful. When we ourselves finally break away from our own comparatively safe detachment and look through Maisie's eyes, we no longer see evil defined in familiar terms. On the contrary, we find a phantasmagoria, sometimes ugly or unpleasant, sometimes apparently beautiful and intensely alluring.

Beale is a handsome man, with a touch of romantic bravado; Ida is beautiful and is adored by at least one man; Mrs. Beale is pretty and cultivated; and Sir Claude can be gentle and courtly. In contrast, Mrs. Wix is homely and colorless. Having been Maisie's nurse, she is a refuge when needed, and she does have for Maisie the merit of loving Sir Claude. In the beginning the girl wants to be loved by all five, and she would be happier if they all loved each other. Since Beale and Ida hate each other, it is at least pleasant that Beale and Maisie's governess are in love. When the governess, now Mrs. Beale, turns against her husband, it is nice that she loves Sir Claude; Maisie would like to think of the two as her father and mother. When rejected by one of the four, Maisie turns hopefully to another. She can always count on Mrs. Wix, but if she must choose between her and Mrs. Beale and Sir Claude, she will desert her for their charm and elegance. Always she is drawn toward the romantically beautiful and exciting. But always, too, she is again cast away into the darkness.

In his study of Maisie, James was trying to get at a problem of primary philosophic and psychological significance. With the most limited help from traditional principles and concepts, Maisie is confronted with interpreting the world in which she is fated to live. She begins at once to build an imagined world which will be pleasant and in which she will be central. When something from the actual world fits, she puts it in; whatever will not she wilfully pushes away. But, of course, she cannot destroy what she rejects, and so she has to hide it in a mental "closet." There is much to hide. Beale and Ida have "wanted her not for any good they could do her, but for the harm they could, with her unconscious aid, do each other." James first summarizes the effect of their hatred on Maisie: "It was to be the fate of this patient little girl to see much more than she at first understood, but also even at first to understand much more than any little girl, however patient, had perhaps ever understood before." Then he expresses the effect in a symbolic image: "The great strain meanwhile was that of carrying by the right end the things her father said about her mother— . . . A wonderful assortment of objects of this kind she was to discover there [in her mental closet] later, all tumbled up too with the things, shuffled into the same receptacle, that her mother had said about her father."

To preserve her illusion against the encroachments of actuality Maisie tries to withdraw and insulate herself, even if she must resort to the pretense of stupidity: "She would forget everything, she would repeat nothing, and when, as a tribute to the successful application of her system, she began to be called a little idiot, she tasted a pleasure new and keen." At the same time that she takes flight into her own secret life Maisie has a yearning to shape the lives of others, and she sometimes tastes an equally keen pleasure in the illusion that she has been successful. But despite her attempts to push things into closets and to live in her illusion, the actual world leaves its record. In the psychological situation faced by Maisie and in her futile effort to evade it are universal implications, for hers is not a unique case; it is merely the human predicament intensified and made objective.

Maisie not only hears her mother called "pig" and her father "beastly"; she witnesses scenes which justify the terms. She soon learns that her mother wants to be rid of her. Yet, when Ida suddenly embraces her, Maisie is instantly converted. Having heard Sir Claude call Ida "You damned old b—," she rejoices to hear Ida's companion, a captain, speak of her as an angel; glad that he loves Ida, she replies, "So do I then. I do, I do, I do!" Later, however, when Masie is again drawn to Ida, she is told, "Your father wishes you were dead . . . ." Dropping the dramatic, concrete method of narration, James summarizes Maisie's bewilderment and precocious insight: "There was literally an instant in which Maisie fully saw [for Ida]—saw madness and desolation, saw ruin and darkness and death."

Scenes with Ida are balanced by others with Beale which for Maisie are equally harrowing. After she has been rebuffed and then petted and again cast out, she is suddenly treated by Beale to what is, for her, an "Arabian Nights" thrill, a visit to a splendid apartment. Maisie does not reason as to the relationship between Beale and the woman who owns the splendor. When he caresses her, Maisie tries once more to forget the unpleasant: "She had such possibilities of vibration, of response, that it needed nothing more than this to make up to her in fact for omissions." But she quickly hears again that her mother "loathes" her and that Sir Claude and Mrs. Beale will "chuck" her; and she pleads fruitlessly to Beale not to desert her. Even then she grasps at any excuse to push aside the bitter facts which have been forced upon her consciousness. She has not liked the ugly Mrs. Cudden, who has joined them; but when the woman showers sovereigns upon her, "it was still at any rate the Arabian Nights." James makes no comment on Maisie's fleeting resurgence of joy. We know, of course, how eager children are to resume happiness, but again it must be remembered that James's story is more than a study of a young girl. Even in the midst of evil there *are* Arabian Nights. One may try to reason about them, even to dispel them as illusions, but they strike the imagination with instant swiftness and one feels that they are realities.

Maisie has been able to hold on to her belief in Mrs. Beale, having felt flattered when the woman remarks to Sir Claude that Maisie has brought them together. She has experienced increasing doubt, but she argues to Beale that Mrs. Beale and Sir Claude "love" her "tremendously." To the homely Mrs. Wix she cries out even later, "She's beautiful and I love her. I love her and she's beautiful!" When Mrs. Wix calls Mrs. Beale "as bad as your father," the now desolate Maisie protests, "She's not!—She's not!" Near the end, however, when she is more knowing, Maisie sees Mrs. Beale as a rival and demands that Sir Claude give her up. The rupture is completed with her hearing herself called by her stepmother "you abominable little horror." Once again James holds to a narrative and dramatic method. It is through Maisie's actions and words—words which only obliquely recognize the new rejection—that we surmise the inner tension which Maisie seeks to disguise even from herself. Mrs. Beale must somehow be tucked away in the closet, for the alternative would be to forsake the semblance of order which Maisie has managed to maintain in her world of the imagination. Maisie has no certainty, here or elsewhere, that it is more than a semblance, but she must assume that it is. By implication James is asking, if what Maisie holds onto is not somehow real, despite the illusions with which she tries to protect it, then where is order to be found?

Maisie has borne much from her parents and Mrs. Beale before finally accepting defeat. But she endures even more from the hand-some Sir Claude. His vile language about Ida—she hears "b—," which she fills out as "brute"—does not accord with her romantic ideal, nor has she enjoyed hearing him describe Mrs. Wix as "the old cat!" And she has wept upon hearing Sir Claude himself called a butterfly. Much as she wants to love him, she is forced to treat him with a secretive aloofness formerly reserved for her father and mother. When he tries to pry from her the captain's words about Ida, she pretends ignorance and is pronounced a dunce: "It brought again the sweet sense of suc-cess that, ages before, she had had at a crisis when, on the stairs, returning from her father's she had met a fierce question of her mother's with an imbecility as deep and had in consequence been dashed by Mrs. Farange almost to the bottom." Gradually she develops a feel-ing of superiority and lofty pity as she sees Sir Claude evade responsi-ble action: ". . . he had unmistakeably once more dodged." One is reminded of the earlier Mary Garland's pity for Roderick Hudson and of Fleda Vetch's compassion for the vacillating Owen Gereth.

With the passing of time Maisie's illusion is given a new element. She is physically not a young woman, but she is becoming conscious of herself as a girl, and the psychological effect is both comic and pathetic. She has tried from the beginning to win Sir Claude's love, and now she hopes that her being a young lady will bring success. Believing herself to be virtually a new person, Maisie naively sees a new world to conquer. It has elements of the old one, but somehow the old frustrations will be gone. In France with Mrs. Wix she meditates upon her mature wisdom: "It came to her in fact as they sat there on the sands that she was distinctly on the road to know Everything. She had not had governesses for nothing: what in the world had she ever done but learn and learn and learn? She looked at the pink sky with a placid foreboding that she should soon have learnt All." When Sir Claude asks her to desert Mrs. Wix, she surprises him by agreeing if he will give up Mrs. Beale. Within the conditions of the story there is nothing immoral in her sudden proposal. As she mistakenly reads Sir Claude's thoughts, Maisie feels with forgiving compassion that he is "afraid of his weakness—of his weakness." She herself is still deter-mined to have life conform at least in part to her will, and if Sir Claude is to be weak, she will be strong for his sake. The illusion, however, has its limits. Sir Claude has been, by our standards, dishonest, cowardly, and, above all, vulgarly crude. Maisie has managed, nevertheless, to force into the closet those things about him which she has wanted to forget. In the end, however, she is confronted with the one fact which threatens the very foundations of her world. Sir Claude proclaims in her presence that he has not given up Mrs. Beale, and he adds, "I never never will. There!" Maisie means and has always meant nothing to him. She has no choice left except to go away with the homely Mrs. Wix.

This is the supreme blow. But Maisie has learned well; Sir Claude, like the others, will have to find his place in the closet. The adjustments that Maisie once again makes are reflected through a dramatic portrait which implies what is going on inside. There is to be no fuss, no admission of defeat, no sentimental outcry. What is the order which keeps Maisie sane? Certainly there is none which can be separated from the illusions which have been smashed. Yet the will toward order appears indestructible; it must perforce create what it does not find. It is still creating—and denying—as Maisie goes away, to no Arabian Nights, with Mrs. Wix.

If the reader is not careful, he will be as much deceived about Mrs. Wix as Maisie has been about the others. She is kind to Maisie, but she does not represent for her an all-protecting love and a perfection of virtue. Mainly her virtue is only the disapproval of vice, and, besides, Maisie does not think in terms of virtue. Near the end Mrs. Wix asks her, "Do you mean to say you've already forgotten what we found together?" Maisie "dimly remembered. 'My moral sense?'" James puts the verdict significantly in question form: "Your moral sense. *Haven't* I, after all, brought it out?" Mrs. Wix can offer Maisie nothing romantic and exciting; and in their last conversation it is quite clear that, having been unable to share her secrets with any of the others, Maisie will make no attempt to share them with Mrs. Wix. On the contrary, she feels herself much the wiser of the two. When Mrs. Wix says that Sir Claude has now gone to "*her*," Maisie replies, "Oh I know!" and the story concludes, "She still had room for wonder at what Maisie knew."

As Maisie returns to England she carries in her mind, not a closet, but rooms full of discordant impressions, most of them unpleasant, indeed dreadful. She will not be able to shut the doors upon them and create a new, unhaunted life. On the contrary, she will have to wander among them, for they make up the only house in which she can live. She has *done* nothing. Far from being a Pippa, she has been a mere convenience for others in their fighting each other and carrying out their odious plans. But she has learned much. Though she will continue to seek insulation, she has been forced to *know* evil—not in the sense of having a rational understanding of it, but in the far deeper sense of having become imaginatively aware of its ubiquity.

III. THE PRESENT-PAST

James stressed repeatedly, as we have seen, the importance of a sense of the past. In story after story, in the sketches of life in Europe, and in the prefaces, he was preoccupied with the recovery of an earlier age. His masterpiece in the recapture of a time gone by was to have been *The Sense of the Past*, not because it would have demonstrated a greater historical knowledge than his other works, but because it would have explored the implications of the title. Once again, however, it is best to approach the theme by way of a crooked corridor.

In "The Last of the Valerii," 1874, the past is evoked mainly as a symbol. When Conte Valerio, living in the nineteenth century, falls in love with a statue of Juno and for a little while is indifferent to his American wife, it is at once apparent that the contrast is between the ideal beauty of a Pagan world and the actual of the present: ". . . she [Juno] seemed indeed an embodiment of celestial supremacy and repose." At the end, after the wife has had the statue again consigned to the earth which once covered it, the Conte still retains one fragment, a perfect marble hand, which he keeps in a cabinet and shows only to those who can perchance comprehend. As the narrator, a painter, recounts the anecdote, we are perhaps most conscious of the symbolic contrast of attitudes toward life. He quotes the strange, uncanny excavator, who philosophizes, "There is a pagan element in all of us,—

I don't speak for you, *illustrissimi forestieri,*—and the old gods have still their worshippers. . . . He's a good fellow, but, between ourselves, he's an impossible Christian!" At one point the Conte's wife laments, "His Juno is the reality; I am the fiction!" The Conte does return to the present, though "he never became, if you will, a thoroughly modern man." As he exhibits the hand he remarks, "It is the hand of a beautiful creature . . . whom I once greatly admired."

The story is rather well told; one accepts the theme, and there is enough about the Conte's ancestral background, the "patrimonial marbles," and the tone associated with the peaceful beauty of the statue to make one feel the pathos and charm. At the same time, the narrative is presented from the outside. We trustfully accept the statement that Juno has become the reality, but we do not penetrate the Conte's mind beyond the general symbolism. When the man comes back to the present world, with the passion quieted but the memory still lingering, we perceive that he will henceforth live in a fusion of the two worlds. We can only guess, however, as to the images, the half-articulated thoughts, the conflicting sensations which must make up the inner drama.

In the same year, in "Florentine Notes," James enunciated in a general way the lure of the past. In a passage cited earlier, he wrote, concerning the Palazzo Corsini, ". . . the past seems to have left a sensible deposit, an aroma, an atmosphere. This ghostly presence tells you no secrets, but it prompts you to try and guess a few. What has been done and said here through so many years, what has been ventured or suffered, what has been dreamed or despaired of? Guess the riddle if you can, or if you think it worth your ingenuity." The passage sets a tone for meditation. It may even lead the reader to a study of Italian history, and it outlines the broad area of inquiry into human passions. Both James and the reader are spectators, looking on, getting hints, perhaps even sensing the ghostly presences of those who used to wander through the rooms and corridors. The mood has been set and the imagination can begin its work. In the sketch, however, we are still not *in* the past; we are still trying to peer in from our vantage points. It was *The Sense of the Past*, left partly written and partly mapped out in one of James's garrulous letters to himself, that was to attempt the magical step. To have laid the scene of a novel in the early nineteenth century would have involved a certain kind of recapture of the past, but nothing different from what James could read in memoirs and published letters or in the typical historical novel, nothing different, in fact, from what he had been doing at times in his own fiction both before and after 1874, when he dipped briefly into a slightly earlier age for the scene of his action. In his unfinished novel, however, he sought to give one more turn to the screw.

The slow unfolding of the theme in the first pages keeps on familiar ground, contrasting Ralph Pendrel, as a "mere thinker," with his American compatriot Aurora Coyne, who likes men of action and wants to make something of America. Ralph has written "An Essay in Aid of the Reading of History" and has spoken to Aurora of "the sense of the past." In contrast to Aurora, he is predisposed toward understanding of the past, but he is still an outsider. His predisposition and his limitation—not that at the moment he recognizes it—appear together in James's commentary as he goes behind his hero to explore his thoughts: "It was when life was framed in death that the picture was really hung up." In short, Ralph wants to go back and study history in the usual manner, knowing the end as well as the beginning. Yet, without quite knowing what would be involved, he wants to recapture the past as if it were present: ". . . he wanted the very tick of the old stopped clocks." At this stage in his career he cannot comprehend that the seeing life framed in death and the hearing the ticking of the clocks can be utterly different experiences.

Ralph is restive, however, because, though he has talked about the past a great deal, he still has not really entered it. The inheritance of a London house dating from 1710 gives him hope, and he feels like Columbus as he sets out to discover what it may offer. It is in the house itself that the miracle occurs, not in one immediate transformation, but in a series of startling experiences, each of which leaves Ralph more receptive than before. First there is a sensation of another presence in the room. The portrait above the mantel seems at first to be his own; then he perceives that, despite the resemblance, it is of another. Next he begins to feel that he is "somebody else." At this point James restates Ralph's anxious feelings in a summary that hints of the future.

In his own words, he has wanted to "cultivate some better sense of the past than has mostly seemed sufficient even for those people who have gone in most for cultivating it . . . ."

This sense comes when he suddenly feels that he has taken the place of the young man of the portrait, an experience that requires his giving the man a new life in exchange, a life which will represent a jump into the future. Ralph is aware of the strangeness which has come upon him, but he is convinced that he is saner than ever before in his life. Before long he finds himself embracing a young woman whom he has never previously seen; and soon, too, he is having to work out a relationship with a number of other persons, all of whom expect him to act consistently with what he is supposed to know and to have done. The girl, Molly, loves Ralph, but he is not drawn toward her in return; instead, he finds himself pitying her absent sister, Nan, whom Molly, her stupid brother Perry, and their mother are evidently trying to force into a cheerless marriage for the family's gain. He has to work out the probabilities. In America he has never heard of any of the group, and he learns that, even now in the new life, he is supposed not yet to have met Nan. In short, he perceives with astonishment that he cannot arrange things to his wish.

As James indicated in the notes, once Ralph uses the latchkey he enters the past. At one point he tells the others helplessly that he is in their "hands." He has become an actor in a drama he did not create. His experience is not unlike what happens in dreams, except that it is sane and logical. He has supposed that the past would be generally pleasant, but Perry is repellently brutal, and Molly and her mother are crudely undiscerning in their willingness to sacrifice poor Nan. The latter is timeless in that, when he meets her, she reminds Ralph of a Van Eyck or Memling virgin, yet is "modern, *modern!*" Paradoxically for this man who has had too much of the present, it is Nan's modernity that is appealing, a modern spirit, not in the sense of a glorying in the things liked by Aurora Coyne, but in the rebellion against the stifling conventions of her age—a modernity which reminds one of that of Nanda Brookenham, in the midst of a family also reminiscent of the Brookenhams.

From here on we are dependent mainly on the notes, though the finished part confirms them. Ralph has to accept "the note of their thrift, a certain hardness of meanness, the nature of their economies, the brutality (I keep coming back to that) of their various expedients . . . ." The essence of his predicament is summed up in one thematic note: "He knows his way so much and so far, knows it wonderfully, finds his identity, the one he wears for the occasion, extraordinarily easy considering the miracle of it all; but the very beauty of the subject is in the fact of his at the same time watching himself, watching his success, criticising his failure, being both the other man and not the other man, being just sufficiently the other, his prior, his own, self, not to be able to help living in that a bit too." Ralph is both somewhat fearful and aware that he causes fear. To help Nan he must let her see his modern identity, for the other young man would have married Molly. That man so enjoys the future that Ralph fears he will not be able to exchange destinies with him again; if not, he will wrong him by not marrying Molly. James's plan called for love of Nan to prevail in that Ralph will expose her family to her and will show her "how poor a world she is stuck fast in compared with all the wonders and splendours that he is straining back to." Since, however, Nan cannot escape to the modern world, she will finally be doomed to the "heartbreak of remaining so far back behind it."

As to method, James wrote, ". . . I see it in images . . . ," and the completed part is presented in scenes and in the thoughts which enter his hero's mind. This is, of course, of paramount consequence in that we see the action as it appears in all its intensity to Ralph; we are not getting it at second hand. Varying slightly his well-known metaphor, James spoke of his task as "the successive driving in of the silver-headed nails." Twice he spoke of keeping "The Turn of the Screw" as his precedent. This can only refer to the perspective, the seeing through the sensations of the hero. Unlike the governess, Ralph does not tell his own story, but, like her, he is concerned with a search for reality, including his own personal identity.

The world into which he has sought cautious entrance, only to find himself entrapped in it, seems in some ways much like the present, and he tries to establish a familiar, plausible pattern. It has essentially the same kind of evil, the same logic of events, the same longing of the imaginative mind to be free. These, however, he is not permitted to contemplate with detachment. Even as Pemberton became a part of the world of the Moreens, he has become a struggling participant, and he has finally to accept the sorrow of being unable to rescue Nan.

His situation is not basically different from that of a novelist, who, if he is sincere, may find himself living in a fictional world which refuses to bend to his will. For the novelist to create his world and for Ralph to trap himself, even for a while, in the past, a disciplined act of imagination is required. For Ralph the consequence is the creation of one particular world—a house and family in one time and place. Had he the capacity, he could live in an infinite number of worlds, each in some way unique, yet governed by the logic which he has come to accept in his actual present. Each world would be a reality in which he would be at one and the same time an actor vigorously engaged in trying to shape events as if they were part of a present and anticipatory of an unknown future, and a critical observer, with a modern vantage, of his own actions. The true sense of the past is thus much more than a spectator's glimpse into a bygone time. It represents one of the most profound—and perilous—adventures of the imagination in its quest for reality.

IV. THE WORLD OF INFERENCE

CERTAIN FACTS CAN BE ESTABLISHED, others appear authentic, and yet others may reasonably be accepted on the basis of hearsay. There still remains, however, the imaginative leap from fact to fact in the search for meaning. Already in this chapter we have been concerned with inferences, for such a story as "Louisa Pallant" or *What Maisie Knew* intrigues us constantly with its enticements to draw conclusions to suit our own desires. The four "fairy-tales" about to be studied happen to be especially, indeed at times exclusively, explorations into the uncharted realm of inference. Three are first-person narratives; and in the fourth, *In the Cage*, 1898, we are also so extensively behind the heroine that we see through her eyes and are as much absorbed as she in her bewildered quest for certainties. *In the Cage* differs from the

173

others in that we also objectively see the heroine as a part of the world which she is trying to understand and to mould to her wishes; we know absolutely at times that she is in error. Nevertheless, in her plight we recognize the universal problem which besets us, too. In the other three—"The Way It Came," 1896, "The Turn of the Screw," 1898, and *The Sacred Fount,* 1901, we perceive the relation of the hero or heroine to the world only through his or her own interpretations and are denied any absolute knowledge whatever on the questions which matter. In all four works the pervading question is: What can one know? Human vanity or other frailties may be motivating forces for the characters, and various emotions may figure in the poignancy of their defeat, but *knowledge* is their abiding need. The quest for it is the one inescapable passion.

The cage where telegraph messages pass before the eyes of the un-named heroine of *In the Cage* is at first nothing more than a place to work. Gradually, however, it develops ironic meaning. By her way-wardness of imagination the girl makes of her narrow quarters the very center of an exciting world of intrigue and romance; yet, as eventually becomes apparent, her mental horizons are the four sides of her cage. The two men in her little world are her commonplace lover Mudge, a grocer, and, contrasting with him, the dashing Everard, who moves in upper society and sends telegrams in pursuit of some clandestine ro-mance. Not only is the girl superior to Mudge and to her mother, who smells of whiskey, but she feels herself much more knowing about the world of society than her friend Mrs. Jordan, who in her line of duty as a flower arranger has entry into upper-class homes. What the girl is seeking is a romantic concept of a universe in which she herself will have an equally romantic role. She chooses to exist as a clever, sophisti-cated confidante who holds human destinies in her hands: "Combina-tions of flowers and greenstuff forsooth! What *she* could handle freely, she said to herself, was combinations of men and women." She is will-ing to share the strange man who uses the telegraph, but not to be a nonentity for him: "The thing in all this that she would have liked most unspeakably to put to the test was the possibility of her having for him a personal identity that might in a particular way appeal." She consequently reads his every gesture, fills in his unexpressed thoughts, and builds up an ecstatic hope: "He did like her!" She even boasts to him of what she knows of the "horrors" of his social set: "I know, I know, I know!"

At the end we perceive that Mudge is a decent, courageous man and that the intrigue of Everard is unromantically sordid, and the clues which lead to disillusionment come largely from Mrs. Jordan. The girl now knows that she has meant nothing to Everard. Her adventure is over and she is ready to marry Mudge, no longer at some vague later time, but the very next week.

James has occasional amusement as the girl puts on an air of shrewdness or tells poor Mudge mistakenly, "You're awfully inferior to him." Mainly, however, the story is a serious drama of her secret adventure in the world of imaginative conjecture. No one who gives her a telegram to transmit would ever guess the intensity of that adventure or dream that his very telegram itself may help to shape it. The telegrams, together with the cage, suggest a universal truth. One does not really know the full thoughts of others; what he has to work with is symbolized by the abridged and cryptic telegrams—fragments which can be arranged in patterns only by an effort of the imagination. And even then, the pattern, however beautifully constructed, may be utterly false to the reality. As for self-knowledge—unlike George Dane, John Marcher, and Spencer Brydon, the girl is not introspective, and yet her own identity is inextricably involved in her romantic vision of the world in which she moves. Though at the end she belives that she has put her adventure behind her in running into marriage with Mudge, she is certainly still in part the romance-spinning girl of the cage; and we may at least be allowed the conjecture that she has merely departed from the precincts of one cage to enter those of another.

Compared with "The Turn of the Screw," the short story "The Way It Came" is slight. It does, however, deal with the same basic problem. A woman records facts and impressions in her diary, and we have no other source of information. She states that, because a friend saw his mother's ghost at the moment of her death and another friend saw her father's, she sought to introduce them to each other. But having become affianced to the man, she experienced a sudden fit of jealousy and lied to prevent the meeting. The other woman died that night, and at or about the same time the man, as he later reported, had a visit from her, during which they gazed at each other speechless for twenty minutes. He insists, however, that she was not a ghost. Later, accused of continuing to receive visits from the dead woman, he once acquiesces —"Well, my dear, what if I do?"—but he later retracts his admission.

Unless we accept the possibility of the supernatural, there is simply no story. The diarist admits to jealousy and, at one stage, to contrition, but beyond this there is no distinguishing feature of her mind. She simply sets down what she knows and also what she infers. She may be mistaken, but she is no more insane than Ralph Pendrel is to be when wandering around in the past.

The time of the visit, as accurately as she can establish it, matches the time of her friend's death, and the visitor's conduct more befits a ghost than a living person. If she came once as a ghost, why should she not come again, especially since the diarist has first built up a spirit of affinity in the two and has then betrayed them? The diarist is in much the same position that Kate Croy will find herself in when she realizes that Densher is in love with the memory of Milly. She has no way, however, of being sure as to the truth. The man's denial proves nothing, and his admission is, likewise, inconclusive, for she prefaces her quotation of his confession with the comment, "He had taken the line of indulgence, of meeting me halfway and kindly humouring me." She tries to be objective, and yet her own personality as it must appear to the man is an indefinite subjective factor, for what he says takes into consideration what he believes her to be.

Had the tale been only a simple ghost story, James might have dispensed with some of its substance and have tried only to make his readers "afraid to go to bed o' nights." Had it been a case study in the hallucinations of a diseased mind, it would have required unmistakable evidence of delusion. Instead, it leaves unanswered what the woman would frantically know. There is nowhere for her to turn to find out whether the other woman's ghost *does* visit the man and whether or not his death six years after the first suspected visit is a suicide to permit him to join her. In short, there is no escape for her from the limitations of subjectivity.

For a good many years "The Turn of the Screw" has been a touchstone in literary criticism. At one extreme is the critic who sees the governess as a virtually angelic being fighting against evil, and at the other is the antipuritan who would make of her a self-appointed vice-gerent of the Lord, driven by a misguided frenzy and guilty of bringing evil into a garden formerly idyllic. Distinct from the second, yet convinced that the governess is a doer of ill, are those who would make her out to be a sexually maladjusted spinstress, who unwittingly records in her first-person narrative the vagaries of a pathological mind. All three types of readers cite the same evidence, and on it all build up substantial superstructures of reason to prove their points.[2]

The trouble with each of the three perspectives is that it is not consistent with economy in storytelling. Had James wanted only to say that a pure, wise, self-sacrificing young woman was at war with evil and that her every act was irreproachably good, he could have written something not unlike a morality play in that, at every turn, the reader would be sure in which direction goodness or evil lay. He could not have justified in his actual story numerous incidents and a good many comments by the governess which are irrelevant in such a narrative and often becloud the issue. If, instead, he had wanted to show what evil the deludedly self-righteous do, he could have omitted other incidents and have left no ambiguity. In this latter type of story he might well have deceived the reader for a while, even as he deceives him about Chad in the early part of *The Ambassadors,* but there should be at the end a general agreement among readers that the governess is evil. Instead, the ending is entirely ambiguous. As to the interpretation of the story as a case study in frustration and neurosis, it offers no justification for the obliqueness with which the presumed pathological condition is presented, and it coerces everything into a stereotype of Freudian preoccupation with sex. If James had wanted to study sexual frustration, he could have written a much simpler tale. Moreover, the sex-starved mortal is merely pitiful. Insofar as he is abnormal he has little universal significance. On the contrary, the themes with which James dealt are uniformly those at the very heart of our being. They include, among other things, love and jealousy,

[2] See Gerald Willen, *A Casebook of Henry James's "The Turn of the Screw"* (bibliography, "The Turn of the Screw").

177

selfishness and generosity, and, above all, bewilderment; and though their presentation in the stories is not in the form of philosophic disquisition, they are the very substance of philosophy.

As to how James himself looked upon his story, we have two significant pronouncements. In the later preface he called it a "fairy-tale," and he also said that he gave the governess "authority." For James a fairy tale was not a case study in pathology translated into fiction; it was as free as possible of any special limitations, being confined only by what one generally accepts as a consistent relationship between the events. It might or might not involve supernatural incidents; it would always have universal implications. As for "authority," James certainly meant that the governess was to be regarded as an accurate reporter; he did not mean that her inferences were necessarily valid.

We need not fall back, however, on what an author says about his work, as the story must be its own testimony. The most satisfactory interpretation of "The Turn of the Screw" need not at all rule out special, indeed esoteric, suggestions which it may have for a reader, but it must not limit the tale to such meanings; and it must justify all the incidents, not merely as psychologically relevant, but as artistically necessary. The fairy tale must be as vast in its meaning as its elements will permit. To allow it such meaning the reader has to accept certain conditions, in this instance above all the authority of the governess. If one concludes that nothing actually happened, that the governess invented the entire account as a veiled expression of her feelings at the time of writing, the story vanishes into idle fantasy.[3] If, on the other hand, we grant that there were children and a housekeeper, we must also accept the reality or the possibility of everything else which the governess reports. This is not to say that she is all-knowing, for she is quite the opposite. But she attempts to distinguish between facts and inferences; and until she has gone beyond the point of return, she includes with each of the latter a self-warning of the possibility of error. If, despite the warning, she reassures herself and continues on her course, building upon hypotheses as if they were truths, this does not impugn her reportorial accuracy.

[3] For such a possible interpretation see Willen, *ibid.*, introduction.

What then must we accept at the outset? First of all, as a parson's daughter, the twenty-year-old governess comes from a home in which she has presumably been encouraged to think about right and wrong and to take life seriously, but a home in which she has not had to come face to face with evil. In a general way she reminds one of Isabel Archer, who expected to find in Europe a kind of freedom and happiness which she had missed at home. The governess sees her new situation at Bly as a wonderful adventure in contrast to her former "small smothered life." She learns to "be amused, and even amusing . . . . It was the first time, in a manner, that I had known space and air and freedom." She is as unprepared as was Isabel for what comes suddenly upon her: "The change was actually like the spring of a beast." Like the Ancient Mariner, she has not specially cultivated an interest in the supernatural or in evil, but has found herself thrust into their midst. Like the Mariner, she has acute sensitivity and the power of language to tell her tale.

At the beginning we are introduced, too, to the feelings of the governess toward the strangely detached yet exacting master who has given her her assignment to care for his niece and nephew and, at the same time, has forbidden her to appeal to him for help. We know that the governess wants to please him. At this point we can, to be sure, decide that, as a frustrated, though very young, spinstress with an infatuation for a handsome man, she begins to perform various self-deluding mental gymnastics to conceal from herself the hopelessness of her love, if not its impropriety. We are then plunged headlong into a case study from which we cannot recover. The fact that Peter Quint appears in his master's clothes, that he is associated with a tower, and that Miss Jessel is associated with a lake becomes evidence for an exercise in Freudian allegory, in which we bring to the tale whatever Freudianism we are willing to accept and enjoy a game of finding incidents which will match.

We can also, however, see the relationship of the governess and the master in a different way, in which normality replaces the abnormal. He is a very real person, and the governess thinks of him as such, but, at the same time, he is an agent of destiny; one does not have to abandon realism entirely and make him into the headman in a Kafkaesque

Castle in order to discover universal implications in the governess's attitude toward him. He has set the conditions under which she must carry out her task, the most perilous of all possible tasks in that she is responsible for the destinies of others. He has refused her any guidance, any touchstones, and has, nevertheless, made her accountable for whatever she may do. If he seems to us to cast more than a mortal shadow, to symbolize a philosophic or theological principle, then the fairy-tale quality of the story is in no way diminished, its implications in no manner curtailed.

As to one of the inhabitants of Bly, the housekeeper, Mrs. Grose, there are a few things which we can say with confidence. She is a matter-of-fact, practical, kindly, unimaginative person; and though she may believe in ghosts, she is not bothered by any philosophical questions which even their possible presence at Bly may suggest. We know this much about her from certain of her own words as they are reported by the governess. What we do not know is her precise feeling toward the governess at crucial moments. Sometimes she disagrees with the governess, but more and more her words appear to concur with the latter's interpretation. We cannot be more definite than this. Does she actually believe the governess's account of the ghosts of Quint and Miss Jessel, or is she only humoring her young companion in acquiescing? She certainly experiences fright, but is it from supernatural causes or from concern for the violent emotion of the governess herself? We have her words and even their intonation—as to these the governess is an authority. But we do not have, because the governess does not really know them, the motives behind the words. The young woman admits to her uncertainty, though she quickly tries to dispel it by rationalization. In her inferences she is, of course, not an authority.

Of the two children, Miles and Flora, we know even less. They undergo such intense exposure to terror, whether from ghosts or from the governess, that the strangeness of their conduct is in either instance plausible. We have no absolute proof that they are at the beginning idyllically innocent; and, on the other hand, despite the fact that Miles has been dismissed from school, no proof that he or his sister is guilty of spiritual sin. If at the beginning they are innocent, we have no certainty as to whether they later become morally corrupt. We do know that each experiences an emotional crisis, during which Flora becomes ill and, according to Mrs. Grose, speaks "horrors," and Miles becomes so overwrought that he dies.

Finally there are the ghosts. Unless one tries to argue that everything was a concoction of a distraught mind, one has to begin by accepting certain premises, among them the possibility that ghosts can exist. Why not? If we are caught up by the story at all we find that the existence of the ghosts opens up avenues for speculation which would otherwise be closed. Nothing of philosophic significance can be made of them as obvious fantasies of a neurotic mind. But once their existence is accepted, they become morally and philosophically significant, for we can then perceive that the governess's concern about them is symbolic of our own philosophic predicaments. The governess reports that she sees them. She makes a distinction between her feeling that there must be some uncanny unseen presence and her visual sensation of the ghosts. She does admit that she is obsessed, that she is tense, that she experiences a "disguised excitement that might well, had it continued too long, have turned to something like madness." But she brings to bear all the evidence she can to prove that she is not mad. Among that evidence is the reappearance of the ghosts. As she surveys the happenings years later, when she is actually recording from memory, she gives to the appearance of the ghosts the same credence as to other things which her eyes saw. If we accept these other phenomena, we cannot well exempt the ghosts.

The moral and philosophic question involves their relation to the children. The governess knows from Mrs. Grose that in life Quint and Miss Jessel were wicked and that they were close enough to the children to influence them. It is a logical inference therefore that they are still determined to carry out evil left incomplete at their deaths. (It may be remembered that the ghost in "The Third Person" is unable to rest until his act of smuggling has been vicariously accomplished.) If the children are already in their power, the governess is morally responsible for counteracting their machinations; indeed, she should take any risk, for all is lost if she does not succeed. If, on the other hand, the children are ignorant of their existence, the governess has no right to unveil their eyes to such evil: ". . . who would ever absolve me,

181

who would consent that I should go unhung, if, by the faintest tremor of an overture, I were the first to introduce into our perfect intercourse an element so dire [as her knowledge of Quint's ghost]." Hence her dilemma. If the children would freely confess to their association with the ghosts, her moral course would be clear. But how can she obtain from them a confession they decline to offer without herself speaking of the "element so dire"? If she does speak first—even if she then secures a confession from the children, who may see only because she has helped them to see—she will never know whether she has offered salvation to captive spirits or whether she is beyond absolution for her sin.

If the young woman could stand aside and watch, she might at least moderate the intensity of her anguish, but she is irrevocably committed to action. Both the command of her employer and her own nature deny her any refuge in neutrality. She is compelled to act, since either revealing or concealing her knowledge and suspicions will affect the children. At the beginning she is quite confident that she is thinking mainly, if not entirely, of Miles and Flora. If she could be sure what was for their good, she would eagerly sacrifice herself to accomplish it: ". . . but something within me said that by offering myself bravely as the sole subject of such experience [seeing the figure again], by accepting, by inviting, by surmounting it all, I should serve as an expiatory victim and guard the tranquillity of the rest of the household." Unable to banish the ghosts from her consciousness, she finds it easiest to believe that they either have or are seeking an evil influence over the children. She realizes that she may be in error, and the thought of her unpardonable guilt if she is makes her acutely conscious of herself. Though she tries to wish that the children are innocent, she actually longs for proof that they are not, for then she will be vindicated. In this she is not a fiendish authoritarian who has set out to play God; she is a deeply troubled person who would gladly find rest. If she cannot have it in knowledge that Miles and Flora are innocent —and she does renew her hope that she may—she must seek it in proof of their guilt. So it is that she watches for every clue and at times actually rejoices when she thinks she has trustworthy evidence. Her frantic desire to be proved right will lead to a momentary emotion of exaltation: ". . . I was blind with victory . . . ."

Meanwhile she takes the step which permits no turning back. When Miles pleads with her to "let" him "alone," she compulsively runs the supreme risk of introducing him, though obliquely and ambiguously, to supernatural evil: "—oh I brought it out now even if I *should* go too far—'I just want you to help me to save you!'" There is a blast of air, followed by a shriek from Miles, both of which could be free from supernatural causes, but such events fortify her suspicion. Soon afterward she assures Mrs. Grose that the children say things about Quint and Miss Jessel which, "if we heard them, would simply appal us." Though the governess assumes still that Mrs. Grose cannot see the ghosts, she believes that she accepts their existence. By now she is so habituated to building inference upon inference that the horror has for her almost a certainty. One may qualify with *almost,* for the impetuousness of her insistence that she is vindicated is a revelation of a flickering doubt.

"Where, my pet, is Miss Jessel?"—for the first time the governess has been so daring as to mention the name to Flora, though she has already said to her strange things which, whether Flora is guilty or innocent, must inevitably have brought her emotions near to the breaking point. Note the accuracy of the governess's record of the outward effect of her words upon her listeners and, at the same time, the complete ambiguity as to the inner one: ". . . the quick smitten glare with which the child's face now received it [the name] likened my breach of the silence to the smash of a pane of glass. It added to the interposing cry, as if to stay the blow, that Mrs. Grose at the same instant uttered over my violence—the shriek of a creature scared, or rather wounded . . . ." Does Mrs. Grose cry out because she wants to shield or rescue Flora from Miss Jessel, whom she herself cannot see, or because she considers the governess deluded and is in terror for the possible effect of her mad influence upon the child? Having gone so far, the governess must build upon her inference concerning Flora's knowledge as if it were an absolute fact. She persists, unsuccessfully, in trying to wring a confession from Flora: "She's there, you little unhappy thing—there, there, *there,* and you know it as well as you know me!" She

THE MADNESS OF ART

tries also, again unsuccessfully, to get an admission from Mrs. Grose. The housekeeper's later "I believe" may be admission that she thinks Miss Jessel was present, or it may be mere compassionate humoring.

The governess by now has no choice. Her words to Flora and her oblique language to Miles are damning if she has been wrong; and so she must believe in the virtue of all she has done and will yet do. When Flora, ill and estranged, leaves Bly, the governess must still save Miles. What is demanded of her is "only another turn of the screw of ordinary human virtue." It is shortly thereafter that she reports that she "was blind with victory." In the climactic moments Miles asks first, "Is she *here?* . . . Miss Jessel, Miss Jessel!" Then "in a white rage" he cries, "It's *he?*" And to her hopeful question "Whom do you mean by 'he'?" comes the answer. "Peter Quint—you devil! . . . *Where?*" His words indicate that he cannot see Quint, and yet they and the "convulsed supplication" of his face show his belief in his presence. It is not necessary, as some have done, to take *you devil* to refer to the governess; Miles has always been courteous, and, besides, the *where?* shows that he is thinking of Quint. But there is complete ambiguity regardless. If he senses the presence of Quint for the *last* time, then the governess has been vindicated; wanting to believe that she is, she exults to Miles that Quint has "lost" him "for ever." If, however, he feels Quint's presence only because the governess has introduced him to the evil, then she has committed the unpardonable sin.

Years later, having recorded the terror and horror, the governess brings her story to a gentle ending, in which all passion is spent: "We were alone with the quiet day, and his little heart, dispossessed, had stopped." She has since been a governess elsewhere, and, as the man who reads her narrative recalls his youthful feelings for her at that later time, he speaks with affection, if not, indeed, love. In short, the woman has survived the experience and gone on to lead an apparently normal life in the world. She has carried with her, however, the secret which she confides to her sheets of paper. She is living an orderly, sensible life, and she is an attractive person. Yet she has gone through the most terrifying of all possible experiences. She has had to choose what to believe and to act upon her belief, with the stakes being salvation or perdition. She wishes to believe that she has morally triumphed;

184

but as she records what happened, she again goes through the anguish of the damned. If her dilemma and her uncertainty are of feverish intensity and if her vision of life includes the very supernatural itself, they are no less universal. She has simply had to do in a superlative way what less harassed minds do in a more subdued fashion.

To turn to *The Sacred Fount* is to leave behind the stuff of tragedy and enter the realm of ingenious and deeply serious comedy. In fact, the novel enunciates a theory which is not comic at all, follows the pattern of a detective story, and ends with the pathetic frustration of the hero. The broad, general concept of a sacred fount was not original with James. He got a general hint from Stopford Brooke. Moreover, he could find almost anywhere evidence of how someone of little moral strength received moral sustenance from a stronger person, and it was easy enough to conceive therefore of one person's aging less than usual in his attitude toward life while the person who took over for him the strain of responsibility became prematurely worn. There is some evidence that James felt that his own father drew strength from James's mother, though the latter seems to have had ample for both.[4] The implication of such a relationship is ordinarily not pursued beyond the casual and obvious. For James, however, it had interesting implications. Like William James, he had long accepted the fact that the clothes a person wore and the environment in which he moved and the books he read were a part of his own personality. What if, in a sense, another's being were to be regarded as the source from which one drank, so that who the other was determined one's own nature and drinking depleted the source from which the sustenance came?

In the novel James gave an additional turn to the screw by letting his narrator—evidently a man—believe that a woman much older than her husband had quickly become younger in appearance while the husband aged rapidly, and that a man notorious for lack of cleverness had become witty while the woman whose sacred fount nourished him wasted away intellectually.[5] Having let his narrator broach the idea, however, James somewhat shifted the direction of the story. *The Sacred*

[4] See Leon Edel, *The Sacred Fount*, xxvi (bibliography, *The Sacred Fount*).
[5] The phrasing makes one person draw from another and the victim then tap his own sacred fount to make up the loss.

Fount is not a psychological study of what happens when such parasitism occurs. Its subject is whether in the given cases it has occurred and even, as regards the second of the two, which person may possess the fount. The narrator becomes a self-appointed detective to ferret out the truth, and his comic bafflement and ultimate retirement from the field constitute the story he has to tell.

The novel is a study in relationships in which the identity of the narrator himself is obscured by the ambiguity of his relation to others. His position is similar to that of the governess in that from what he sees and the impressions he acquires he must leap to inferences. It must be remembered that Dencombe, in "The Middle Years," immediately began to imagine the relationships among the persons who were coming toward him; he accepted his penchant as an attribute of his novel-writing trade. The narrator-hero in *The Sacred Fount* is no novelist, except that the story he sets down amounts to a novel, but he is a questioner. When he sees something, he must work out a logical explanation. Mrs. Brissenden, about forty-two or forty-three years of age, strikes him as much younger and prettier than he remembers her being, and Gilbert Long, her travelling companion on the way to a party at Newmarch, seems much more intelligent than before. It is Mrs. Briss who provides the cue to speculation by suggesting that a "very clever woman" has given Long "steadily, more and more intellect." Though he asks her if she means Lady John, the hero is soon off on a trail of his own. When, before dinner, he sees Mrs. Server and his artist friend, Obert, together, he is at first aware that she is "extraordinarily pretty, markedly responsive, conspicuously charming"; but, though she seems happy, he is soon afterwards impressed with Obert's comment, "She's too beastly unhappy." Shortly thereafter he meets Briss, who seems to have become old. Here are the principal facts, which soon become pillars to hold up the world of inference which our hero creates. To use his own metaphor, "I was just conscious, vaguely, of being on the track of a law, a law that would fit, that would strike me as governing the delicate phenomena—delicate though so marked—that my imagination found itself playing with. A part of the amusement they yielded came, I daresay, from my exaggerating them —grouping them into a larger mystery (and thereby a larger 'law') than

186

the facts, as observed, yet warranted; but that is the common fault of minds for which the vision of life is an obsession."

He now has his theory—Briss is his wife's sacred fount, and May Server is Long's—and when facts are seemingly at variance with it, he must work out an explanation to re-establish consistency. To be sure, Long insists that he sees no change in Briss, but since Long himself is drawing upon another's sacred fount, he may be lying to discourage suspicion of himself. On the other hand, Obert states that Mrs. Briss is evidently much younger than her husband, and Obert is presumably objective. To be sure, the couple are new to him, and so he is not speaking of any change; but at least he listens with apparent sympathy to the hero's theory. In time Mrs. Briss appears to confirm his secret belief that May Server is Long's "mystic Egeria." Despite his initial sense that she was "markedly responsive," he has quickly modified his portrait of May: "She was like an awestruck child; she might have been herself—all Greuze tints, all pale pinks and blues and pearly whites and candid eyes—an old dead pastel under glass." Here it is to be noted that every objective detail fits equally with the concept of May as a dead pastel and with the image of a delicately sensitive and charmingly responsive woman.

By now the narrator begins to find dissent on the part of Mrs. Briss, but this is plausible. She knows that he suspects her, for he has recklessly implied as much; and so, like Long, but much more cleverly, she will try to lead his suspicions astray. It is almost safe to conclude that whatever she says is confirmation of its opposite. After all, he is concealing his own thoughts to protect May. What he can surely rely on, however, is people's looks and unconscious gestures, for these can hardly deceive. It is at about this time that a painting is introduced which really symbolizes the theme of the book. In the picture a young man holding a mask has "a pale, lean, livid face and a stare, from eyes without eyebrows, like that of some whitened old-world clown." [6] The mask is not distinct, but "on a second view becomes a representation of a human face." May calls the mask "the Mask of Death," but the

[6] For the possible connotation of *old-world*, cf. "It was an old-world garden . . . such a garden as one does not see this side of Moscow." (*Virgin Soil*, tr. by Constance Garnett, 1901, I, 72–73.)

narrator replies, "Isn't it much rather the Mask of Life? It's the man's own face that's Death. . . . The other one, blooming and beautiful . . . is Life, and he's going to put it on; unless indeed he has just taken it off." Who is right, May or he? And if he is right, he is still unsure about an all-important point. The appearance of the painting—like the looks and gestures of people—is the same for May and for him, but how different the meaning!

Before long the hero finds Obert apparently accepting his theory, but shifting its application, for he asks "who's paying for Mrs. Server?" Obert must be kept "on this false scent," and so the narrator will help to deceive him. Soon it is clear that all the others are building up their own theories about one another, even about the narrator himself, though he gets only faint hints of what they may think about him. The earliest is Mrs. Briss's "Perhaps what you don't like is that my observation may be turned on *you*. I confess it is." At one point the hero takes "a lively resolve to get rid of my ridiculous obsession," but he cannot. When May is unmistakably charming, he concludes that she is exhausting herself "to create, with intelligence rapidly ebbing, with wit half gone, the illusion of an unimpaired estate." With such reasoning there is no possible phenomenon which cannot, with some effort, be made to support his theory. He does respect Mrs. Briss and Obert as, like himself, "consciously infernal" observers, and his problem is to remain convinced that his own deductions are correct, however unlike theirs.

Like the governess, he has his moments of exaltation and feels "a mild artistic glow." Tasting the romance of his adventure, he compares it to "roaming at close of day in the grounds of some castle of enchantment." He even gloats: "The state of my conscience was that I knew too much—that no one had really any business to know what I knew"; and again, "*I* alone was magnificently and absurdly aware— everyone else was benightedly out of it." We are, of course, to be excused if we suspect that not only Mrs. Briss and Obert but some of the others feel much the same about themselves; at least, Obert echoes Mrs. Briss with "Oh, I've watched *you*." Though Mrs. Briss tells him he is "crazy," our hero takes pride in his unemotional objectivity. He cannot, however, win affirmation, now that Obert has assured him that May is really not unhappy and Mrs. Briss has returned to her first theory, that, after all, Lady John, whom she no longer considers clever, is Long's friend—this because Long himself has not really become clever. Her last words are indeed cruel, as she repeats her charge, "My poor dear, you *are* crazy, and I bid you good-night!" She has already made him feel a thousand years old, and her casual dismissal is the end. He cannot linger where he cannot win. Yet, as he decides to leave, he still holds on to what he dare not give up, for to yield his theory would be like relinquishing life itself: "I *should* certainly never again, on the spot, quite hang together, even though it wasn't really that I hadn't three times her method. What I too fatally lacked was her tone."

Had James been interested only in the comedy of mistaken identities, he could have arranged objective evidence that his hero was absurd. The comedy, however, which he provides is much subtler. The narrator is denied even the relief of certainty that he is in error, and, indeed, he may still be on the right trail. Or, most dreadful of all, since he feels old and exhausted, can it be—she hints as much—that he himself has suddenly become Mrs. Briss's sacred fount? The comedy is as deep as life itself. Despite the quantity of objective fact in the world around us, we interpret it in the only way we can, from our own subjective consciousness. We are the architects of our own castles of inference. We are highly comic, and yet pathetic too. And when we consider that the narrator chose to regard himself almost as an all-seeing providence, there may be in our curiosity, at least if it becomes obsessive, an element, too, of the sinister.[7]

V. THE SEARCH WITHIN

ALL JAMES'S STORIES ARE, in some degree, concerned with the identification of the self. Three distinguished exemplars come from the 1900's—"The Great Good Place," 1900, "The Beast in the Jungle," 1903,

[7] See Ralph A. Ranald, *"The Sacred Fount:* James's Portrait of the Artist Manqué," and James K. Folsom, "Archimago's Well: An Interpretation of *The Sacred Fount"* (bibliography, *The Sacred Fount*). Oscar Cargill, *The Novels of Henry James,* 295 (bibliography, General Criticism), concludes that "the story of the narrator is a bizarre tragedy of self-destruction."

and "The Jolly Corner," 1908. The first two are not ambiguous when summarized in general terms, and yet their implications stretch on and on into the realm of mystery. The third has experienced great diversity of interpretation.

In a general way the theme of "The Great Good Place" belongs in the tradition of Wordsworth's sonnet telling us that "the world is too much with us" and of Marvell's portrayal of the mind's withdrawal "into its happiness." The world has been far too much with George Dane, who wakes up to a day of commitments which his literary success has brought him: "He must reap as he had sown. It was a thing of meshes . . . ." Dane has a busy social life, even as James had, and, it may be, with the same justification, for James recognized his debt to the social world which supplied him with hints and insights. At least Dane has not been trapped by mere vain folly. He is a hard-working author, and the meshes have come into being because his success has brought responsibility and he has not been able to call a halt to commitments, still less reduce them. There is no single item in the day's schedule which by itself is intolerable; it is just that the accumulation has destroyed his freedom of choice. Unlike St. George, he is not a cynic, and yet, as he later recalls his feeling when the young and enthusiastic visitor came to his room, he speaks of "my littered room, my shattered day, my bored face and spoiled temper." He is a sensitive man and he knows that something is wrong. From this point on the problem is to achieve a cure. Dane would certainly be willing to settle for a neutral condition, for ordinary mental health with the fever gone. What he is actually to get is infinitely better. Even as tottering from a bed to a chair may have for a convalescent a sensation almost miraculous, so will Dane's dream bring a freshness of appreciation into his life.

Only at the end are we told that it is in a dream that he has found the great good place, but suspense does not hang on whether we shall suddenly be told that he has only been dreaming. For what happens to Dane is very real, and the convention of sleep is but a device, as with Chaucer, for the clearer vision of reality. How does such a man as Dane manage to extricate himself from his unfortunate predicament? According to James's story it would appear that two things are requisite. One is something which in secular terms is akin to grace. For months and years Dane has gone on his steadily narrowing way with no apparent hope for change. Then he suddenly finds himself in a quiet monastic garden, conversing with a brother whose manner and wisdom lead him further and further from the tone of the life he has left behind. He feels he is in a "broad deep bath of stillness." James lets the brother draw an analogy with the ideal of Catholic monasticism, though he is careful to keep a distinction: "It's as simple a story as the old, old rupture—the break that lucky Catholics have always been able to make, that they're still, with their innumerable religious houses, able to make, by going into 'retreat.' I don't speak of the pious exercises—I speak only of the material simplification. I don't speak of the putting off of oneself; I speak only—if one has a self worth sixpence—of the getting it back. . . . So it was high time that we—we of the great Protestant peoples, still more, if possible, in the sensitive individual case, over-scored and overwhelmed, still more congested with mere quantity and prostituted, through our 'enterprise,' to mere profanity—should learn how to get off, should find somewhere *our* retreat and remedy."

At this stage the emphasis is on escape from the material-too-much, but the cue to the future action is in the reference to the getting back of the self. There is no hint of anything akin to religious ecstasy, but the vista developing before Dane invites sensitive appreciation and an emotion intense, yet sustainable. The first sensation, which has been mainly one of relief and relaxation, is replaced by another as Dane perceives that the new world is not only removed from "the wild waters . . . of our horrible time." Though there will continue to be tranquil experiences, soothing to a troubled spirit and having, for Dane, the quality of an act of grace, he becomes increasingly conscious of the second requisite, the discipline involved in the creation and the appreciation of the great good place: "The mere dream-sweetness of the place was superseded; it was more and more a world of reason and order, of sensible visible arrangement." Dane recognizes the inspiration and care which have created the place: "There was no daily miracle; the perfect taste, with the aid of space, did the trick. What underlay and overhung it all, better yet, Dane mused, was some original inspiration, but confirmed, unquenched, some happy thought of an individual breast. It had been born somehow and somewhere—it had to insist on being—the blest conception." In the dramatic context it is another who has created what Dane enjoys; but the dream is his, and one may properly refrain from making a distinction between the other and Dane himself, for the creative act belongs to both. In fact, Dane has lost a sense of a separate identity: "The real exquisite was to be without the complication of an identity . . . ." He exists simply as an appreciative consciousness, with no egoistic desire to assert himself, only with a passion for selfless appreciation.

Thus, a major transformation has occurred. If not to be called a miracle, it has nonetheless a fine suddenness. Once Dane has experienced it he can bring all his energies to the single task of appreciation. As he watches a shower of rain he is, according to our usual concept, passive, but he is actually absorbed intently in his awareness of it. So with everything else—nothing is conducive to mere idle reverie, for everything invites to creative meditation. Even the absence of things is significant: "One by one he touched, as it were, all the things it was such rapture to be without." His mental "detachment" assumes for him a physical sensation—"the sense of a great silver bowl from which he could ladle up the melted hours." In short, every capacity of mind and sense is brought into play, and relationships form in the imagination which have no chance to develop in one's ordinary purblind existence. Detachment in one respect becomes involvement in another.

Though the unknown person to whom Dane attributes the origin of the great good place worked for the sheer joy of creation, without thought of other reward, the fact is repeated that the guest must pay and that the price is indeed dear. The precise coin with which one pays may presumably vary, but it is some form of creative meditation. For James himself it was the very act of writing the story, with all the rigorous discipline and all the bold flights of imagination which it exacted and permitted. The attempt to pay or the illusion that one was paying would not insure the wonderful transformation. On the other hand, however, no one could achieve the experience who had not paid, that is, readied himself for it.

The rain symbolizes the purification which has occurred, and it is also the connecting association by which, reminiscent of Keats in "Ode to a Nightingale," Dane comes gradually back to consciousness of his own room and learns from his young visitor, not only that he has "slept all day," but that "everything's done." One is reminded of the inner self in "The Private Life," which has kept its secret, inviolate existence as creative artist even while the social man has been on public display. We do not need to try to work out the realistic details that would be required for the getting everything done. It is sufficient to believe, with James, that in the very midst of the obligations which one is required to meet he can still partake of the innermost life of the spirit, where he sees things in their elemental beauty and where social life becomes the affinity of kindred spirits. The last words of the story fuse the dramatic, the narrative, and the lyric: "Everyone was a little someone else. . . . the face was the face turned to him by the good Brother . . . . Dane rose and looked about his room, which seemed disencumbered, different, twice as large. It *was* all right." What Dane's eyes tell him about his room and about his visitor is, of course, the measure of the transformation of his inner vision, his inner self. The man who emerges from the great good place is, for ordinary practical purposes, the same man who fell asleep; the world will perhaps discover no differences. But the real George Dane will remember stillness and rain, an interested face, and a voice that spoke for two.

Dane has begun with some preoccupation with self, some hope that he can cease to be the man he seems; but he has been interested mainly in the conditions of his life, and, once he is in the great good place, he has no longer any self-concern. John Marcher, of "The Beast in the Jungle," on the other hand, is obsessed with the question of his identity. Not that he is seeking to determine just what kind of inner nature he has, but that he must believe that he is a very special being, destined for an unusual if indeed not a unique fate. Marcher is at the beginning in the absolute center of his own universe, and only tragedy can shatter his world to let him build anew. Though it would not be proper to call Marcher Everyman, yet his predicament is only an accentuation of that in which any sensitive person may be entrapped.

Marcher is not a philosopher, and he is, likewise, not a psychologist. He cannot work out possible systems of metaphysics and choose the one which will give maximum rein to a creative imagination, nor is he interested in probing into the strange ways of the mind. Instead, he is possessed by a feeling that something much greater must be in store for him than appears to suffice for ordinary mortals. Worldly success would be meaningless; in fact, he is quite contented with his obscure office in the government. It is not the adulation of men that can prove to him who he really is; what is wanted is something he can feel. Indeed, he has already become so immersed in his pursuit of his special fate that he no longer believes he is seeking it; rather, it is something which he is convinced he cannot escape. To doubt its inevitability would be to destroy his universe. What alone remains is to seek for clues as to what the fate may be and how it is to present itself.

Because we have come to accept the belief that to find oneself one must lose oneself, and because we are confident that egoism is a prison, we have no trouble with the general pattern of Marcher's history. When he cannot see that May Bartram loves him so selflessly that she devotes her life to trying to help him, we can easily label Marcher a supreme egoist; and when, at the end, he comes to a bitter awareness of the love he has failed to perceive, we agree that the lesson is valid. He should have known. What, then, differentiates his tragedy from the commonplace? The answer is to be found in James's overtreatment, or what might again well be called one more turn of the screw. For what James gives us is not a mere warning that we must be unselfish, but something much deeper and subtler. The story becomes a quest into the nature of life itself. We dare not condemn Marcher lest we condemn a part of ourselves. Instead, we pity him exceedingly without danger of maudlin self-pity, and this because our emotions are aroused slowly as we come gradually to see the intellectual nature of his problem.

Marcher is acutely sensitive and intently conscientious. True, when he again sees May Bartram ten years after their previous meeting, he has remembered almost all the facts wrongly, whereas she has a most accurate recall. True, he misses the significance of her attempts, both by word and gesture, to tell him that she loves him. But he is, nevertheless, a man worthy of his fate. There are many things which he does intellectually notice and seek to understand, and he repeatedly thinks of May and tries to be kind to her. He is, indeed, fully her

194

equal in capacity for comprehending and in sensitivity; there would be no point in narrating the story of a crude, arrogant boor.

Marcher's history is interpreted in reference to one single theme, and that theme is studied unwaveringly until its vastness has filled James's created universe. We need not go to abnormal psychology to realize that a mind can withdraw from the world outside and construct a dream—or nightmare—realm of its own. The normal man who is seriously introspective sometimes feels himself alone, possibly terrifyingly alone, and preoccupied exclusively with his own isolated being. We generally cut ourselves loose from such supposedly morbid thoughts or find them suddenly shattered by the encroachment of the external world. But what if we were not to be released or by a sheer act of revolt to release ourselves? Then we should have to meet the issues honestly and fully and submit ourselves to the schooling which isolation would bring. James does not grant to Marcher a breaking down of a prison wall by a mere display of will, nor does he make his preoccupation so weak that the exigencies of daily life will shatter his world of thought. He must live within it until he has understood its nature and is ready to depart.

The measure of Marcher's isolation is to be found in the contrast provided by the thoughts and emotions of May. May is not without an awareness of her own personal self, and she cannot escape from deep loneliness and sorrow. She falls into moods of sadness, however, only when her efforts to live in a world outside herself have failed, and she is quick to recover hope and excitement until the final overthrow. Having learned from Marcher ten years before of his strange absorption, she has found it a center for her own thoughts, and upon their meeting again she is caught up in a great romance of adventure. She will watch with him, and, naturally, she hopes that she can somehow play a part in shaping the fate which is to come; for she recognizes that it is something that must happen within Marcher's own mind. Having perceived that he is a man of uncommon sensitivity and depth of feeling, she has no reservation in identifying her own life with his. She is completely in love with him simply because she lives only with concern for penetrating his mental universe, seeing life as it must, she believes, seem to him, and trying to work out an interpretation of it from his perspective. In a sense she has accepted precisely the conditions which James himself accepted in creating Marcher, and all the creative power of her imagination is brought into play as it could not have been by a lesser task. Having early told him, "I'll watch with you," she can much later, after repeated disappointments, say to him, "If you've had your woman, I've had . . . my man."

Her statement is not to be misunderstood. He has not belonged to her in the usual sense, as she has had illusions both as to his nature and his fate; and she is yet to suffer most acutely at his hands. She has had him, however, in a much deeper sense. She has lived because of him as she could never otherwise have done, for she has "let this association give shape and colour to her own existence"; and her own ultimate identity, both for herself and for him, will be the product of her adventure. At the beginning she would sell that adventure short. Though sympathetic, she asks Marcher whether what so vaguely haunts him may not be "but the expectation—or at any rate the sense of danger, familiar to so many people—of falling in love?" Ironically, of course, her words are prophetic, but she cannot yet know how tragically accurate they are. Unlike Marcher, who can see his fate only as a beast which will sometime jump, she sees it as something always at work. When he assures her that it is "in the lap of the gods," she replies, "Yes, . . . of course one's fate's coming, of course it *has* come, in its own form and its own way, all the while." She is only human, however, and she cannot see the end of the affair; she can read only what she has seen, and her most imaginative conjecture cannot transcend the evidence. Consequently, she once mistakenly tells Marcher, in veiled reference to his quest and to her own secret, "You'll never find out."

In the last scene between them her emotions range from fragile hope to despair. As we first see her through Marcher's eyes she appears detached from life: ". . . she was the picture of a serene and exquisite but impenetrable sphinx, whose head, or indeed all whose person, might have been powdered with silver. She was a sphinx, yet with her white petals and green fronds she might have been a lily too —only an artificial lily . . . ." We must accept Marcher's portrait as describing what May herself has tried to seem, as she has gradually

196

become more secretive in expressing her feelings toward him and pre-sumably in acknowledging them to herself. In accord with her with-drawal, she tells him, "I've shown you, my dear, nothing." Suddenly she admits to a hope of yet showing him, though her words are still sphinxlike in ambiguity—". . . if it should happen"—and, with those words, she suddenly, though fatally ill, seems youthful again. She is still not an infallible prophet; for, when asked by Marcher whether he will "consciously suffer," she can only reply, from what she knows, "Never!" She has revised her earlier view: "What I mean isn't what I've always meant. It's different." It would appear that she is trying to say that, whereas she had once thought that he would come to miss her, she now realizes that he will not. But even now she refuses to mind her own prophetic words and moves toward Marcher timidly in one last effort to reverse the pattern of fate which she has tried so hard to accept. When he still does not see, she can do no more. "Don't you know—now," she asks, and she gets in reply, "I know nothing."

May's adventure has ended. When asked, "What then has hap-pened?" she can only lament, "What *was* to." For her the beast has jumped. For Marcher, however, recognition is yet to come. His obtuse-ness seems complete, and the reader, no more than May, can see how light can ever penetrate. And yet the preparation for enlightenment has been going on "all the while," for the last stage in his history is to be no arbitrary verdict by James; it will result from all that has gone before.

When one thinks of May's attempts to reveal her love and the cruel effect upon her of Marcher's blindness, one is tempted to consign him to outer darkness. Yet there have been very significant clues which are unobtrusive simply because Marcher himself does not perceive their drift. He *has* had his woman, even as May has had her man. She may have meant only to express her loyalty, but, ironically, her words are profoundly true in a very different sense. Marcher has been constantly aware of her, even though in an oblique way. He has acted out his role with concern for how it will seem to her. In the very be-ginning he singled her out as the only person to whom he could reveal his innermost thought, and, while wearing a mask before all others, he has later been unashamed in his dependence on her. Almost immediately after they have met anew he senses an affinity: "He had thought of himself so long as abominably alone, and lo he wasn't alone a bit. . . . So he had endless gratitude to make up." He wants to believe that he is carrying his burden alone, yet he is willing to be "selfish just a little" in having May's understanding. He buys her birthday presents, and whenever he fears that he has been selfish, he tries to atone. As the years go by, he fears that he may lose her, and he feels sorry for her: "What if she should have to die before knowing, before seeing—?" At the moment and for a long time to come he cannot, to be sure, make her more than a helpmate in the search for his fate, and he must believe that her own death cannot be the thing fated, for this would be "an abject anticlimax."

In the last meeting, however, despite his blindness and the excruciating cruelty he commits, Marcher has his woman more than at any time before. He is under a partial illusion, of course, when he sees her as a sphinx or an artificial lily, and he is self-centered in believing for a moment that she will be "capable even yet of helping him." When he senses, however, that she is dying, he feels that his own life will end, indeed that her death represents, after all, the leap of the beast. Such a fate would be the "common doom" rather than something rare, "but poor Marcher at this hour judged the common doom sufficient."

There is no reason why May's death should suddenly bring recognition; reflection is needed for its meaning to take form, and loneliness is required to complete the sense of loss. At first Marcher feels a lack of any mark of distinction such as bereavement should presumably bring. Then there comes a realization that all else is "vulgar and vain" in comparison with what he once knew. The shift from looking inward comes in a dramatic manner. In his imagination Marcher creates a second, "his younger self." He can see things as they ought to seem to this other person, and as his thoughts turn more to May he has a "sense that he once *had* lived." On this sense he is "dependent . . . not alone for a support but for an identity." In short his true identity begins to reveal itself to him only as he finds his imagination playing upon a reconstructed past in which Marcher lives in the imagined younger self and is no longer oppressed with consciousness of his present self. It is May who has given him whatever identity he values. There is still

198

some egoism, but it is rapidly departing. When at May's grave he sees another man whose face cannot conceal his grief, Marcher is at last ready to respond to what it has to reveal. Here James adds a significant author's comment: "We allow him at any rate the benefit of the conviction, struggling up for him at the end, that, whatever might have happened or not happened, he would have come round of himself to the light." Chance has provided the immediate impulse, but Marcher is responsible for the ensuing vision: "He had seen *outside* of his life, not learned it within, the way a woman was mourned when she had been loved for herself. . . . and what he presently stood there gazing at was the sounded void of his life."

As James interprets Marcher's thoughts we must remember that the judgments are not precisely James's own, for Marcher condemns himself unreservedly: "The fate he had been marked for he had met with a vengeance—he had emptied the cup to the lees; he had been the man of his time, *the* man, to whom nothing on earth was to have happened." Actually his verdict is untrue, for he has at last seen May Bartram and appreciated her excellence. Indeed, his recognition and his deep sense of loss are the more poignant because he now knows what it means to love May for herself. In his recognition he sees the beast in not one but two symbolic images. Thinking again of the last parting, he sees the beast as having then sprung: ". . . it had sprung in that twilight of the cold April when, pale, ill, wasted, but all beautiful, and perhaps even then recoverable, she had risen from her chair to stand before him and let him imaginably guess . . . ." It is only now, however, that the full consciousness of that farewell comes to him, and so it is now that the spring actually occurs: "He saw the Jungle of his life and saw the lurking beast; then, while he looked, perceived it, as by a stir of the air, rise, huge and hideous, for the leap that was to settle him. His eyes darkened—it was close; and, instinctively turning, in his hallucination, to avoid it, he flung himself, face down, on the tomb." The final gesture is especially fitting, for he has once more turned to May for compassion and help.

John Marcher may not understand more than the sorrow-ravaged man, and in a general sense his love for May is common. If it were not so, it would lack universal significance, but commonness is not cheapness. How universal, however, is the rest of his experience? Here and there the Ancient Mariner recognized a man who could comprehend his rime, and presumably Marcher's fellow in bereavement is among those who can read his desperate gesture aright. What has happened to Marcher has come through his own arduous struggle, and yet it is, at the same time, essentially like an act of grace. He has had at the beginning to be a man capable of profound feeling, and he has had to suffer much before purification could come. Yet the gift of May's love and excellence is completely free once he has the perspective to understand. In "The Liar" the artist says that he likes to paint men at the end of their lives, when the portrait is complete. Whatever may hereafter happen to Marcher, his true portrait is now finished. It is the portrait of a man who has experienced remorse, pity, and, most of all, wonder. In these is his identity.

One interpretation of "The Jolly Corner" makes of the story an autobiographical rationalization by James to justify his living abroad. There are, to be sure, feelings attributed to the hero, Spencer Brydon, that match impressions recorded in James's nonfictional works—particularly the annoyance with the new New York and the nostalgic tolerance of even the ugliness of the city of Brydon's and James's childhood. The story could have been told differently, however, if James had wanted only to discuss the pros and cons of his own way of life. Moreover, there are reported incidents in Brydon's past in Europe that do not parallel James's own experience and are not complimentary to Brydon. Insofar as the story is autobiographical it is so in the manner of "The Great Good Place" and "The Beast in the Jungle." As we saw earlier, James stated that to create certain of his heroes and their histories he had to look within and virtually to turn himself inside out. This he certainly did in "The Jolly Corner," not to rationalize anything, but just to try, with the aid of imagery and symbolism, to convey the intimations that came from somewhere in the recesses of his mind and took possession of his imagination.

Accepting the fact that Brydon's nightly wanderings through the upper rooms of the house known to him as the "jolly corner" and his pursuit of a ghostly alter ego are symbolic, one must still treat them as literal facts, for only then does one actually feel what James was trying to express. The mind must give concrete embodiment to its own inner workings. This is what happens in the story until the next-to-last scene, when the supernatural fuses with the psychological and then finally yields to it entirely.

The subject of the story may be stated as a simple question: Who is Spencer Brydon? That is what Brydon himself sets out to discover. In the beginning we learn a good deal about the man as he has ordinarily seen himself. He has liked an earlier New York and has, in fact, cherished certain memories of it. He has also, however, enjoyed the life he has had abroad; and, unlike Alice Staverton, who has remained at home, he has been a "wanderer," at times guilty of "infidelity" to the values she has preserved from their youth. It becomes clear quite soon that he has been absorbed far too much in his own egoistic indulgence, even as was Marcher. He is fond of Alice, but he thinks of her as one might of a precious possession: ". . . she was as exquisite for him as some pale pressed flower (a rarity to begin with), and, failing other sweetnesses, she was a sufficient reward of his effort." He values her because she has retained the grace of the earlier time, but upon his return home he is still preoccupied with himself. What happens, first of all, is that he finds himself in an unfamiliar world: "Proportions and values were upside-down . . . ." The ugly things from his youthful days now have a charm for him, and, in contrast, the new buildings are big, queer, and monstrous. He is actually lost in a strange world, though he is not yet conscious of that fact. If he is not to remain lost, he will have to search for his own identity. If he is homeless, we may conclude that the cause is in part that the world has not stood still while he himself has changed from youth to late middle age. It is evident that, if he is to search, he can best begin at the jolly corner, his boyhood home, for it will have the most associations with the past.

Before he has consciously framed his problem, however, a new element appears.[8] Having come into possession of a second house, which is being converted into profitable flats, he soon discovers and actually likes "this lively stir, in a compartment of his mind never yet penetrated,

---

[8] James leaves obscure the precise sequence of Brydon's thoughts, but his first interest in wandering through the rooms of the jolly corner apparently precedes his awareness of his latent talent and is then augmented by it.

of a capacity for business and a sense for construction." His imagery
for expressing his awareness prepares vaguely for what is to come; there
is a latent self which he has never had occasion to recognize. Consequently, a hint from Alice that, had he stayed home, "he would have
anticipated the inventor of the sky-scraper" lingers in his memory and
sounds a "small silver ring" over the "queerest and deepest of his own
lately most disguised and most muffled vibrations." It is thus that the
image of a haunted house is born. His "wonderment" takes concrete
form, as if "he might have been met by some strange figure, some
unexpected occupant, at a turn of one of the dim passages of an empty
house. The quaint analogy quite hauntingly remained with him, when
he didn't indeed rather improve it by a still intenser form: that of his
opening a door behind which he would have made sure of finding
nothing, a door into a room shuttered and void, and yet so coming,
with a great suppressed start, on some quite erect confronting presence,
something planted in the middle of the place and facing him through
the dusk."

It is noteworthy that Brydon's talent for business is particularly for
"construction." It is the new construction in the city that has most distressed him, for those who have created new buildings have destroyed
the tone he has cherished. In contrast, while wandering about Europe,
Brydon has ostensibly destroyed nothing. At the same time, of course,
he has never really created. When now he is suddenly confronted with
the only kind of creative activity for which, so far as he knows, he has
talent, it is the task of remodeling, which, in essence, means a destruction of the past. It is with the scarcely admitted excitement of finding
a latent aspect of his nature that Brydon becomes absorbed in the introspective adventure symbolized by the prowling at night through the
upper chambers of the jolly corner.

At the beginning Alice's perception, more prophetic than Brydon's,
anticipates the final revelation. She sees two men—the one she loves,
who, she nevertheless feels, has been "leading, at any time these thirty
years, a selfish frivolous scandalous life"; and an alter ego, who would
have achieved something "quite splendid, quite huge and monstrous."
She is evidently dimly aware, however, of yet another possible Brydon,
for when asked whether Brydon is "as good as I might ever have been,"

she replies, "Oh no! Far from it!" She is certainly not thinking merely of the alter ego, though that man is inseparable from her concept of the true Brydon. She provides a vague clue to what she *is* thinking of when she immediately adds, ". . . you don't care for anything but yourself."

In the dramatic action which follows we may discover certain paradoxes which are fundamental to James's ingress to reality. Brydon has as yet the ability to imagine only the alter ego, and it is that man whom he is determined to bring to bay. But soon a leap of the imagination occurs which James merely illustrates in a dramatic context, free from commentary. It is easily overlooked, and yet it starts Brydon on the way toward final revelation. Having begun as one man, Brydon suddenly becomes a second; that is, he sees himself as if through the eyes of the man he is tracking, for whom he must be "in the apparitional world, an incalculable terror." [9] At the moment his focus is still on himself, but in an utterly new way; and soon he becomes sufficiently detached to see himself, not only in a game of chase, but in one of counterchase. In his excitement he builds up the alter ego as a man who, if necessary, will "fight." The dramatic detachment represents a step towards self-knowledge, for Brydon sees himself in terms of the roles played by both the man called Brydon and the other man, who is also somehow Brydon and will fight for the right to his identity. In his bewilderment he feels that he is "slipping and slipping," and he yearns for something to which to hold fast. Certainly James is trying here, by way of the images in Brydon's mind and even his physical sensations, to suggest how, through introspection itself, the mind, at first haltingly and then swiftly, releases its hold on the inadequate, though hitherto apparently safe, world it has always known when a new, even though forbidding, world opens before it. Brydon does not know into what abyss he may be slipping, but he senses that the familiar daylight existence which he has never previously questioned may be doomed.

The story is told alternately in a dramatic or narrative manner and in an ordered description of the images or articulated thoughts in Brydon's mind. The thoughts are the nearest James comes to offering a

[9] This parallels Ralph Pendrel's sensation in the notes for *The Sense of the Past.*

commentary, and they provide only clues. The rest the reader has to work out for himself, and what follows is one reader's interpretation. Words and phrases must be read in the total context, for, no matter how positively Brydon may assert that he has made a discovery, the meaning of his adventure must await the final scene. That scene, how-ever, is not sprung upon him or the reader out of nothingness. Every-thing ultimately takes its beginning in Brydon's initial malaise, his feeling that the self he has known is not the complete reality. As he slips downward, fearing his descent, he tries to struggle back; yet, ironically, the slipping is what brings him nearer to what he seeks.

By way of Brydon's thoughts and mental images, James summarizes certain changes in his condition. The man suddenly perceives his situation in terms of a romantic adventure: "This was before him in truth as a physical image, an image almost worthy of an age of greater romance. That remark indeed glimmered for him only to glow the next instant with a finer light: since what age of romance, after all, could have matched either the state of his mind or 'objectively,' as they said, the wonder of his situation?" Thus, even though the quest is egoistic in origin, it is becoming something to be wondered at for its own sake. Once again Brydon is like a spectator studying a Brydon involved in a romantic role. The detachment gives him a perspective from which to get a better picture of himself. Shortly thereafter the unreal takes on an authority of its own. Even as Ralph Pendrel was to be unable to make the past behave to suit his will, so Brydon can-not make the imagined. He feels suddenly that a door has been "sub-sequently closed." The unreal must have its own life. The feeling is reiterated when he seems to see "the two, the opposed projections of him, in presence." The alter ego is not specifically defined, of course, but he has a reality which awaits only identification; and Brydon's con-sciousness, which cannot see itself, can see both the supposed Brydon and the alter ego with about equal interest. Our hero even feels that the alter ego, as well as he, has suffered, and, not unlike Withermore of "The Real Right Thing," he would fain retreat from what may be a trespass on the rights of another: "I retire, I renounce—never, on my honour, to try again. So rest for ever—and let *me!*"

The last phrase heralds a reversal, still not clearly understood and subject to attempts to turn back. From this point on Brydon is increasingly in retreat. Here, of course, we have a paradox reminiscent of Chaucer's "Pardoner's Tale" and of many others in that it is when he would gladly abandon the quest for his true self that Brydon hurries, indeed plunges, toward self-knowledge.

Where everything takes place at night there is a mysterious strangeness about each event, but one can find distinctions even within what is strange. While Brydon is cautiously making his way from room to room on the upper floor he is employing the utmost power of reason which he possesses. Much of what comes to him there is imaginative, but he is, nevertheless, determined to keep rational control. His retreat, on the other hand, is not a rational matter at all. When he opens a casement to try to break the spell by letting in the presumably rational outer world, the spell remains unbroken; the "hard-faced houses" have nothing to offer, for they are alien. Only descent is possible, and James's representation of the flight is both literally and symbolically plausible. The author keeps before him constantly the actual physical scene as it would appear to the eye. Under the skylight the stairway seems to lose itself in a "deep well . . . which might have been, for queerness of colour, some watery under-world." James reinforces the image: "This was the bottom of the sea . . . ." Here reason is helpless; the experience is entirely in the form of images and sensations. Moreover, the images refuse to remain fixed. As a faint light reaches Brydon, now near the foot of the stairs, it takes the shape of "a cold silvery nimbus that seemed to play a little as he looked—to shift and expand and contract." The picture is phantasmal, and yet the queer wateriness and the unquiet light are as much a reality as rooms whose doors open into yet other rooms, and, for Brydon, a much more immediate reality than the houses he saw through the casement.

As for the symbolic meaning—it need be nothing beyond what our own sensations suggest as we see the physical picture. Images enter the mind; we try to sort them out and hold one or another fast, but at some point, if we become sufficiently captivated by them, they do "shift and expand and contract" as of their own volition. Since Brydon's quest is for himself, the ultimate symbolic suggestion is, of course, that he, too, may be as phantasmal as what he looks upon. We are thus prepared for the climactic event which will dissolve the world and the personal identity he has believed in and make way for a new creation.

Much conjecturing has been done about the spectral man who confronts Brydon at the very moment when a few more strides would bring him to the outer door and what he fancies would be freedom. One may let his speculations range far and wide, but there are some conclusions which seem more immediately suggested than others. It must be remembered that Brydon was astonished by his suddenly discovered talent for construction. It must be recalled, too, that his discovery gave impulse to his search for the alter ego. That being was at first vague in Brydon's mind; he felt only that it must be utterly unlike himself. Then the other became a man who would fight and later one who had suffered. Now the image becomes much more definite, though not yet fully seen, for the man between Brydon and the door does not at first reveal his face. Brydon is aware of "his grizzled bent head and white masking hands, his queer actuality of evening-dress, of dangling double eyeglass, of gleaming silk lappet and white linen, of pearl button and gold watch-guard and polished shoe." We are entirely dependent on our own interpretation, as James rightly refrains from comment. Obviously the figure represents some form of material success. The only other side of Brydon that has been revealed is that of the potential constructor of buildings, and the appearance of the alter ego is not inconsistent for such a man. The stranger is dignified and impressive; he must have struggled and endured. In conceiving of what he might have been, even though he may prefer his present existence, Brydon cannot want that other to be unworthy of his quest. But, of course, he cannot admit that he has misused his life, and so, the first shock having passed, he comes back to self-conscious comparison and feels himself superior—"he, standing there for the achieved, the enjoyed, the triumphant life."

Then comes the final blow, the unmasking of the face, as the figure removes his hands, one with two fingers missing: "Horror, with the sight, had leaped into Brydon's throat, gasping there in a sound he couldn't utter; for the bared identity was too hideous as *his*, and his glare was the passion of his protest. . . . It was unknown, inconceivable, awful, disconnected from any possibility—! . . . the face was the face of a stranger. . . . the stranger, whoever he might be, evil, odious, blatant, vulgar, had advanced as for aggression, and he knew himself give ground." This is, in short, a man who will fight.

It is, of course, evident that in a different set of circumstances the spectral man might have stood where Brydon was and, had he by some miracle entered upon the quest for *his* other self, he might have confronted the present Brydon. But although external circumstances or some trick of fate would have brought the reversal, James is surely not finally concerned, as some would conclude, with what might have been. The dramatic representation is to illuminate what *is*—"the bared identity was too hideous as *his*." What was unsuspected as Brydon wandered about in Europe and then became recognized as a latent possibility is now seen for what it is, a part of Brydon's very nature.

Yet the discovery cannot be the end of Brydon's search. If the spectral is as much a part of the real Brydon as the man who confronts it, the choice is not to be between the two. A transformation must occur. To bring it about, James dropped, not only the dramatic method by which Brydon confronted his second self, but, for a little while, conscious awareness itself. As George Dane straightened out his life in a symbolic sleep, so Brydon is to be reborn from a swoon. There is actually no rational means of reconciling the two egos that have come face to face, and the recognition of the second self is too overpowering for Brydon by himself to endure. In the succeeding scene, as he returns to consciousness with his head on Alice's lap, he is outwardly the man who came back from Europe, but a great change has begun to take place within. He is responsible for having carried through the adventure which has brought it about, but it is Alice who has been the inspiration and who is finally to help him to live with his new self-knowledge.

Unhesitatingly using symbolism, even in the form of prophetic dreams, James, sometimes in general summary, sometimes in concrete images, explores the essence of Brydon's change. The man sees his experience as a journey home: "He had come back, yes—come back from further away than any man but himself had ever travelled; but it was strange how with this sense what he had come back *to* seemed really the great thing, and as if his prodigious journey had been all for the sake of it."

Again, in semiconcrete form, combining images and reflection: "It had brought him to knowledge, to knowledge—yes, this was the beauty of his state; which came to resemble more and more that of a man who has gone to sleep on some news of a great inheritance, and then, after dreaming it away, after profaning it with matter strange to it, has waked up again to serenity of certitude and has only to lie and watch it grow." The two passages assume greatest significance if one takes them to refer to Brydon's entire life. Certainly, to read the second as referring only to his search at the jolly corner would mean that he had come back to what he was before he began his search, a man guilty of "infidelity," who, as Alice told him, was not at all the man he could be. But the passages do include the nightly prowling, for during it Brydon has been so completely introspective that he has, indeed, lived for a little while in a condition of almost total nihilism.

Significantly, James does not let the swoon and the awakening make of Brydon a paragon of virtue. He is, instead, very human. He would still like to believe that the "awful beast" is not he "even as I *might* have been"; and when Alice assures him that she accepts and pities the other man, whom she has seen in a dream, Brydon becomes comically jealous. So for the first time in his life he admits his dependence on Alice. He has, indeed, come a long way since he saw her as a delicate but pressed flower. When to comfort him she replies, "And he isn't— no, he isn't—*you!*" she could add, were she not merciful, that neither was the earlier Brydon, who wandered rootlessly and thought only of himself. Indeed, the alter ego is really no worse than that Brydon. Alice has accepted both men, with all their imperfections; she is neither ashamed of the one nor horrified by the other. It will take Brydon a while longer to get over the shock of discovery, and he needs Alice's help. They both know that the man who now, for the first time, has admitted his need of her love will always be in part both men, and Brydon must live with that fact. But the man to whom Alice is speaking is not just a dual personality made up of two incongruous elements. As a result of his insight into his latent self Brydon has seen, too, in proper perspective what he once thought was his only self; and as a consequence, he has risen from his swoon ready to become a new man.

It is this new being who humbly appreciates Alice's love as he embraces her. Brydon has at last come home.

Before James wrote the three great stories he had carried on his experimentation for the theater, from which had come his guiding pronouncement: "Dramatise, Dramatise, Dramatise!" The stories are really much more than ordinarily dramatic; indeed, they make use of a special dramatic perspective. Each of the heroes is both himself and one or more other selves, and all the selves are personae in a drama. Dane is the man who falls asleep and also the guest in the great good place, and the young writer who has replaced him at his desk is really Dane, too. Marcher comes to know himself only when he talks with a second, younger Marcher, and Brydon only when his alter ego brings him to bay. James seems to be saying that one cannot see himself by merely trying to look within. To find who one is one must from within look out, even to the extent of projecting oneself into multiple roles upon a stage, where one seeks to perform his parts freely, and yet is subject to the relentless artistic logic which the well-made play demands.

CHAPTER FIVE

THE FUSION OF THEME AND ART:
A MATTER OF WEAVING
AND TAPPING

". . . in all the weaving of silver threads and tapping on golden nails . . ." (Preface to *The Princess Casamassima*)

IN JAMES'S DOUBLE METAPHOR there is no intent of separating technical proficiency from artistic insight. The first commandment for the artist was to see his subject; if he saw it fully, what he perceived was the relationship of all the parts to one other and their general relationship to spiritual experience. As we have seen, James often began with a commonplace motif, perhaps in the form of an unusual or ingenious anecdote. As he mulled over the implications, the motif might become forgotten in the abundance of new suggestions that streamed through his mind—witness the long monologues in which he talked to himself in the notebooks. Eventually there evolved the pattern of the fabric, but even that was tentative until executed in detail; and, as studies of his revisions have demonstrated, a clearer insight into a specific scene, a sharper view of an image, might result in changes which heightened the tone. In short, the weaving—and tapping—was not the means of art; it was the thing itself. As the artist wove, he saw better the design he was trying to find. And with no thought of exhausting the figure in the carpet, the reader may still take pleasure in following the tracery as James left it, to see the interweaving of the strands.

I. AFFINITY: "THE ALTAR OF THE DEAD"

ONE LIVES THE MORE INTENSELY as he projects himself imaginatively into the minds of others, either the living or the dead. James's hero, Stransom, like his creator, would find life flat or, indeed, meaningless

211

if he did not with every faculty of his sensitivity and understanding submit himself to this belief. Like the author who was yet to write "The Great Good Place" and who had already described peaceful retreats from the bustle of human affairs, Stransom cherishes meditation, not only to free himself from the chaos of daily existence, but to feel with intense awareness and deep emotion. As a man to whom experience comes with poignant distinctness, he sees life in images and, like a novelist, creates concrete symbols to give intensity and singleness to his visions.

It is with these primary attributes of a sensitive mind that James began his story, one of several in which, as he said, he had virtually to turn himself inside out. For though the story is not autobiographic in the usual sense, it is an enquiry by its author into the inner recesses of his own thought and feeling, a quest for an orderly understanding of reality.

At the beginning Stransom already appears to possess a condition of mind which, according to James's customary view, one must work hard to attain, and we wonder what is left for him to achieve.[1] He has so loved Mary Antrim that a visit to her grave, though sad, amounts to a "feast of memory." Somewhere or other he goes about his daily work and the routine of external existence, but in his mind there is a churchlike retreat where he worships, not in the conventional tradition, but in reverence for the dead. And since his feelings are at moments almost ecstatic, he conceives in his mind's eye of an altar lighted with candles, one for each dead friend. As we enter his thoughts we are given quick summaries of their general tenor, enlivened by sudden flashes of thematic images. The summaries keep the pattern before us, but it is the images and the resultant actions that are the substance. At first these are lyric in nature in that Stransom wishes merely to preserve precious sensations. There is, as yet, no indication that his present, apparently philosophic, state of mind should not continue.

[1] The notebook entries do not go beyond the mere beginning. In fact, they offer even less, as James noted only Stransom's losing a mother or dear friend, whose death would be a reminder, and his seeing an old woman in a church. Mary Antrim's death means much more. In the notebooks there is nothing suggestive of Acton Hague or of the role of the unnamed woman.

As he was to reveal, however, in *The Sense of the Past,* James knew that one cannot maintain even a private mental experience except through struggle, if at all. So it is that we find Stransom's mind is really not so calmly composed as he would wish. His state of tenseness is revealed by his bitter revulsion when he meets Creston and his noisy second wife, so unlike the dead Kate Creston. We perceive at once that, though Stransom is far superior to Creston, he is, nevertheless, far short of having the philosophic detachment which he would like to possess. He is actually a long way from the great good place, from any state of completely self-forgetful meditation. Indeed, the scene is already in preparation for inner conflict, for dramatic action.

That conflict begins when Stransom reads by chance the small headline "Death of Sir Acton Hague, K.C.B." He must, of course, have thought sometimes of his original friendship with Hague and of their quarrel, but death is a touchstone for Stransom, and James implies the problem which Hague's presents: "He went cold, suddenly and horribly cold, to bed." Memory should be inclusive, and in Stransom's memory Acton Hague should have a prominent role. Even as Maisie, however, was to cast unpleasant things into her mental closets, Stransom will try to obliterate the bitter experience of his wrong by wilfully pushing it out of sight. Hague cannot be accommodated at any altar for Stransom's dead. If it takes effort to consign him to the darkness, it must be recognized that no mere arbitrary effort would effect the opposite. In the world Stransom has sought to preserve there is simply no place for Hague. No wish to follow moral precepts, to be forgiving, to become godlike in dispassionate tolerance could avail. The mind works by its own logic; Stransom's has constructed a world that seems to hold together, and he cannot introduce a destructive force without the certainty of ruin. Thoughts of Hague will recur in Stransom's mind, for he is soon troubled by the instability of his universe; but for a time he will manage, by anxious effort, to keep his mental altar generally under the control of his conscious will.

It is while Stransom is returning from Mary Antrim's grave, the very next day after he has read the headline, that the second intrusion occurs into his private world. The art with which it is presented is an example of James's economy in framing his story. What Stransom recognizes in the bowed worshipper in the church where he has sought rest is the expression of a mood akin to, but much more intense than, his own. The presence of the woman in deep mourning gives him a sense of "community." The scene will be paralleled outwardly at the end of the story, but Stransom has no hint that this quiet incident is to lead to the shattering of his fragile world and to the miraculous creation of a new one. The experience is of a lyric nature, and the story is to end on a lyric note. Between the two there is to be drama, heightened by lyric overtones. It is a drama in which the virtues Stransom has tried to preserve will be lost, then recovered, and finally transformed.

At first Stransom is inspired to greater devotion to his religion. He relegates the ghost of Hague to the periphery of his consciousness and makes the complex arrangements to have an actual array of candles before an altar. Hence his course seems to run more smoothly than before and with increased intensity of feeling. In a passage that reminds one of James's later description of the effect upon him and William of the death of Minny Temple, James summarizes the condition in which the elderly Stransom sits before his shrine: ". . . he found the years of his life there, and the ties, the affections, the struggles, the submissions, the conquests, if there had been such, a record of that adventurous journey in which the beginnings and the endings of human relations are the lettered mile-stones."

The fact that James is always sympathetic toward Stransom must not be construed to mean approval of his every act. Quite the contrary. Stransom is humanly selfish, and James merely recognizes his humanity. There are to be times when the man will almost wish that his friends were dead so that he might have them completely in his possession. If the wish is recorded as a matter of fact, with no expression of moral shock, James is not commending it; he is merely admitting its naturalness. Stransom wants order and harmony. What living people do is disturbingly unpredictable—as he is yet to discover beyond his wildest expectations. If they are dead, they will conform to the dictates of one's will, except, of course, Hague, who, consequently, even in death, must be excluded.

What follows in the story is a weaving of the threads to create a figure and a tone far different from the image and the mood with which

Stransom's adventure began, yet with no loss of their identity. The introduction of Hague has revealed a flaw in Stransom's spiritual world, and it is obvious that, if the story is to be artistically complete, this flaw must cease to exist. One is therefore prepared to await a reconciliation. What occurs, however, is much more. The new life which Stransom is to attain will not be merely the old one purified, but will be a very different one, in which the past and present will become as one and he will live timelessly in the experience of the moment. In short, his is to become a great positive adventure, even against his will, with a sudden new discovery during the final scene. How this occurs is the action of the story—an action which, to turn again to another of James's favorite metaphors, will involve passage through a long crooked corridor before one comes into the "presence."

Stransom's renewed awareness of the second worshipper, who has chosen to sit before his candles, is at first a mere confirmation of the validity of his religion. Very quickly, however, he finds himself thinking specifically of her and wondering about the nature of her sorrows. He knows, so he believes, the essentials, and he is actually never to be proved wrong about these; she is sad, she worships the dead, she is exquisitely sensitive, and she is, as he soon perceives, "pretty." So it is that he is drawn toward what he feels is an infidelity to the dead; he must not go to the church in the hope of seeing his fellow-worshipper —"He went only for *them*—for nothing else in the world." Yet there must be a place in his mind for pity, and he can at least contemplate what he is sure must have been the sacrifice of her youth. Then he comes to feel that, though he has not yet learned her name, what matters is "only their perfect practice and their common need." And then, to give an epic touch, James makes reference to ancient religion—". . . you might have taken them for a pair of pagans of old alluding decently to the domesticated gods." By now we perceive that there is a second adventure which must find its conclusion, a conclusion which must also, however, involve the memory of Acton Hague.

There will never be a contradiction of the initial impression; the woman will fulfill all Stransom's expectations—but in a manner he cannot foresee. First there comes the discovery that her dead "are only One." Her loyalty to that one makes her the more wonderful; but

215

without consciously realizing what he is doing, Stransom would make her disloyal. True, his language is that of friendship, but when he hints that he wants finally among the candles one taller than all the rest and, in answer to her puzzled inquiry, replies, "I mean, dear lady, my own," he is actually inviting a shift in allegiance. Her reply, like all her words, appears to be simple and honest—"And who will kindle one even for me?" We are not inside her mind as we are in Stransom's; we know only that she seems now and later to be clear-eyed and to treat Stransom as if he were, too. What follows, as we trace it through Stransom's thoughts and feelings, is in broad outlines universal. Though Stransom is elderly, he goes through mental gyrations as radical as those of an adolescent. This is only to say that he has come upon something which in its newness is enthralling and yet frightening, and his accustomed way of thinking is under constant assault. At every opportunity he seeks refuge in his old egoism. So it is that, when the woman admits him into her own room in her modest home, he feels "at last in real possession of her." It does not matter that he has in mind something subtler than an inferior mind would feel; the point of view is the same. Her mind, her whole life is of such finite limits that he essentially comprehends it. One recalls Lyon, of "The Liar," who felt equally sure of Mrs. Capadose. Unlike Lyon, Stransom is kind and tender, but he is still naïvely human. It is precisely when he is relishing his sense of possession that he is to find himself staring at the portrait of Acton Hague.

Stransom is trapped. He cannot put out of his mind what has happened, some of it so precious; yet he cannot fit the parts together and accept them. At first the discovery is almost like the revelation of a loved one's infidelity, and yet he has no right to accuse the woman. He tries to find escape in pity, which will preserve his rejection of Hague—"Good God, how he must have used *you!*" She does not, however, require it, and Stransom's refusal to forgive Hague as she has forgiven him brings a quarrel, sad rather than violent in manner—"And she closed the door, shutting him out." There follows a mad whirl, in which Stransom reverts to self-pity, then admits to jealousy and finally to loss of faith as he finds that his devotion to the dead has "ceased like a dropped watch." Only a week has passed, in contrast to the long months before, but time is to be measured in events. In her presence again, he is sobered by her "simple submission to hard reality, to the stern logic of life." Still he cannot resolve their conflict—"Acton Hague was between them—that was the essence of the matter . . . ." In the turmoil Stransom feels helpless; yet we perceive that he is slowly achieving some understanding of his problem even though he cannot tolerate the thought of forgiveness.

Again he escapes from jealousy to pity, but pity intensifies his hatred for Hague: "In one way or another this creature had been coldly sacrificed. That was why at the last as well as the first he must still leave him out and out." Nothing short of forgiveness, however, is acceptable, and so he must reject everything together: "Practically, at the end of six months, he had renounced the friendship once so charming and comforting." The quarrel parallels that of any very young lovers; it differs only in that philosophic meaning is implicit. Stransom again flees to his religion. At first the dead remain dead, but he does succeed in reviving something of his former feeling for them. So, if we could suppress all that has happened since, we should be again about where we began.

The dead do have a reality, indeed in a much greater sense than Stransom can yet perceive. He has turned to his religion for consolation, but it is to offer him much more. For it is when he begins to experience comfort before his altar that he comes to sense a "sharper and sharper pang in the imagination of her darkness." And so he is drawn to the woman in a new way, as he thinks of her wandering in "*exile*," unable to use the altar because of him. The phrase "Just one more" begins to take possession of his mind. It once referred to a candle for himself, but the candle needed for completeness can have no importance after his death if the woman is not there to attend the altar; and when in his illness his mind wanders, the phrase appears to be taking on an even more definite meaning. The obsession with the phrase and the illness itself are not unlike the madness of Lear in sorting out irrelevancies and leaving the possibility for clarity of vision.

Mary Antrim has not been mentioned since the beginning; and the loss of faith in the dead can mean only that the man who felt scorn for the fickle Creston has not been nearly so faithful as he had expected

217

to be to the memory of Mary. But when he finds himself alone before the altar and too weary to care to leave, he is, for the first time, wholly in the power of his religion: "He had given himself to his Dead, and it was good; this time his Dead would keep him." What follows is in the pattern of miracles, but it is possible only because Stransom's mind is prepared. In what seems a "dazzling and blinding" light he sees "human beauty and human charity" expressed by the face of Mary, and in that very moment he is struck with the contrast of his "rapture with the bliss he had refused to another."

In the succeeding moments we are reminded of the much earlier scene. The woman has asked about him during his illness, and her presence now in the church implies that she, too, must have experienced a change. We recall that she has forgiven Hague despite his injury to her. Though she has never admitted that she had reason for forgiving Stransom, maintaining that he had never wronged her, yet she was certainly unable to accept him as he was; the shutting of the door symbolized her refusal. Now, as Stransom becomes aware of a "prostrate figure, a figure he had seen before," and tries in his weakness to make the necessary association, we, too, come slowly to a consciousness that something akin to forgiveness must have occurred. We are struck also with the fact that James has omitted all except the essentials. At the beginning it was affinity of feeling that Stransom imagined; now he is to find it beyond all doubt. The woman's own words amount to a renunciation, not of her religion, yet of what was selfish in it. She herself uses the term *miracle* to describe the transformation which has taken place, and she adds, "It's not for my own—that's over. But I'm here for *them*." In the reconciliation Stransom offers her the candle she has asked for, and we know that, for him, peace has come.

The very last paragraphs, however, bring a new insight, expressed by a shift in the perspective. We have felt that we have known the woman, perhaps almost that we have had "possession" of her, but the point of view has been, nevertheless, from outside her mind. The next-to-last paragraph is still from outside, but the phrasing indicates a certainty as to her feelings beyond what has preceded: "'Ah no more—no more!' she wailed, as with a quick new horror of it, under her breath." The earlier scene in the church was lyric in nature, with the emotion depending on our general and familiar associations. The present emotion has sprung from the action itself. And now the bold leap to a new recognition is completed, with all the emotion it brings. For note the daring shift in the perspective: "'Yes, one more,' he repeated, simply; 'just one!' And with this his head dropped on her shoulder; she felt that in his weakness he had fainted. But alone with him in the dusky church a great dread was on her of what might still happen, for his face had the whiteness of death."

As we enter the woman's mind, now, at last, the affinity is complete. As the result of all that has gone before, Stransom and we *are* in possession. Such is the miracle of art.

II. BETRAYAL AND SORROW:
THE WINGS OF THE DOVE

THE IMAGE OF THE DOVE'S WINGS suggests immediately, of course, both the popular tradition and the passages in the Psalms, and the connotations of the allusion dominate James's novel increasingly as it progresses toward its climax and end. In time it becomes evident that the image symbolizes, not just one narrative action, but a story of dramatic complexity, with an interweaving of themes. The artistic interest is in that weaving, by which each theme gains from its ultimate inseparability from each of the others. The course and resolution of each can be traced, but along the way its development is heightened by the presence of the other themes, both for support and contrast. Though the patterns can be identified, they are not readily apparent. A character's attitude may be presented first in reference to one situation, only to become significant at a later time in a new relationship. Thus Kate's feelings toward her father and Aunt Maud prepare for her treatment of Milly, and Densher's deception of Aunt Maud for his deception of Milly; and seemingly casual remarks in the earlier conversations of Densher and Kate become of major importance as we enter the final scene. The unity of the novel is never explicitly indicated; instead, it is suggested in the nuances and implications of each separate action, even the most minute.

Theoretically, James could have begun his novel with either of his three main characters—Kate Croy, Merton Densher, or Milly Theale. There was, however, the matter of economy. Densher's problem could not be stated fully without reference to Kate; and, though Milly's initial attitude toward life could be presented separately, what happens to Milly depends on Densher and Kate. So it is that we are introduced first to Miss Croy.

We quickly learn that all is not well with Kate, that because of her own nature she may be headed toward, if not absolutely destined for, tragedy. We learn also that she is worthy of compassion, indeed, in certain respects, of admiration. Whatever tragedy may come will be the greater in magnitude because of the greatness of the spirit which will suffer. James portrays Kate by placing her in an environment which is evil and by unfolding her rebellion against its standards and her self-entrapment within them.

At the beginning Kate seldom thinks in moral terms; it is mainly after she has done wrong that she becomes concerned with ethics, and then, of course, with much rationalization. At first she is drawn by family ties and driven by her determination to be free. Her feelings about her widowed sister Marian and her shamelessly base father are confused. Since she does not love Marian, whose poverty and narrow existence she finds oppressive, it is with a mixture of loyalty and annoyance that she has given her half of her own £200 annuity. And while she is waiting in Croy's squalid quarters she tries futilely to work out a satisfactory attitude toward the man who made life wretched for her now dead mother: "She tried to be sad so as not to be angry, but it made her angry that she couldn't be sad." Despite her generosity to Marian she has been rebuffed; and now, when she offers to share her remaining £100 with Croy, she is told cynically that she must instead keep the favor of her rich Aunt Maud. As she soon confesses to Densher, she has offered to live with Croy "to save myself—to escape," and she adds that she would join Marian "in a moment if she'd have me. That's all my virtue—a narrow little family feeling." Kate is moved neither by affection nor by generosity. When she recalls her father's treatment of her mother she has to "smother" her "shrieks." Indeed, she can think of Croy only with a sense of humiliation and resentment and of Marian only with a strong mixture of contempt. James does not probe into the nature of her attachment; it is sufficient that the two relatives do represent the familiar, that they still symbolize what ought to be Kate's home.

She is not only drawn, but compelled, toward Croy and Marian, for the immediate alternative is complete submission to the will of Aunt Maud. If Kate were to submit, she would be rich and respected and could even do something for Croy and Marian; but the price is more than she can bring herself to pay, for it includes the giving up of Merton Densher. Kate is no shallow, giddy girl; she has not fallen in love with Densher because of any quality in him of glamor. He is not rich, nor is he brilliant. He does, however, love her devotedly, and she senses the value of his devotion. At the same time, with the memory of her mother's suffering and the object lesson of Marian's poverty, she cannot bring herself to give up wealth for Densher. At this point we are not permitted by James to find an easy solution. Kate is impelled by powerful sensations. She is not a mercenary creature or she would never offer to go live with her father. But she cannot bear to look forward to a lifetime of hardship and uncertainty as the wife of a struggling journalist.

What then can she do? Though she loves Densher, she has too independent a spirit to let him influence her decisions. She is therefore essentially alone in a world filled with sordidness and egoism. She has been frank with her father and in reply has been counselled to deceive Aunt Maud. She thinks of her aunt as a lion, with herself the kid about to be devoured; again, her title for her is "Britannia of the Market Place"; and yet again, Maud is an "unscrupulous and immoral" besieger of a citadel inhabited by Kate. As we accumulate information about Aunt Maud our sympathy for Kate increases. Under the pretense of wanting Kate's happiness, which a good marriage and Maud's money would somehow assure, she demands absolute obedience. Even as Marian and Croy typify aspects of reality which are oppressive to a person of Kate's sensitivity, so Maud comes to represent a sinister, relentless force determined upon the destruction of Kate's soul. Except for one thing, we could rejoice in Kate's success in deceiving her, for she deserves to be deceived. That one thing, unfortunately, is central in importance. Kate knows that Aunt Maud is using her and that she therefore owes her nothing; but she herself has gone a step beyond mere rebellious evasion, for she is going to use Aunt Maud. The effect on the latter need not worry us, but we begin to fear for Kate.

In touches here and there we have already sensed the fact that Kate is dreadfully alone. James obliquely emphasizes her loneliness by revealing that, even in her love for Densher, she has her own secret motives and makes her own private decisions: "What she felt was that, whatever might happen, she must keep [Densher's 'long looks'], must make them most completely her possession; and it was already strange enough that she reasoned, or at all events began to act, as if she might work them in with other and alien things, privately cherish them and yet, as regards the rigour of it, pay no price." This summary is properly free from specific moral comment. At the same time it hints of tragic error and of eventual moral isolation; the fitting together of alien things implies a defiance of racial experience to the contrary, and we traditionally assume that all things demand a price.

We can see early in Kate's career that, if all persons were to achieve such independence as she seeks, the social world would disintegrate, and we begin to anticipate tragedy. The significance of her story will not depend, however, on the mere repetition of attested truths. Rather, it will lie in discovering afresh the capacities of the human mind, above all the capacity for sorrow. While remaining a person with a specific history and identity, Kate will come to epitomize a range of experience which man must comprehend. At the same time, too, that she is demanding our compassion we suspect that she may become a force for evil in the lives of others.

One of those others is inevitably Merton Densher, like Kate, a person of sensitivity and refinement, and, like her, bewildered. In temperament he contrasts strongly with her, being more a philosopher than a doer, more an idealist than a realist. Because of the dynamic role played by Kate, Densher seems at first almost a minor personage. James had to resort to explication to define his character: "The difficulty with Densher was that he looked vague without looking weak—idle without looking empty." For him, Kate is a remarkable woman; she has brought romance to his life, and, like a knight of chivalry, he would fain please his lady. Yet he dislikes the part she allots him. In his acquiescence to her demands is his tragic error, in his resultant malaise the possibility of his self-discovery. Kate once tells him frankly that she has learned to do things which she does not like. Densher is less honest with himself and attempts to disguise the unpleasantness of what he feels he must do. Knowing, for example, that Aunt Maud actually likes him, though not as a moneyless husband for Kate, and trusting that somehow Kate will gain by concealing their love, he consents to the deception; yet he cannot face it for what it is: "He wouldn't grovel perhaps —he wasn't quite ready for that; but he would be patient, ridiculous, reasonable, unreasonable, and above all deeply diplomatic." Aunt Maud is a very different kind of adversary from the traditional foe of knights, and the weapons must be chosen to fight guile with guile. To consent to be ridiculous—not in Maud's eyes, but his own—is to pay a high price, but the concluding word with which James sums up his thoughts shows how determinedly he turns his face from the reality. Not only does *diplomatic* nicely push aside any moral considerations, it even puts the stamp of cleverness on his proposed conduct, no matter how ridiculous. And having begun with deception of Maud, he will, in the course of time, find it the easier to rationalize Kate's and his betrayal of Milly Theale.

Still, Densher is a much better fellow than the preceding paragraph would suggest. He has a dream of beauty, and he is, by nature, kind. He could like Aunt Maud if he did not see her tyranny to Kate. Even his exquisite taste is combined with a feeling which is humane, perhaps moral. Thus, as he contemplates the expensive ugliness of Maud's home, he senses it emotionally as "operatively, ominously so cruel." In every fiber of his nature Densher shrinks from ugliness; and cruelty is inseparable in his mind from uncouth and vulgar behavior. He is therefore inevitably on the side of beauty and gentleness and, above all, consideration for the feelings of others. Indeed, diplomacy toward Aunt Maud is an expression of good taste and of kindness; he could hardly act otherwise than he does without being ashamed. And, of course, he will never wish anything unkind to Milly.

At the same time, Densher is restive. He has relinquished whatever independence he previously had, and he cannot think of Kate without sensations that are far removed from idealistic adoration. Hypocrisy, however rationalized, involves intrigue and constant preoccupation with practical, indeed petty, details of conduct. Densher is, by temperament, indifferent to such matters and inclined toward heroic action and exalted emotion. Though he has not the passionate singleness of mind which we expect of a great tragic figure, he is nonetheless sensitive and thoughtful; and, if he can escape corruption, he may yet do something impractical—and essentially heroic. He will need inspiration, however, and it cannot come from Kate. We are thus ready for the introduction of Milly Theale.

Without the presence of Kate and Densher a beautiful and pathetic story could have been told of Milly, even as in actual life such a story was to be told of Minny Temple. It is, indeed, a most serious error to regard Milly as a mere symbol of virtue or religious grace, even though she may eventually represent an ideal for Densher. She is a young woman of sensibility, the "potential heiress of all the ages," doomed to die and conscious of the sweetness of life and of her own mortality. Her sorrows and her fears as to her health have not led her toward asceticism, and she has not needed to sacrifice herself for the sake of others. On the contrary, she wants to live and to enjoy. Despite the friendship of Susan Stringham, however, Milly is in "romantic isolation," having lost all her immediate family. Because of her isolation she yearns for friends, but in the great crisis of her life she will have no one to whom to turn. We quickly become aware of her wistful longing for romance of adventure and, at the same time, of her loneliness. She is found sitting on a precarious mountain seat, and James provides an author's chorus: "She was looking down on the kingdoms of the earth, and though indeed that of itself might well go to the brain, it wouldn't be with a view of renouncing them."

It is at this point that Sir Luke Strett's pity betrays to his patient that she is gravely ill, and with the discovery Milly joins the ranks of the dissemblers, in her naïveté choosing Kate for her accomplice. The deception which she determines upon is, of course, of a praiseworthy nature, to spare Susan the truth about her illness. It is an escape of a sort from the thought of death itself. Milly manages to find some excitement in the intrigue, revealing how frantically she wants to live. She is now, more than ever, concerned that she must not waste the remainder of her life, that she must "go in for pleasure" and get the "highest" kind. She does not yet know what is the highest, but, as she tells Kate, "Well, it's just our chance to find out. You must help me." Before, with Kate's help, she finds out that it is love, she gets what seems to her a very high form through acting her part and working at appreciation. When, for example, Kate calls her a dove, Milly perceives the danger implied in the image, but she decides to enjoy the prerogatives of a dove. She accepts Kate's respect as being "in the manner of an *accolade;* partly as if, though a dove who could perch on a finger, one were also a princess with whom forms were to be observed." She likes the attention shown her by Sir Luke, wanting to imagine he is in love with her; and for a time she will get all the pleasure she can out of the consideration which her great wealth brings her.

It is important to keep in mind that, even though the pretense to Susan is a kindness, Milly is not presented in moral terms. She does not think in the language of right and wrong, because she has no need. She does not even want to see the evils around her. Lord Mark tells her quite early that "no one among them did anything for nothing," and Kate soon adds that Mark "was working Lancaster Gate [Maud and her associates] for all it was worth: just as it was, no doubt working *him,* and just as the working and the worked were in London, as one might explain, the parties to every relation." Milly is so utterly absorbed, however, in her fragile adventure in search of the highest pleasure that she has no thought for evil. It could never occur to her that, for the sake of her money, Kate and Densher might ever use her.

Thus, we have the three—Kate, Densher, Milly—with Susan and Sir Luke typifying imaginative understanding of Milly; and Croy, Marian, Maud, and Lord Mark, the various manifestations of the world best known by Kate. By the end of volume one there has been some interplay, but mainly the points of view have been presented and the dramatic relations are just beginning. The small group of characters constitute a complete world. It is sufficient, for James, to trace their relations to each other, for both exaltation and tragedy are encompassed therein.

The career of Milly, which is told in part through dramatic action, in part through the thoughts of Densher and Kate, follows a rather simple pattern. From believing that she is deceiving Susan, Milly goes on to fancy that she has actually become a kind of guardian-confidante of Sir Luke, and then to believe that Densher loves her rather than Kate. Established expensively in the Venetian palace, she sees herself paying for happiness and liking to pay. Susan treats her as a princess, and she tries to enjoy the role. When she finds her freedom increasingly restricted by illness, she manages to work out a view of life that will make a virtue of her forced retreat: "The romance for her, yet once more, would be to sit there for ever, through all her time, as in a fortress; and the idea became an image of never going down, of remaining aloft in the divine dustless air, where she would hear but the plash of the water against stone." There are numerous images which suggest both the fragility and the beauty of the life Milly imagines and attempts to live.

The pathos is revealed in hints here and there, but especially in one scene, the full account of which is not completed till later. Because Milly does not love Lord Mark, she has no need to dissemble to him, and so she tells him frankly, "I'm very badly ill." Then comes the supreme shock, Lord Mark's exposure of the truth that Densher loves Kate. Milly denies the possibility, but her subsequent decline shows that she has acknowledged the blow. Soon afterward Susan is to report, "She has turned her face to the wall."

Though Milly has not been active, even in encouraging Densher's love, her very existence has influenced and, after her death, is to continue to influence, not only the actions of Kate and Densher, but their very beings. They have plotted to deceive her, have, in fact, shaped their whole view of life in reference to her, and must finally see themselves in the light of her excellence. In this sense the lyric representation of Milly becomes a dramatic force. She is most present when absent, and death but intensifies her reality for the others.

What has this American girl known, and what is it that remains after her death? She has experienced intoxicating exaltation, despite the shadow upon her of death. She has determined to make of life the highest adventure, and for a brief while she has had that adventure in the world of imagination and dreams. She has also been subjected, not merely to sobering realities, but to humiliation. She has finally to recognize that it is her money that has been loved, with a love that has assumed her early death—that she has been cruelly *used*. Even so, she cannot bring herself to contemplate evil; she does not condemn Densher. As her last days are reported, it appears that she has admitted that her life has been an illusion; but she does not entirely accept defeat. She has enjoyed being treated as a dove, and she plays out the role by making Densher her heir. Here we are given only the external fact, but the action is consistent with her thoughts as we have come to know them. The gesture amounts to a final pathetic attempt to keep alive, even after her own death, a joy she has lost. Ironically, of course, without her knowledge, she is at last loved, more wonderfully than she could ever have imagined.

The progress of Kate is also toward disillusionment, but with no exaltation along the way. There is much that she never makes articulate, but which we sense from the feelings which she does acknowledge. At all times we have justification for pitying Kate, though she brings her own undoing. She herself does not ask for pity, nor does she ever blame others. Recognizing the crass egoism of Lancaster Gate, she never asserts that she is forced to subscribe to its cynical code. What she does, she is convinced, is of her own decision. She wants to hurt no one, and very early she feels a deep and sincere compassion for Milly, a feeling she is to remember as "precious." Lacking moral touchstones, however, she would effect both Milly's happiness and her own eventual pleasure by doing something unpleasant, persuading Densher to woo and even marry the girl. It is in justifying her conduct that she tells Densher that she is accustomed to doing things she does not like. Kate has not the imagination to understand that the game is perilous for Milly, as she may become undeceived, and that she is playing with the soul of her reluctant accomplice, who may sometime rebel.

We could, of course, say simply that duplicity is always bad; but James keeps to his own rules, and in the history of Kate he is concerned with her view of the world and of herself. Once the deception has begun, Kate tries to free her mind of any qualms by arguing that it would be wicked to break Milly's heart by telling her the truth. She admonishes Densher, "Do you want to kill her?" and after telling him that the girl is "worse," she adds, "We're doing our best for her. We're making her want to live." Her words are, of course, factually accurate, but she belies their spirit by reminding Densher why he is to marry Milly: "You'll in the natural course have money. We shall in the natural course be free." It is not she or Densher who is to bring sorrow to Milly; indeed Kate must know that feeling she is loved may well lengthen the girl's life. She stakes her trust on the "natural course"; there can be no guilt in that. As for her own and Densher's freedom, she can have no possible conception of what Milly's death will ironically do to that.

It is paradoxically true that, even though Kate is responsible for her own conduct, she cannot remember a time when she was free. Her offer to accept penury with Croy was an effort at freedom. Her deception of Aunt Maud has been to preserve some individuality, to keep from being spiritually destroyed. By her own definition she can be free only when she is independent of others. She is unable to see that the freedom that matters is from one's own self-concern. Her feeling of compassion for Milly was precious because, for the brief moment, she *was* unconsciously free, living outside her own isolated life and seeing the world from a new vantage. What she expects from the death of Milly could not possibly bring freedom, for it could only increase her spiritual isolation.

In the closing scenes, after Kate has done much that she has disliked doing, she hopes at first to take full advantage of the natural course. She reasons that she and Densher have "squared" Aunt Maud; and, as for Milly, she has had her "peace." She amplifies for Densher, "Of having *been* loved . . . . She had all she wanted." Kate's actions, however, reveal her uneasiness. Marian's home is a poor refuge, and Kate's escape to it from Lancaster Gate shows how seriously she is disturbed. She is, nevertheless, of a sturdy spirit, even when her world is in danger of collapse. She tries to persuade Densher that Milly still believed that he loved her, that Mark was convinced that she so believed, and that she herself at all times played fair with Milly. She is patient with Densher, going on tram rides and proving an excellent companion. Indeed, she has never before been so apparently in command of herself.

The truth, however, will not be hidden forever. Kate has not been sincere with Densher; she has used him, too. But in the final scene she is forced to admit reality, both to Densher and to herself. After one last futile attempt at deception, she tears away the veil. When poor Densher loyally denies that he was ever in love with Milly, she replies, "But your change came—as it might well—the day you last saw her; she died for you then that you might understand her. From that hour you *did*." Again for a moment Kate is self-forgetful as she sees life through Densher's eyes, but she returns to her lonely self. When told she can have Densher or the money, but not both, she can only reiterate, "Her memory's your love. You *want* no other." And when he says that he will marry her "in an hour . . . . As we were," the very words are the measure of her loss. She pronounces her own sentence: "We shall never be again as we were." In that tragic cry is an admission of the contrast between herself and Milly. It is not a confession of remorse and a yearning for atonement; but it is a stark, abject recognition of tragic loss.

The focus in the novel is, at one time or another, on Milly or Kate, and the story of each is fully told. The career of Densher is no more important than their histories. It is, however, somewhat more complex, and it serves indirectly as a commentary on the other two. For Densher is drawn toward both Kate and Milly, even while he is struggling to work out a destiny for himself.

Repeatedly, and even in the last scene, Densher takes moral refuge in the thought that he has been and is still willing to be loyal to Kate. Yet he gets no satisfaction from his allegiance. Once he tells her, "You keep the key of the cupboard, and I foresee that when we're married you'll dole me out my sugar by lumps." Soon he is embarrassed to realize that Aunt Maud considers him "bribeable." Having acquiesced in the plan of deception, he feels he must endure the humiliation it brings: "Not to give away the woman one loved, but to back her up in her mistakes—once they had gone a certain length—that was perhaps chief among the inevitabilities of the abjection of love." So it is that, having permitted the betrayal of Milly, Densher lies to her: "He had so rounded his corner that it wasn't a question of a word more or less." Like Kate, he would shift the issue from the main problem to a less unfavorable one. Instead of contemplating his deception of Milly, he continues to think rather of his subjection to Kate. He feels a "sensible sharpness of irony as to her management of him." With a "special smothered soreness, his sense almost of shame," he wonders "whether he hàd really no will left." It is under the naïve illusion that an assertion of manliness will solve his problem that he drives his bargain with Kate —"to tell any lie you want"—on condition that she come to his rooms, a contract which only binds him the more tightly.

At this very time, ironically, Densher finds himself increasingly drawn toward Milly with a dim sense of wonder, which will grow and bring with it a new sense of shame. He feels that she is "indeed a dove" and that her wings may offer protection to others. Having become uncreative in his profession and being unhappy in his role, he would welcome protection. When his growing awareness of his wrong to Milly threatens remorse, he tries at first to shift the guilt to Lord Mark, who, for his own selfish interests, has exposed him. Having already regarded himself as more delicate and honorable than Mark, he now bestows upon him the epithets of "idiot" and "ass." Nevertheless, he cannot escape; he must finally admit to himself that he is afraid and ashamed. The objective expression of his feeling is the fact that it is two weeks after his return to London before he visits Kate. When he talks with her he is much confused, for he has begun to be conscious of strangely discordant images. We learn of the change partly from his own words, partly from his not denying Kate's. Even while protesting his fidelity to her he condemns himself. When, for example, she speaks of their having squared Aunt Maud, he replies, "What a brute then I must be! . . . To have pleased so many people." He is beginning to glimpse something better than he has known before: "He had been, to his recovered sense, forgiven, dedicated, blessed; but this he couldn't coherently express." He even becomes ashamed of his deception of Aunt Maud, which has been a part of his betrayal of Milly. Still unaware, however, of the price he must pay, he seeks to pay no more: "We've played our dreadful game and we've lost. . . . Our marriage will— fundamentally, somehow, don't you see?—right everything that's wrong . . . ." He once tries to find solace by entering a church, and he enjoys

Kate's society when they go riding on the trams. These attempts at escape, however, do not avail. In the last scene he reaffirms his loyalty, but acquiesces when Kate tells him that Milly's memory is his love. It is then that, at long last, he asserts his independence in saying that he will marry Kate only "as we were."

Densher is not a spectacular tragic figure; he does not express his passions in a traditionally heroic manner. Here at the end he is not a magnificent sinner. Rather, he is a resigned and lonely person, who, through coming to wonder at the excellence of Milly, has attained also to as much as he is capable of achieving of self-knowledge.

In thinking of the three histories that James has presented, one is, of course, aware of mythic types. In the forgiveness by Milly, for example, there are inevitably resemblances to Christianity, but only because both traditional Christianity and James begin with the nature of human life. Despite the several references to the image of the dove, Milly is not intended to personify an abstraction; she is a very real young woman, aspiring and suffering, beautiful and pathetic. If Kate is doomed to some kind of hell, it is one which she herself has discovered, no matter how many others have descended to similar self-knowledge in the history of religion or myth. Though she is not devoid of shame, what she senses most is a loss, an emptiness. She has nothing on which to construct a new life. Under the shadow of the wings, she is yet an outcast from happiness and hope. As for Densher, his sin has been only more accentuated than that of most people; his puzzlement is utterly human. He has experienced and will continue to experience remorse, but he has also had glimpses of beauty. If the wings have extended to protect him, he must nonetheless suffer that he may achieve understanding.

As we have followed the action of the novel, we have seen, on the one hand, the longing of the human spirit to be free, and, on the other, the human predicament. We have become immersed in a world of ugliness, of animal strife, and, indeed, of animal fears; and we have realized that we must accept the predicament even while seeking the most ethereal freedom. We have come to pity both Milly and Kate, and to see life through the tragic eyes of Densher. There has been a completeness, and there has been a unity. In the last scene we come back to the title with a recognition of new implications. Relations, as James remarked, stop nowhere, but a vast and complex action has been brought to an artistic conclusion, and human passions have been resolved.

III. INITIATION: *THE AMBASSADORS*

WITH EQUAL APPROPRIATENESS *The Ambassadors* might have been called "The Education of Lambert Strether," for the other ambassadors from America to Europe serve mainly to contrast with Strether; and we are interested in his ambassadorial mission only because it is basic to his acquisition of knowledge. Indeed, a somewhat similar title might be "What Strether Knew," for there are parallels between the perspectives of the middle-aged American and the young Maisie, in that each is eager for adventure, yet afraid, and each must finally accept a reality different from his romantic dream.

The limited point of view in *The Ambassadors* has repeatedly been praised. Except for minor departures, the action occurs in the presence of Strether or is seen through his consciousness. This fact by itself would be of no value were it not for the nature of Strether's mind and problem. To illustrate, we may start by giving a summary of the novel which, superficially, more or less covers the entire action. A New Englander with a puritan moral background goes to Europe to disapprove what he expects to find, instead becomes attracted by what he discovers, and then must finally admit to disillusionment and act in accord with his initial moral views. Such a summary bears the same relation to the actual narrative as many of James's notebook plots bear to the tales that grew from them; it in no way suggests the significance of the novel. But since we have, as hero, a man who is not narrowly puritan, who is not naïvely gullible, and who does not settle for easy solutions, the plot becomes less simple. Since, moreover, we have a man endowed with sensibility, a rare imagination, and a latent passion for experience, we see at once that, instead of a linear narrative of what comes to his consciousness, we have the possibility of a complex drama. All kinds of conflicting images and ideas come into Strether's mind. If each were allowed unrestricted authority, there would be anarchy. If, on the other hand, any of them were completely suppressed, the effect would be narrowness of understanding. The technical—and philosophic—problem for James was to present a mind in which powerful contradictory forces would be at work and yet in which there would be a unifying principle sufficient to maintain consistency of personality and integrity.

One may say that in the novel there are two stages, with an invisible separating line. The consciousness of Strether is one. At times James lets us look directly into his hero's mind to see the struggle between impressions, between wishes, between ideals. The social world in which Strether acts is the other. In that world the various characters illustrate objectively the conflicting views with which he must reckon. There is added intricacy in that the reader perceives some things about the other characters that remain at least partially obscured to Strether, and yet, in judging them, must see them for what they mean to him. Thus, we see them on the outer stage and draw our conclusions about them in hard, perhaps inflexible terms, only to see them again in Strether's consciousness and to accept his tolerant view. Who are they finally? Or, in a larger sense, what is life? It is not exactly as Strether sees it, and yet it is also not what it might seem to us if we lacked his help in discrimination and appreciation. So we are concerned with Strether for his own sake and perhaps even more for what he helps us to see.

As we have seen, James stated that he had to turn himself virtually inside out to create such characters as Strether. What did he gain by imagining a hero who perceives only from his limited view what James himself could see more inclusively? Actually Strether was his means of exploring life with a consistent perspective and attitude. As Strether finds his way among events, he is confronted persistently with the problem of fitting new knowledge with the old. His difficulties are those of Henry James and of all other sensitive, imaginative persons, who inevitably find themselves in the midst of comparable adventures. The complexity of his career stems from the complexity of his own mind, its clarity from his passion for order. The story of his adventure contains variety because it is an inquiry into diverse, incongruous things. Its suspense resides in the nature of what Strether will climactically recognize and what he will then feel compelled to do. The doing will, of course, be only the overt expression of the seeing.

The unfolding of Strether's story is both technically and psychologically subtle. Instead of trying to give a full portrait of a complex person at the very beginning, James recognized that things remain latent in the mind until called into life by circumstance. So it is that, after his arrival at Liverpool, Strether, stage by stage, discovers or rediscovers things about himself which become increasingly important in his new adventure. In short, what takes place is essentially self-discovery, which comes through his capacity for appreciation. Who Strether is, is a matter of what he can become, that is, of what he can come to appreciate.

We have already discussed the forms which the puritan impulse took in nineteenth-century New England. His home town of Woollett appears to represent for Strether primarily two aspects of puritanism. It values hard work which leads to success, and it has a fear of pleasure. As Strether remarks to Maria Gostrey, "Woollett isn't sure it ought to enjoy." He respects Woollett; he may have sport about its standards, but in his comment to Maria he is actually speaking of himself. Moreover, Waymarsh, of Milrose, who exemplifies both the working for success and the suspicion of pleasure, is his good friend. Waymarsh could easily have been presented in the manner of a caricature; instead, he is treated with respect. Strether is amused with his friend's "sacred rage"—his mingled frustration and fascination before things European—and he tries sometimes to escape his oppressive solemnity; but he recognizes in Waymarsh a side of his own nature.

What individualizes the man from Woollett, however, is, first of all, the basis of his moral preoccupation. If, like his fellow townsmen, he subscribes to negative commandments, he does so, not because they are easy rules of thumb, but because they seem in general accord with his consideration for others. Like Fleda Vetch, he cannot endure an image of himself engaged in selfish enjoyment. Since there is nothing wrong with such a standard of conduct, Strether would be guilty of a moral decline if he were to abandon it, and he never does.

What then makes for complications and suspense? Simply the fact that Strether has also come to identify enjoyment itself as having virtually a moral claim upon him. To fail to live is wrong. In the course of time he is to pronounce this verdict to Little Bilham, but he has already felt its truth before embarking for Europe: life must not be wasted. The tension between the two feelings comes out repeatedly in his first association with Maria. Having visited Europe many years earlier, he wants to immerse himself in its charm, even to the point of trying to push aside whatever is ugly in his new surroundings. Yet he is again and again frustrated by what he feels is the Woollett side of his nature: "I'm always considering something else; something else, I mean, than the thing of the moment. The obsession of the other thing is the terror."

Though Strether uses *Woollett* as a symbolic term and wishes to draw sharp distinctions between the town and Europe, we ourselves must be wary. Contrasts are apparent between the general tone of the life Strether has known in New England and the tone of European life which he sees as an outsider, a visitor. The significant distinctions, however, are between the two forces in the man's own nature. If he compares Mrs. Newsome to Queen Elizabeth and Maria to Mary Stuart, we must remember that Maria is an American. We must note, too, that Strether will come to identify some of the best qualities of Paris with Little Bilham, also an American. Most of all, we must keep in mind that, if our hero feels that he has not fully lived in America, he has nonetheless brought to Europe a far more refined sensitivity than that of any of the Europeans whom he meets there.

We must be careful not to define precise boundaries between Strether's ethical concepts and his cultural appreciation. His remark to Maria implies that Woollett would make such delimitations, that it would even suspect an antithesis; and while he is still in the elementary stages of his new adventure he has to employ his native manner of thought. From the beginning, however, Strether is hopeful that he can free himself from restrictive, negative attitudes and begin to see life as an appreciative experience. He seeks escape from Waymarsh, James implies, because his friend reminds him of the constriction of his own previous ways of viewing life. It is from the same motive, we soon conclude, that he is actually fleeing from Mrs. Newsome, though he is her ambassador to Chad. In fact, he hints as much to Maria by asking whether she thinks he is "running away" from Mrs. Newsome and soon afterward suggesting that she will probably never marry him.

His flight, however, is not a simple matter, for we must see Mrs. Newsome herself through his eyes. Before we label her a tyrannical matriarch or a soul devourer, we must remember that she is a handsome, intelligent woman, for whom Strether has a high admiration. To treat her as if she were a caricature would be unjust both to her and to him. In her nervous intensity, however, he recognizes an inability to break free from a rigid sense of duty and to see life as he himself wishes. He is in awe of her, we gather, simply because she does represent ethical values and he himself is not sure how to get what he wants without sacrificing them. Yet, somehow, he hopes to manage.

Though James does not spell out his definition of *ambassador*, it is evident that the ideal condition of an embassy is one in which the representative has a loyalty to the country which has sent him and a love of the nation to which he has come. He must also have the freedom to make his own decisions consonant with both. Strether's coming to Europe on behalf of Mrs. Newsome to rescue her son from presumed disaster is only the apparent ambassadorship, and he is under no moral obligation to be a mere messenger. But a way of life is something quite different. Merely to cast it off because one has fallen in love with a new one might amount to betrayal—in Strether's case treachery to a precious part of himself. The only satisfactory resolution of his problem must encompass both loyalty and love. The philosophic significance of his career comes from the extreme tests to which each is put, tests that might well cause a man to seek escape in rationalization or cynicism.

At times the two worlds seem completely incompatible, and yet Strether cannot think of the one without being affected by the other. Though he is free of Waymarsh's initial rigor, we come gradually to realize that he is much more exacting than the man from Milrose or, indeed, Mrs. Newsome in his sense of what is right; and he has to recognize, even against his will, that all is not right in the Parisian lives which at first seemed so excellent. Meanwhile he continues, as at the beginning, to feel how empty his new life makes the old. There is to be no easy, joyful solution. On the contrary, there will be increasing disillusionment, climaxing in a sudden stroke in which the last veil is stripped away and, in the haggard face of Madame de Vionnet, he perceives naked reality.

When we first see Strether he is both eager to like Europe and fearful of what he may find. He tries to discover in everything new a quality of romantic charm. The shops and dining rooms, the very streets themselves, become for him expressions of a leisurely, appreciative manner of life, the product of a long cultural heritage. When he first meets Chad, he is thrilled by the poise and air of refinement which the young man has acquired. If Chad had been obviously corrupted by life abroad, Strether's immediate mission would have been simplified, but at the cost of his romantic dream. He is determined to hold onto his dream, even though he suspects that it is fragile. In the succeeding events he cherishes it, at times without effort, but again by sheer determination. In the garden at Gloriani's, for example, what we see is a mixture of elegance and crudeness, of graciousness and bad manners. Strether is too observing to miss the unpleasant, but he quickly puts it out of his mind. He is soon almost enchanted by the manners of Madame de Vionnet and the cultivated gentleness of her daughter. Everything about Madame de Vionnet's home has for him a magic which Maisie would have associated with the Arabian Nights.

The hope of nourishing his appreciation stays with Strether even in the midst of anxiety. Even after he has become so enmeshed in Chad's affairs that he has grave fears for the outcome, he tries to give himself one more treat, an adventure reminiscent of James's own excursions in Europe. What is noteworthy as he sets out on his short train ride is his preconception. James once wrote, as we have observed, that one developed his impressions of Europe from picture books read in childhood, and that a trip abroad did not greatly change them. Strether was once so moved by a Lambinet landscape seen in Boston that he sees the countryside of France in terms of the painting—"the oblong gilt frame." [2] In his European sketches, as we have noted, James maintained that the very eggs and butter served at an inn contributed to the pastoral loveliness. Strether does not know where he will eat, but he is convinced that the inn and the hostess will be charming. Though he does not know precisely what he will have for dinner, he counts on

[2] He also sees it as a scene on a stage.

237

"something fried and felicitous." In that single, utterly vague phrase, as we have observed, is the concrete epitome of Strether's romantic dream. And however unrealistic the dream may appear, it represents a quality in Strether which will sustain him when all illusion is gone.

In holding to his preconceptions Strether is generally helped by Maria Gostrey and Little Bilham. Because we are so much concerned with Strether himself, we may easily scant the extraordinary excellence of Maria. It has commonly been noted that she serves as a confidante, asking the right questions to draw forth illuminating responses and in other ways technically facilitating the narrative. She is, however, significant in her own right. She combines integrity with an appreciative sense of adventure. With little money, she has nonetheless cultivated a taste in art. She is able to live imaginatively in the lives of others, even the unhappy tourists whom she introduces to Europe and then sends home again. Most striking is her unselfish devotion to Strether. Though she comes to love him, in accepting his final verdict, which leaves her out, she speaks with a subtle playfulness that generously disguises the hurt. It is one of the ironies of Strether's life that at first his loyalty to Mrs. Newsome restrains his interest in Maria and that his appreciation is later bedimmed by his concern for Madame de Vionnet. It is to Maria, however, that he turns for understanding.

From the beginning Strether finds much more of real excellence in Little Bilham than in Chad. Like Maria, Bilham has integrity; he does lie to protect his two friends, but Strether approves. He also shares Maria's view of life as an adventure; indeed, he does not need Strether's advice to live all he can. As nearly as it is possible for serious, responsible persons to do so, both Maria and Bilham live in a fairyland of appreciation, the kind of realm Strether would like to enter. He can accept their ways without reservation.

In maintaining his love of the new, Strether at first experiences no trouble from Sarah Pocock and Jim. In his crude way Jim utters common sense about the narrowness of the mercantile life which awaits Chad in Woollett, and he himself is the best evidence that he speaks truth. The frank, charmless rudeness of Chad's sister does not invite one to desert a milieu in which she seems a barbaric interloper. Of course, though for the wrong reasons and in a manner of low comedy,

Sarah comes to introduce some jarring notes of reality before she her-self falls victim to an illusion and sets out to gulp up culture as a tourist. Her narrative function is to state blatantly ideas which Strether has been reluctant to acknowledge. Her dramatic role provides comic contrast and irony.

The central figures in Strether's new world, however, play more com-plex parts, and we need to see them both without and with our hero's help, or, more precisely, as he is conscious of their actions and as he interprets them. Piece by piece we put together a portrait of Chad which becomes increasingly unfavorable. We learn that Little Bilham liked him better before his Parisian education had done its work. We see him, at first in casual matters, then in serious ones, fleeing responsi-bility at the expense of others. What at first would seem decorum and consideration for Madame de Vionnet turns out to be evasion of un-pleasantness. Even his urbane acquiescence when Strether lectures him on his moral obligation to her is in reality an act of deceit. Before the end we discover two things about him which might at first seem unequal in importance, but are really not. He is growing tired of Madame de Vionnet, and he is beginning to show some curiosity about the techniques of advertising. It is unfair to blame Woollett for Chad. The town would approve his returning to a mercantile career and it would sacrifice Madame de Vionnet, but it does not condone cowardice or deceit. Europe, on the other hand, has only taught him how to dis-guise his initial weaknesses and saved him from having to stand trial. As Little Bilham recognizes, he *is* worse than Madame de Vionnet found him.

Nevertheless, for Strether, Chad for a long time symbolizes excel-lence. He has an easy, gentlemanly manner, an apparent self-assurance free from perplexities. He is handsome and he appears to enjoy a wonderful friendship. Strether admires in Chad what he mistakenly thinks he himself lacks, and he feels that he must go to school to him. We must realize, of course, that the qualities in themselves are good, and we must remember that Chad owes them to Madame de Vionnet.

When we turn to Marie de Vionnet, we again find a discrepancy be-tween the facts that are known to both us and Strether and his inter-pretation of them. Her conduct toward him in Gloriani's garden is not

239

considerate. Though Strether admires her home and furnishings at the expense of Maria's, she has come into possession of them through no special talent of her own. Having groomed her daughter to please, she offers her on the marriage market, all the time trying to believe that her own wishes are Jeanne's. Her equivocations to Sarah amuse us, but her lies to Strether do not. He appreciates her covering up for Chad and sparing everyone from the confession of her adultery, but she goes beyond the requirements of decorum. She likes Strether, but she also flatters and deceives him in order to use him. Her most serious flaw is, of course, exposed in the revelation of her relations with Chad. At first when Strether is assured that their love affair represents a "virtuous attachment," we are aware that he is thinking in the conventional terms of Woollett. Before the end, however, the attachment is revealed to be lacking in virtue because it is fundamentally dishonest. Chad keeps his own mental reservations, but so does Marie. She has tried, irresponsibly, to have him for herself without regard for him or others; and when, at last, she unashamedly sobs out to Strether her despair at losing him, she is paying a price which was from the beginning inevitable.

Nevertheless, his devotion to Marie de Vionnet has transformed Strether's life. His own attachment to her has certainly been virtuous in the highest degree. Capable of overlooking her faults, he has found inspiration. Marie with her elbows on the table, with her willingness to defy practical considerations, with her heritage of culture, has symbolized the romantic world which Strether fearfully hoped to discover. In reminding Chad that he owes her everything, Strether is ironically speaking for himself. For his debt does not stop with recognition of the aura of beauty Marie has cast around him; it includes insight into tragedy as well. When the truth finally comes to him, when he sees his lady like a "maidservant crying for her young man," he is "conscious of some vague inward irony in the presence of such a fine free range of bliss and bale."

Strether's spiritual voyage has, indeed, been a long one, much farther than from Woollett to Paris, for it is neither of time nor of place. It has encompassed the wildest yearnings and the deepest compassion of a sensitive mind. Along the way it has even subjected Strether to terrible loneliness in an unfamiliar universe. As he tells Bilham, before the final revelation, he has been "sacrificing so to strange gods" that his hands have been "imbrued with the blood of monstrous alien altars—of another faith altogether." In the last scene he puts the matter more composedly to Maria Gostrey, "I'm not . . . in real harmony with what surrounds me." Where has he finally come out?

Certainly he has done little to change the course of other lives. Maria and Bilham have benefited from knowing him, but they were journeying free from peril when he first met them. If anything, Chad may have been adversely influenced, as his knowledge of Strether's original mission may have encouraged him to make the flight he was already contemplating. Marie de Vionnet will be able to recall his friendship, but she is emotionally lost in her personal tragedy. It is his own life that has been altered. Like George Dane and Spencer Brydon, at the end he has come back to the life he left, but with a great change of vision. He is saddened, yet grateful for what he has had. At the beginning he expected to pay, and he has done so. Even if he knew how deeply Maria loves him, he would still insist on his "logic. Not, out of the whole affair, to have got anything for myself."

In the things to which Strether's consciousness has been exposed there is little that is new. Outwardly much is commonplace, some is melodramatic, and some is tawdry. What matters is what he himself has seen within or because of it. At the end he knows Chad for what he is, and he knows more about Marie de Vionnet than would embitter a lesser man. Yet he has made of his terrible knowledge something which is morally right and esthetically beautiful; and there is finally no conflict between his loyalty and his love. He could not have had his imaginative insights had it not been for the world around him, but what he has attained to he himself has created.

Thus we come back to the concept of life as a creative activity. Of all his characters, Strether is the most completely like James in the range of his experience and the philosophic order which he achieves. He has been troubled by conflicts and battered by assaults that threatened destruction of his spiritual universe. He has had to accept the existence of bliss and bale, not as separate phenomena, but as the two inseparably joined faces of a medal. As we think back over his career, we come to recognize more and more the significance of the Lambinet frame, for it really symbolizes what has saved Strether. During the long years which he fears have been wasted he has developed a way of looking at life. The adultery he finds at the end of his trip to the French countryside is utterly foreign to the subject matter, so nicely ordered as to pattern and tone, within the Lambinet frame; but what he discovers he disciplines until it, too, fits into a frame. At first the experience seems madly chaotic, but Strether brings to it a sense of pictorial logic and a rich, compassionate tone. What he, in short, creates is a new picture which may serve the reader even as the Lambinet served him.

For it was through his artistic perspectives that James saw reality. In his portrait of Lambert Strether, the man from Woollett, he created one of his finest frames.

IV. LIFE AS A FINE ART: *THE GOLDEN BOWL*

MAGGIE VERVER AND HER FATHER ADAM exemplify the evil which James identified with American puritanism and materialism; they use their wealth to buy a husband for Maggie and a wife for Adam, and they draw upon a ruthless moral code to hold the two victims, Charlotte and Amerigo, in subjection—such is one extreme interpretation of James's *The Golden Bowl*. Maggie is a virtual saint, who, in her love and wisdom, symbolizes a divine compassion that can even rescue such sinners as Amerigo and Charlotte—such is the opposite view.[3] The two agree in accepting the novel as a symbolic, metaphorical vision of life. Since the story is filled with metaphors, and since the golden bowl itself is a symbol, James certainly intended his novel to possess symbolic implications.

The trouble with the two opposed interpretations, however, is that each would allow the novel merely to depict a narrowly restricted aspect of life and to reproduce observations which James had made more or less briefly in his other works. As we have seen, James recog-

[3] See Walter F. Wright, "Maggie Verver: Neither Saint nor Witch," footnotes (bibliography, *The Golden Bowl*), for a summary of conflicting views.

nized that puritanism could become a stifling religion when the puritan made of it a negative code; and he, of course, concurred with Hawthorne, as we have noted, in regarding as a supreme evil the attempt to play god to another human soul. We have seen, too, that he appreciated the angelic quality in life; indeed his words concerning Minny Temple are as moving as anything in the *Divina Commedia*. Since we can lift sentences from the novel to support either extreme, what are we to believe?

Though the full meaning is clothed in the language of fiction, with complex characters and situations, the perspective is discernible. James was not attempting to assert a thesis about puritanism, though his novel provides evidence of moral tyranny. Nor was he writing a hymn in praise of divine pity and love, though the novel is concerned with the wonder of human love. He was doing something much greater in scope, which encompassed both extremes. There is very great evil in *The Golden Bowl*, but there is also wondrous good. What is more important is that the evil and the good are not typified by separate characters; they exist in each. The story is romantic and mythical, even as are Dante's epic and *The Faerie Queene;* but it is also realistic and specific. All four of the principal characters, and, for that matter, such minor ones as Fanny Assingham, are perplexed human beings, prone to err, but struggling toward enlightenment. The major ones are, in a sense, autobiographical—in the same way that Stransom and Marcher and Strether are autobiographical. For the one thing that pervades all James's autobiographical writing is the awareness that life is ideally an unending effort to overcome in oneself the lassitude of mind which permits one's drifting toward meaninglessness and to transform all experience into a romance of adventure.

In *The Golden Bowl* the temptation to relax, to find an easy way out of one's predicament, is omnipresent, even till the end of the final scene. It takes various forms, including the allurement of moral despotism, but also the very different attraction of moral indifference. All four of the major characters are in grave danger as they become aware of seemingly overwhelming forces. The most inviting solution is to drift, yet each of the four finds in himself a spirit that forbids drifting. Each has an individuality which is not to be thrown away, a sense that may be called creative. It includes a moral consciousness, and yet it is larger than that. It is a sense, even as was Strether's, that life must somehow become a creative adventure, a fine art.

In all James's works life is primarily a social matter. Even when Spencer Brydon sets out to discover himself, he makes his discovery in reference to Alice Staverton; and Strether's personality at the close of his story reflects his feelings toward all the persons he has met. As we have seen, too, we cannot identify any of the characters in *The Awkward Age* except in reference to the others. So it is that in *The Golden Bowl,* though we may speak of each of the four whose lives are unfolded, we cannot really separate any one of the four from the others. Moreover, the lives are not definable in static conditions.[4] Like Yeats and, indeed, like any writer of narrative, James saw the inseparability of the dancer and the dance. The Maggie Verver of the last scene is not the girl of the first book, nor even of the next-to-last scene. And the changes that have come to her are not the consequence of her learning more clearly the nature of her father, her husband, and Charlotte as we first knew them. They are, in part, the product of the changes which each of these has undergone, changes for which Maggie herself has been partially responsible. The story of all four is a narrative of perplexed, fallible human beings whose relationships at the beginning are superficially as perfect as the seemingly flawless gold-covered crystal bowl, but which, like the bowl, possess a hidden crack. Like the bowl, their world must be recognized for what it is. Like the bowl, it will split into fragments which by themselves are meaningless, but which by a supreme effort of imagination can be fitted together again into a thing of beauty which all four will have helped to create, and which they must henceforth work together to maintain.

The artistic problem for James was, as always, not separable from his theme itself. He had to identify the fragments, as each character has his own special quality and his own peculiar predicament; and yet he had to keep always before him the total concept, to see each frag-

[4] A frequent error in criticism of James has been to quote statements by a character early in a story as if they represented his final view, without recognizing that he may grow in understanding. *The Golden Bowl* has suffered much from this practice.

ment both as it threatened to split away and as it could contribute to the unity of which the bowl is the lyric symbol.

If the light is most on Maggie and secondly on Amerigo, it nonetheless illuminates Adam and Charlotte. In the first of the two books, "The Prince," Amerigo is the most prominent, but all four characters are introduced. The presentation is mainly from without. What we learn about Adam and Charlotte is almost exclusively from their own words and actions, and what we discover about the prince and Maggie is mainly so. In the second half the first three are again depicted in dramatic scenes, but James enters into the thoughts of Maggie. By "going behind" Maggie, to use his own term, James indirectly goes behind the others as well, for Maggie's own thoughts are preoccupied with what she believes to be theirs. The method is intricate and precarious. Maggie is confused about herself, and it would be impossible to make her a perfect witness as to the hidden thoughts of the others. James keeps his problem under mastery, however, through the nature of Maggie's concern and through support from other sources.

We and Maggie see and hear the others, and we come to suspect that, whatever other thoughts may cross their minds, they are much more concerned even than in Book One with the question of their mutual relationships. For additional evidence we have Fanny Assingham's speculations as she tries to explain to her husband, and rather more to herself, the changes in those relationships as she senses them. Fanny has been accused of stupidity. Were she really stupid, she would be irrelevant and tedious. Actually, her discernment, though limited and at times comic, is always pertinent. Of course there are things beyond her power to comprehend, but it is she who rightly smashes the bowl as a warning to Maggie; and though she, too, has erred very widely in her earlier guesses, she points the way to a solution. With the dramatic representation of the others and with Fanny's choral observations to serve as a general commentary, we are willing to believe that the others are deeply absorbed with the questions which Maggie attributes to them. At the same time, the major concern on Maggie's part comes to be whether they know what she would earnestly conceal from them—her own knowledge of Amerigo's and Charlotte's secret as she imagines it. Thus, we have for a long time, not a complete insight into their minds, but an increasing appreciation of the central question, the answer to which unfolds first to reveal what Amerigo knows and then what is possibly known by Charlotte and Adam. In the meantime Maggie's own interpretation of the relation of Amerigo and Charlotte has also begun to undergo a transformation which will be completed only at the end, when she will finally see it as a part of the relationship of Amerigo and Maggie herself.

Put crudely, the theme of *The Golden Bowl* is the triumph of altruism over egoism. Though the characters, however, do speak of ethics and specifically deplore their own selfishness, the subject is not at all so simple as a mere conscious choice between self-concern and concern for others. Moreover, ethics is only part of a still larger concept. One can more accurately think of the forces that tend to bring disintegration to one's universe and those which hold it together, or, from a slightly different perspective, of that which diminishes one's life and that which expands and enhances it. Each of the four major characters illustrates some special variation of the theme.

The enormously rich Adam, whose name has led to attempts to equate him with the Biblical Adam, is like the latter only in the general sense that he finds himself in a strange world and that he has to come to knowledge through suffering.[5] At the beginning and for a long time thereafter he is shallow and occasionally cruel despite his yearning for serious experience and his wish to be considerate of others. Having decided to spend his money for works of art and having moulded his own manners in accord with what he believes to be refinement of taste, he thinks in terms of acquisition, and, in effect, he buys Maggie a husband who will measure up to his standards. Indeed, he uses the language of an art connoisseur in talking to the prince himself about his excellence: "As it is, for living with, you're a pure and perfect crystal." To which James soon adds the comment, ". . . the instinct, the particular sharpened appetite of the collector, had fairly served as a basis for his acceptance of the Prince's suit." Even at the end Adam still appreciates the prince and Charlotte in artistic terms; he cannot be expected to revolutionize his habits of thought. The unconscious cruelty

[5] To push the symbolism of Adam's name is to overemphasize his position among the four.

of his words to the prince is obvious enough. Even more glaring is the suffering imposed by Adam upon Charlotte. Though Maggie sees herself responsible for Charlotte's being confined as in a cage, she also muses on Adam's unconscious heartlessness toward her: ". . . the likeness of their connexion wouldn't have been wrongly figured if he had been thought of as holding in one of his pocketed hands the end of a long silken halter looped round her beautiful neck." Again, Charlotte's voice, as she acts as art cicerone among Adam's treasures sounds to Maggie "like the shriek of a soul in pain."

If we had only such passages as these, we should unequivocally condemn Adam. The fallacy of such condemnation, however, would lie in the fact that, like the other three, Adam has a complete story. He is not a static character, but a man worthy of serious study because he is capable of making a profound discovery.

The discovery is not to come as a mere surprise. It is prepared for. First of all, Adam himself is a philosopher of sorts, who spends some time examining his own life. Early in the narrative he sums up his and Maggie's situation in language which is accurate because imagina· tive: "There seems a kind of charm, doesn't there? on our life. . . . A kind of wicked selfish prosperity perhaps, as if we had grabbed everything, fixed everything, down to the last lovely object for the last glass case of the last corner, left over, of my old show. That's the only take-off, that it has made us perhaps lazy, a wee bit languid—lying like gods together, all careless of mankind." His conduct bears out his admission, and yet he is also correct when, much later, he protests to Maggie, "I ain't selfish. I'll be blowed if I'm selfish." The objective evidence provided through Maggie's contemplation of him is by no means uniformly in accord with the halter image. Rather, it emphasizes his self-discipline and his search for understanding. It is a reasonable conclusion to Adam's adventure, therefore, that at the end he has come to regard Charlotte no longer as a useful possession of whom he earlier remarked, ". . . one finds that she only wants to know what *we* want. Which is what we got her for!" Instead, he has for her an intense admiration. Repeating Maggie's comment that "Charlotte's great," he soon adds, "She's beautiful, beautiful." At long last he has journeyed a great distance from his initial godlike insulation and from seeing life entirely in reference to himself and Maggie. In the revelation that has come to him he has not consciously rejected egoism. It has simply ceased to exist. He admires his wife, not merely as a work of art, but as an artist; for he now sees the beauty of the life she has helped create.

In the eyes of some readers Charlotte is the innocent victim of Adam's and Maggie's cruel obsession. We must allow her, too, however, to have a story which has a beginning, a middle, and an end. Otherwise she becomes little more than the waxen image which, upon need, she can resemble. We must remember that Charlotte initially renounced thoughts of marriage with the prince because they lacked money, that she marries Adam after he has told her that he needs her for the sake of Maggie, and that she continues to share secrets with the prince, even to taking with him an unchaperoned excursion which, whether or not it involves physical adultery—a point on which James is deliberately obscure—most certainly amounts to deception of Maggie and Adam. James is interested in what Charlotte's conduct will mean to Maggie when the facts are learned, but equally in the conflict it reveals within Charlotte's own mind.

Superficially her motives remind one of Kate Croy's. Though she has lived frugally, she is impelled by concern for money, and she consents to marriage almost as to personal enslavement from an ulterior and unexalted motive. Yet there are differences, and these widen toward the end. Kate has to rationalize that she is doing good for Milly; Charlotte is much more frank in self-questioning. When told by the prince that she is "very, very honourable," she replies, "I can't not ask myself, I can't not ask *you* . . . if you're really as much at liberty as your universal generosity leads you to assume. Oughtn't we . . . to think a little of others? Oughtn't I, at least, in loyalty—at any rate in delicacy—to think of Maggie?" She has resented Maggie's dominance over Adam, but she has disciplined herself to endure it. Her kinship of feeling has been with the prince, and she is surely not to be blamed for cherishing it; for Maggie treats her as a friend to be taken for granted, and Adam seems to have affection mainly for Maggie. Yet she and the prince are always aware of their duty; James speaks of "a mystic golden bridge between them, strongly swaying and sometimes almost vertiginous, for that intimacy of which the sovereign law would be the vigilance of 'care,' would be never rashly to forget and never consciously to wound."

The law is not accepted cynically, nor are the two moral cowards. They genuinely do not want to be guilty of lack of delicacy. They want to believe in a virtually ideal mode of conduct by which they will daily repay Adam and Maggie for marrying them and giving them freedom to be together. If they are discreet, no one will have been hurt; indeed, Adam and Maggie will have been shown great consideration. At the same time, though not free and happy, they can at least share an affinity with each other which they can find nowhere else. Such is their reasoning, and the evidence for it is so strong that there seems for a time no adequate alternative. The direction of their conduct is, nevertheless, toward disaster. There is the excursion, and there are later meetings; but the affinity weakens and the two are more and more alone. Meanwhile the obligation which Charlotte has assumed becomes a voluntary servitude; Maggie, as we noted, pities her. That disaster is finally averted is due in part to her efforts.

In the late pages of her history we see Charlotte from outside, often through Maggie's thoughts. For a time Maggie is sure that she is concealing her own suspicions from her, and rather late the prince calls Charlotte "stupid," to imply that she has guessed nothing. The objective evidence, however, is ambiguous; for if Charlotte has guessed, she will be as concerned as Maggie to disguise her feelings and preserve decorum. When, for example, she tells Maggie that she wants to return to America to have Adam to herself, she may be sincere or only aware that, after what has happened, she must go. The very end has exciting ambiguities, along with some certainties. Charlotte has toiled faithfully to be a conscientious wife, even to the point of lecturing to the tourists. At the farewell call on Maggie and the prince, she and the prince perform their decorous roles with scrupulous care, making "an ampler submission to the general duty of magnificence; sitting as still, to be thus appraised, as a pair of effigies of the contemporary great on one of the platforms of Madame Tussaud."

We cannot say, even now, how much Charlotte loves her husband, for her manner may denote only self-discipline. It is clear, however, that Maggie gives her credit for greatness. Somewhat earlier she has remarked to the prince, "How can we not always thinks of her? It's as if her unhappiness had been necessary to us—as if we had needed her, at her own cost, to build us up and start us." And when, during their praise of Charlotte, Maggie comments to her father that he knows his wife best, James gives his reply—"Oh, but naturally!"—and then, re-entering Maggie's thoughts, he adds, "On which, as the warranted truth of it hung in the air . . . she found herself lost, though with a finer thrill than she had perhaps yet known, in the vision of all he might mean." That Adam admires his wife we have remarked. How well he really knows her thoughts we can only surmise, but of the nobility of her conduct we are sure.

In speaking of Charlotte we have inevitably in part characterized Prince Amerigo. The clue to his psychological problem is suggested in his early admission to Fanny that he lacks a "moral" sense. His full explanation is put metaphorically: "I've of course something that in our poor dear backward old Rome sufficiently passes for it. But it's no more like yours than the tortuous stone staircase—half-ruined into the bargain!—in some castle of our *quattrocento* is like the 'lightning elevator' in one of Mr. Verver's fifteen-storey buildings."

Without a moral sense, how is the prince to escape tragedy? Well, at first he is helped along somewhat by his severe concept of his personal dignity and by the exquisiteness of his taste. He may seek Charlotte's companionship, but, like Charlotte, he will try to preserve the amenities. Then a new element comes into his life. One faint clue after another reveals that he is beginning to love Maggie and to need her love in return. Long before the final scene he has tried to be frank with her, but she has been slow to perceive his feelings. As with Charlotte, it is mainly through Maggie's thoughts that we surmise how lonely he is and how splendid in adversity. Then, after a much more rapid revelation, as we approach and enter the final scene, we comprehend, with Maggie, the depth of his understanding. He is speaking from his own suffering when he philosophizes to Maggie, "Everything's terrible, *cara*—in the heart of man." Between the beginning and the end he has come to see the poignancy of Maggie's anguish and the genius of her imagination. In his love for her there is a feeling of wonder that

250

is, in itself, ennobling. At the end he has no need for a "moral" sense as a guide to conduct, for he has transcended its province.

James's subject was the search for creative personal freedom, with all the ironic paradoxes involved. Adam, Charlotte, and Amerigo are all engaged in the adventure. All are conscious of evil in themselves, and all come to accept even the most restrictive conditions imposed by their marital relationships. Each emerges nobler, more appreciative, and freer than when his history began. Only in their recognition of the conditions that would seem to inhibit freedom have they found opportunity for the creative exercise of imagination.

The person in whom James most extensively studied his theme is, of course, Maggie. We see her through the comments of others and her own words, but most significantly through the images and sensations which come into her mind. There is, in her story, a general pattern from ignorance, through a conviction of evil, to enlightenment. Since she is at no time omniscient and since she is moved by human impulse, the pattern is not a steady one. Instead, there are leaps and regressions.

Maggie's initial state is revealed in a remark by Fanny, "She wasn't born to know evil. She must never know it." The point is reiterated in variant form in Maggie's own comment to Adam and his reply: " 'Do you realize, father, that I've never had the least blow?' . . . 'Who *should* realise if I don't?' " We have no knowledge of what harm Maggie has heretofore caused to others, but we soon discover that her naïveté permits her to engage in thoughtless cruelty. Later Adam speaks of their living like gods, but in the meantime Maggie has repeatedly played the part of careless tyrant to Charlotte and Amerigo, and even to Adam himself. The fact is that, although she has a background of American mores to guide her, mores according to which adultery is condemnable, she actually has no more *real* moral sense than Amerigo. She has simply never thought about moral problems. What then is later to keep her from a career of narrow-minded, unmitigated persecution of Charlotte and Amerigo? Something in part like what supports these two themselves. At one moment of dire temptation, for example, she remembers that she is her father's daughter. Adam has set a standard of decorum, and she would be ashamed to fall below it.

Such support is not exhilarating; it does not lead to a sense of adventure. It does, however, rescue from error.

Marking the opening of a new stage in Maggie's progress, Fanny remarks that her "sense will have to open. . . . To what's called Evil —with a very big E: for the first time in her life." Fanny is thinking of evil done by others, and it is to this evil that for a long time Maggie directs her attention. The evil which most matters, however, is that which threatens from within—the temptation to smash a world to bits merely because it is strange and not to her liking.

Having assumed that she could possess the affections of others almost as if by purchase, and that she could establish relationships to suit her will, she now experiences disillusionment: "Of course they were arranged—all four arranged; but what had the basis of their life been precisely, but that they were arranged together? Ah! Amerigo and Charlotte were arranged together, but she . . . was arranged apart." During the following scenes all kinds of discordant thoughts and images throng into Maggie's mind. At times she wishes that Amerigo and Charlotte would do wrong as vindication of her suspicions. Again, to keep a husband whom she is not sure she loves, she would sacrifice Adam—tenderly, to be sure, but irrevocably—by sending him away with Charlotte. She gets a perverse pleasure out of her suspicions and the belief that she is playing a subtle, deceptive role: "I go about on tiptoe, I watch for every sound, I feel every breath, and yet I try all the while to seem as smooth as old satin dyed rose colour." There are better moments, when she appreciates the kindly deference of Amerigo and of Charlotte; but her feeling of isolation and personal humiliation grows. During the card game at Fawns, as from a distance she watches the three others and Fanny, she reminds one of the vengeful wife in Browning's "The Laboratory": "Yes, under that imputation, to her sense they sat—the imputation of wondering, beneath and behind all their apparently straight play, if she weren't really watching them from her corner and consciously, as might be said, holding them in her hand."

In this wilderness of envy, self-pity, and twisted pride Maggie wanders for a long time. Little by little, however, a new kind of experience comes to her, and it grows out of her very obsession itself. She finds herself more and more wondering what the lives of Charlotte and

Amerigo are like, both when they are together and when they are apart; and she begins to feel first pity and then a timid admiration. She goes through a stage of ambivalence, of fluctuating hate and compassion; but as her imagination continues to rearrange her chaotic impressions, a new order slowly begins to take form. In time she reaches a point where she can be frank with Amerigo and where she tries to deceive Charlotte from a desire to spare her suffering.

As the separation of Amerigo from Charlotte approaches, she compares him to a French aristocrat nobly awaiting the guillotine. She does give up her father, but not by sacrificing him; and she realizes at the end that, in growing up, she has owed much to Charlotte. In the final scene she admits to herself that her happiness depends upon her husband's love, and she is moved almost to terror as she awaits the verdict. In praising Charlotte to him she has accepted his view of life, has, indeed, entered as fully as she could into his world. The last words reveal that he has likewise accepted hers: " ' "See"? I see nothing but *you*.' And the truth of it had, with this force, after a moment, so strangely lighted his eyes that as for pity and dread of them she buried her own in his breast."

And so we have finally a bowl without a flaw, a perfect crystal covered with gold. It has not been a gift, however, for it represents the most intensive and imaginative efforts of all four. The highest experience for each of the four has been made possible by all the others. Maggie has grown from thoughtless adolescence to womanhood because of the example of each of the rest, and of this she is thrillingly aware. What might have disintegrated into fragments through the carelessness of any of the four has first escaped such tragedy and has then become something positively good. The result is almost as if a miracle had occurred, but one of human origin. As we reflect on Maggie's history, we perceive that she—and the others—is an artist. She has submitted herself to doubt, and she has imagined with audacity. She has also woven delicately with silver threads and tapped carefully on golden nails.

To be sure, Maggie could not put together a book or a picture, but in the grand art of life itself she has achieved some proficiency. If she were capable of philosophic speculation, she might well say with Dencombe, "We work in the dark—we do what we can—we give what we have. Our doubt is our passion and our passion is our task." And if she were to try to describe the wonder of the love and awe she has come to know, she might perceive that it has surpassed her conscious dreams—that it partakes, indeed, of "the madness of art."

A SELECTED BIBLIOGRAPHY

BIBLIOGRAPHY

Edel, Leon, and Laurence, Dan H. *A Bibliography of Henry James.* London, 1957. Definitive.

Hamilton, Eunice C. "Biographical and Critical Studies of Henry James," *American Literature,* XX (1949), 424–435. A checklist.

GENERAL CRITICISM

Allott, Miriam. "Symbol and Image in the Later Work of Henry James," *Essays in Criticism,* III (1953), 321–336. Regards James's symbols as "almost always connected with his theme of appearance and reality."

Anderson, Charles R. "James's Portrait of the Southerner," *American Literature,* XXVII (1955), 309–331. Shows the limitations of James's knowledge of the South and his acceptance of myth about it.

Anderson, Quentin. *The American Henry James.* New Brunswick, 1956. Stresses symbolism; is sometimes controversial.

Auden, W. H. "Henry James and the Artist in America," *Harper's Magazine,* CXCVII (1948), 36–40. Stresses James's integrity as artist.

Bantock, G. H. "Morals and Civilization in Henry James," *The Cambridge Journal,* VII (1953), 159–181. Seeks to find discrepancies between morals and manners in James.

Barrett, Laurence. "Young Henry James, Critic," *American Literature,* XX (1949), 385–400. Notes that aspects of James's later thinking are revealed in his criticism 1864–1878.

Beach, Joseph W. *The Method of Henry James.* New Haven, 1918. Still one of the best introductions to James.

Beach, Joseph W. "The Sacred and Solitary Refuge," *Furioso,* III (1948), 23–27. Stresses theory.

Beach, Joseph W. *The Twentieth Century Novel.* New York, 1932, 177–228.

Beebe, Maurice. "The Turned Back of Henry James," *The South Atlantic Quarterly,* LIII (1954), 521–539. Rejects the Freudian approach; shows the artistic function of James's detached view.

Blackmur, R. P. "The Loose and Baggy Monsters of Henry James: Notes on the Underlying Classic Form in the Novel," *Accent*, XI (1951), 129–146. On theme and form.

Booth, Bradford A. "Henry James and the Economic Motif," *Nineteenth-Century Fiction*, VII (1953), 141–150. Discusses numerous examples.

Bowden, Edwin T. *The Themes of Henry James; A System of Observation through the Visual Arts*. New Haven, 1956. Focuses on the arts in James.

Brooks, Van Wyck. *The Pilgrimage of Henry James*. New York, 1925. Presents a thesis now partially discredited.

Brown, E. K. "James and Conrad," *The Yale Review*, XXXV (1946), 265–285. Maintains that the late novels lack vitality; a minority view.

Canby, Henry S. *Turn West, Turn East: Mark Twain and Henry James*. Boston, 1951. Title indicates point of view.

Cargill, Oscar. "Henry James's 'Moral Policeman': William Dean Howells," *American Literature*, XXIX (1958), 371–398. On the literary relationship of the two authors; James found Howells too restricted.

Cargill, Oscar. *The Novels of Henry James*. New York, 1961. A criticism and review of critical opinion; especially excellent on sources.

Cary, Elizabeth L. *The Novels of Henry James*. New York, 1905. A judicious early criticism.

Clark, Edwin. "Henry James and the Actress," *The Pacific Spectator*, III (1949), 84–99. Surveys James's adventures in the drama.

Crews, F. C. *The Tragedy of Manners, Moral Drama in the Later Novels of Henry James*. New Haven, 1957. Explicative.

Dupee, F. W. *Henry James: His Life and Writings*. New York, 1951. Controversial in judgments.

Dupee, F. W., ed. *The Question of Henry James*. New York, 1945. Essays by various critics.

Edel, Leon. *The Complete Plays of Henry James*. New York, 1949. Includes criticism.

Edel, Leon. *The Ghostly Tales of Henry James*. New Brunswick, 1948. Includes introductions.

Edel, Leon, and Ray, Gordon. *Henry James and H. G. Wells; A Record of Their Friendship, Their Debate on the Art of Fiction, and Their Quarrel*. Urbana, Ill., 1958.

Edel, Leon. *Henry James the Untried Years, 1843–1870*. Philadelphia, 1953. Biographical and interpretive.

A SELECTED BIBLIOGRAPHY

Edgar, Pelham. *Henry James, Man and Author*. London, 1927. A general summary of plots and themes.

Falk, Robert P. "Henry James and the 'Age of Innocence,'" *Nineteenth-Century Fiction*, VII (1952), 171–188. On the American-European background of James's thought.

Firebaugh, Joseph. "The Pragmatism of Henry James," *The Virginia Quarterly Review*, XXVII (1951), 419–435. Interprets James as a pragmatist.

Firebaugh, Joseph. "The Relativism of Henry James," *The Journal of Aesthetics and Art Criticism*, XII (1953), 237–242.

Foley, R. N. *Criticism in American Periodicals of the Works of Henry James from 1866 to 1916*. Washington, D.C., 1944. A survey and summary.

Forbes, Elizabeth. "Dramatic Lustrum: A Study of the Effect of Henry James's Theatrical Experience on His Later Novels," *The New England Quarterly*, XI (1938), 108–120. Calls attention to the greater use of dramatic method after the 1889–1896 playwriting experience.

Frierson, W. C. *The English Novel in Transition, 1885–1940*. Norman, 1942. Chapter Eight discusses James's experimental method.

Gale, R. L. "Art Imagery in Henry James's Fiction," *American Literature*, XXIX (1957), 47–53.

Gale, R. L. "A Note on Henry James's First Short Story," *Modern Language Notes*, LXXII (1957), 103–107. Reveals the consistency in James's use of imagery throughout his career.

Hoffman, Charles G. *The Short Novels of Henry James*. New York, 1957. Covers all periods.

Holder-Barell, Alexander. *The Development of Imagery and Its Functional Significance in Henry James's Novels*. New York, 1960.

Jefferson, D. W. *Henry James*. New York, 1961. A survey of biography, literary career, and reputation.

LeClair, Robert C. *Young Henry James, 1843–1870*. New York, 1955.

Lerner, Daniel, and Cargill, Oscar. "Henry James at the Grecian Urn," *Publications of the Modern Language Association*, LXVI (1951), 316–331. Shows that James "knew the Greeks."

Lerner, Daniel. "The Influence of Turgeniev on James," *The Slavonic Yearbook*, XX (1941), 28–54. Gives extensive evidence.

Levy, Leo B. *Versions of Melodrama: A Study of the Fiction and Drama of Henry James, 1865–1897*. Berkeley, 1957. Treats the works as profound melodrama.

Marks, Robert. *James's Later Novels: An Interpretation*. New York, 1960. Explicative.

Matthiessen, F. O. *Henry James, the Major Phase*. New York, 1944. On the later works.

Matthiessen, F. O. *The James Family, Including Selections from the Writings of Henry James, Sr., William, Henry and Alice James*. New York, 1947.

Matthiessen, F. O., and Murdock, Kenneth B. *The Notebooks of Henry James*. New York, 1947.

McCarthy, Harold T. *Henry James: The Creative Process*. New York, 1958. Excellent on theory and method.

McElderry, Bruce R., Jr. "Hamlin Garland and Henry James," *American Literature*, XXIII (1952), 433–446. Makes clear that James's laments to Garland are not evidence of a feeling of guilt for leaving America.

McElderry, Bruce R., Jr. "Henry James and 'The Whole Family,'" *The Pacific Spectator*, IV (1950), 352–360. Shows James at work.

McElderry, Bruce R., Jr. "The Uncollected Stories of Henry James," *American Literature*, XXI (1949), 279–291. Notes that those laid in Europe are generally better than those laid in America.

McIntyre, Clara F. "The Later Manner of Mr. Henry James," *Publications of the Modern Language Association*, XXVII (1912), 354–371. Represents the early objections to the later style.

Murray, Donald M. "Henry James and the English Reviewers, 1882–1890," *American Literature*, XXIV (1952), 1–20. Demonstrates the provincialism and stupidity of the reviewers.

Pacey, W. C. D. "Henry James and His French Contemporaries," *American Literature*, XIII (1941), 240–256. On the French influences.

Parquet, Mary E. "Henry James: the Bliss and the Bale." Unpublished doctoral dissertation, University of Nebraska, 1959.

Poirier, Richard. *The Comic Sense of Henry James*. Oxford, 1960. A study of six novels before 1881.

Rahv, Philip. "The Heiress of All the Ages," *Partisan Review*, X (1943), 227–247. On the American heroines.

Raleigh, John H. "Henry James: the Poetics of Empiricism," *Publications of the Modern Language Association*, LXVI (1951), 107–123. Interprets James in reference to Locke.

Roberts, Morris. "Henry James and the Art of Foreshortening," *The Review of English Studies*, XXII (1946), 207–214. Discusses the narrative function of the dramatic method.

A SELECTED BIBLIOGRAPHY

Rosenzweig, Saul. "The Ghost of Henry James," *Partisan Review*, XI (1944), 436–455. A Freudian approach.

Short, R. W. "Henry James's World of Images," *Publications of the Modern Language Association*, LXVIII (1953), 943–960. Traces the shift away from conventional images.

Short, R. W. "The Sentence Structure of Henry James," *American Literature*, XVIII (1946), 71–88. Demonstrates the suitability of the sentence structure to James's purpose.

Slabey, Robert M. "Henry James and the Most Impressive Convention in All History," *American Literature*, XXX (1958), 89–102. On James's interest in Catholicism, especially 1869–1874.

Theobald, John R. "New Reflections on *The Golden Bowl*," "*Twentieth-Century Literature*, III (1957), 20–26. Considers the motivation inadequate.

Tintner, Adeline R. "The Spoils of Henry James," *Publications of the Modern Language Association*, LXI (1946), 239–251. On James's interest in art.

Vivas, Eliseo. "Henry and William," *The Kenyon Review*, V (1943), 580–594. Compares their ideas; does not consider Henry a pragmatist.

Wagenknecht, Edward. "Our Contemporary Henry James," *College English*, X (1948), 123–132. Good condensed interpretation of James's ideas.

Ward, J. A. *The Imagination of Disaster: Evil in the Fiction of Henry James*. Lincoln, Nebr., 1961. Explicative.

Wegelin, Christof. *The Image of Europe in Henry James*. Dallas, Texas, 1958. A careful explicative study; stresses the relation of "the fine consciousness and the fine conscience."

Winters, Yvor. "Henry James and the Relation of Morals to Manners," *The American Review*, IX (1937), 482–503. Illustrates especially from the major novels.

"The Altar of the Dead"

Tate, Allen. "Three Commentaries: Poe, James, Joyce," *The Sewanee Review*, LVIII (1950), 1–15. Considers it "James's greatest failure in spite of its own great tone."

Wagenknecht, Edward. *Ibid.* (above, General Criticism). Regards it, with "The Beast in the Jungle," as one of James's "two greatest short stories."

The Ambassadors

Berland, Alwyn. "Henry James," *The University of Kansas City Review*, XVIII (1951), 94–108. Especially good on the point of view.

Durr, Robert A. "The Night Journey in *The Ambassadors*," *Philological Quarterly*, XXXV (1956), 24–38. Suggests archetypes.

Gerber, John C., and Sampson, Martin W. *The Ambassadors*. New York, n.d., introduction.

Tilford, John E., Jr. "James the Old Intruder," *Modern Fiction Studies*, IV (1958), 157–164.

Watt, Ian. "The First Paragraph of *The Ambassadors*," *Essays in Criticism*, X (1960), 250–274. Detailed explication.

Young, R. E. "An Error in *The Ambassadors*," *American Literature*, XXII (1950), 245–253. Corrects the order of chapters 28 and 29; unconvincing in critical inferences.

The American

Gettmann, Royal A. "Henry James's Revision of *The American*," *American Literature*, XVI (1945), 279–295. Shows that the revisions were more concrete and explicit.

Schulz, Max F. "Bellegardes' Feud with Christopher Newman: A Study of Henry James's Revision of *The American*," *American Literature*, XXVII (1955), 42–55. Demonstrates James's retention of the romanticism.

Traschen, Isadore. "An American in Paris," *American Literature*, XXVI (1954), 67–77; "Henry James and the Art of Revision," *Philological Quarterly*, XXXV (1956), 39–47; "James's Revisions of the Love Affair in *The American*," *The New England Quarterly*, XXIX (1956), 43–62. Detailed examinations of the revisions and their effects.

"The Aspern Papers"

Edel, Leon. "*The Aspern Papers*: Great-Aunt Wyckoff and Juliana Bordereau," *Modern Language Notes*, LXVII (1952), 392–395. Finds indebtedness for the portrait of Juliana.

"The Beast in the Jungle"

Cambon, Glauco. "The Negative Gesture in Henry James," *Nineteenth Century Fiction*, XV (1961), 335–344. On renunciation by Catherine Sloper and May Bartram.

Lucke, Jessie R. "The Inception of 'The Beast in the Jungle,'" *The New England Quarterly*, XXVI (1953), 529–532. Finds a parallel in *The Blithedale Romance*.

Stone, Edward, ed. *Henry James: Seven Stories and Studies*, New York,

A SELECTED BIBLIOGRAPHY

1961. Pp. 241–259. Excerpts from studies by Knights, Smith, Wertham, Kerner, Tate, Dupee, O'Faolain, Dawner, Stone, Rogers.

The Bostonians

Anderson, Charles R. *Ibid.* (above, General Criticism). Especially discusses Ransom.

Trilling, Lionel. *The Bostonians*. London, 1952, introduction.

Confidence

Levy, Leo B. "Henry James's *Confidence* and the Development of the Idea of the Unconscious," *American Literature*, XXVIII (1956), 347–358. Considers it a "landmark" in James's "study of human consciousness."

Daisy Miller

Dunbar, Viola. "A Note on the Genesis of *Daisy Miller*," *Philological Quarterly*, XXVII (1948), 184–186. Shows a parallel with Cherbuliez's *Paule Méré*.

Dunbar, Viola. "The Revision of *Daisy Miller*," *Modern Language Notes*, LXV (1950), 311–317. Finds the revision more poetic than the original.

The Golden Bowl

Anderson, Quentin. "Henry James and the New Jerusalem," *The Kenyon Review*, VIII (1946), 515–566. Maintains that "Adam is Divine Wisdom, Maggie, Divine Love."

Blackmur, R. P. *The Golden Bowl*, New York, 1953, v–xxi. Holds that Maggie "is in intention rather like Beatrice, and suffers the pangs of the highest human love."

Cox, C. B. "*The Golden Bowl*," *Essays in Criticism*, V (1955), 190–193. Sees Maggie as battling for her rights.

Fergusson, Francis. "*The Golden Bowl* Revisited," *The Sewanee Review*, LXIII (1955) 13–28. Sees it, *The Ambassadors*, and *The Wings of the Dove* in Swedenborgian terms.

Firebaugh, Joseph J. "The Ververs," *Essays in Criticism*, IV (1954), 400–410. Severe on Adam and Maggie.

Gordon, Caroline. "Mr. Verver, Our National Hero," *The Sewanee Review*, LXIII (1955), 29–47. Sympathetic to Adam; calls Charlotte a "monster."

Krook, Dorothea. "*The Golden Bowl*," *The Cambridge Journal*, VII (1954), 716–737. Considers Maggie "the scapegoat and redeemer."

261

Kimball, Jean. "Henry James's Last Portrait of a Lady: Charlotte Stant in *The Golden Bowl*," *American Literature*, XXVIII (1957), 449–468. Compares Charlotte with Milly Theale, Isabel Archer, and Minny Temple.

Leavis, F. R. *The Great Tradition*. London, 1948. Finds an "element of distaste" in Maggie and Adam; unconvincing.

Nuhn, Ferner. *The Wind Blew from the East*. New York, 1942. Calls Maggie a witch.

Spencer, James L. "Symbolism in James's *The Golden Bowl*," *Modern Fiction Studies*, III (1958), 333–344. A careful study of symbolism and realism.

Spender, Stephen. *The Destructive Element; A Study of Modern Writers and Beliefs*. Boston, 1936. Discusses the theme.

Stevenson, Elizabeth. *The Crooked Corridor*. New York, 1949. Sees Maggie as paying for the wrong done by others.

Warren, Austin. "Myth and Dialectic in the Later Novels," *The Kenyon Review*, V (1943), 551–568. Considers Maggie triumphant over disloyalty.

Wegelin, Christof. *Ibid.* (above, General Criticism). A sound study of the theme and art.

Wright, Walter F. "Maggie Verver: Neither Saint nor Witch," *Nineteenth-Century Fiction*, XII (1957), 59–71. Includes a summary of criticism.

"The Impressions of a Cousin"
Havens, Raymond D. "Henry James's 'The Impressions of a Cousin,'" *Modern Language Notes*, LXV (1950), 317–319. Warns of the danger of reading the final versions in terms of the notebooks.

In the Cage
Friend, Albert C. "A Forgotten Story by Henry James," *The South Atlantic Quarterly*, LIII (1954), 100–108. Seeks symbolic parallels, Everard being Jove.

Knights, L. C. "Henry James and the Trapped Spectator," *The Southern Review*, IV (1939), 600–615. Sees the girl as typical of James's trapped spectators.

McFarlane, I. D. "A Literary Friendship—Henry James and Paul Bourget," *The Cambridge Journal*, IV (1951), 144–161. Notes that both wrote on the subject of James's story.

"The Jolly Corner"
Blackmur, R. P. "*The Sacred Fount*," *The Kenyon Review*, IV (1942), 328–352. Sees Brydon as exorcising a partly living self.

A SELECTED BIBLIOGRAPHY

Stone, Edward, ed. *Ibid.* (above, "The Beast in the Jungle"). Pp. 292–308. Excerpts from studies by Wilson, Rosenzweig, Honig, Schroeder, Allott, Beebe, Rogers, Anderson, Stovall, Wegelin.

"The Liar"

Stone, Edward, ed. *Ibid.* (above, "The Beast in the Jungle"). Pp. 102–106. Excerpts from studies by West and Stallman, Bewley.

"Madame de Mauves"

Bewley, Marius. "Henry James and Life," *The Hudson Review,* XI (1958), 167–185. Finds resemblances to Hawthorne.

"The Middle Years"

Westbrook, Perry D. "The Supersubtle Fry," *Nineteenth-Century Fiction,* VIII (1953), 134–140. Considers the story a satire; unconvincing.

"The Next Time"

Lind, Ilse D. "The Inadequate Vulgarity of Henry James," *Publications of the Modern Language Association,* LXVI (1951), 886–910. A thorough account of the New York *Tribune* affair.

"A Passionate Pilgrim"

Gegenheimer, Albert F. "Early and Late Revisions in Henry James's 'A Passionate Pilgrim,'" *American Literature,* XXIII (1951), 233–242. Finds that the revisions reduced the ornateness and increased the concreteness.

The Portrait of a Lady

Krause, Sidney A. "James's Revisions of the Style of *The Portrait of a Lady,*" *American Literature,* XXX (1958), 67–88. Finds that the revisions sharpened and clarified the meaning and gave greater flexibility of style.

Leavis, I. D. "A Note on Literary Indebtedness: Dickens, George Eliot, Henry James," *The Hudson Review,* VIII (1955), 423–438. Notes the weakness of the description in Isabel's visit to the Roman ruins.

Matthiessen, F. O. "The Painter's Sponge and Varnish Bottle," *The American Bookman,* I (1944), 49–68. Finds the revisions subtle and more concrete.

Millett, Fred B. *The Portrait of a Lady.* New York, 1951, introduction.

The Princess Casamassima

Berland, Alwyn. "James and Forster: The Morality of Class," *The Cambridge Journal,* VI (1953), 259–280. Considers aesthetic experience to be moral for James.

263

Cargill, Oscar. *"The Princess Casamassima:* A Critical Reappraisal," *Publications of the Modern Language Association,* LXXI (1956), 97–117. A review of earlier criticism and a new interpretation.

Oliver, Clinton. "Henry James as Social Critic," *The Antioch Review,* VII (1947), 243–258. Regards the novel as principally on social reform.

Woodcock, George. "Henry James and the Conspirators," *Sewanee Review,* LV (1952), 219–229. Holds that James depended on journalistic views of anarchists.

"The Pupil"

Stone, Edward, ed. *Ibid.* (above, "The Beast in the Jungle"). Pp. 183–198. Excerpts from studies by Nuhn, Rahv, Dupee, O'Faolain, Martin, Hagopian, Stein.

Wagenknecht, Edward. *Ibid.* (above, General Criticism). Objects to a Freudian interpretation.

"The Real Thing"

Stone, Edward, ed. *Ibid.* (above, "The Beast in the Jungle"). Pp. 131–141. Excerpts from studies by Anderson, Munson, O'Faolain, Lainoff, Wright.

The Reverberator

Anderson, Charles R. "Henry James's Fable of Carolina," *The South Atlantic Quarterly,* LIV (1955), 249–257. On James's limited background of knowledge for his Carolina characters.

Roderick Hudson

Dunbar, Viola. "The Problem in *Roderick Hudson," Modern Language Notes,* LXVII (1952), 109–113. Notes James's stress on freedom of the will.

Gardner, Burdett. "An Apology for Henry James's 'Tiger Cat,' " *Publications of the Modern Language Association,* LXVIII (1953), 688–695. Suggests that Christina was modeled after Violet Paget.

The Sacred Fount

Beach, Joseph W. (*The Method of Henry James*). New Haven, 1918. Notes that James "failed to develop the idea of the 'sacred fount.' "

Blackmur, R. P. *Ibid.* (above, "The Jolly Corner"). Considers James the sacred fount for the characters.

Edel, Leon. *The Sacred Fount,* New York, 1953, v–xxxii. Notes resemblances to "The Turn of the Screw" and other stories.

Folsom, James K. "Archimago's Well: An Interpretation of *The Sacred Fount*," *Modern Fiction Studies*, VII (1961), 136–144. Sees the narrator as a spiritual vampire.

Hinchcliffe, Arnold P. "James's *The Sacred Fount*," *Texas Studies in Literature and Language*, II (1960), 88–94. Regards the novel as transitional and not fully successful.

Perlongo, Robert A. "*The Sacred Fount:* Labyrinth or Parable?" *The Kenyon Review*, XXII (1960), 635–647. Sees the narrator as a tragic figure valuing life not for itself, but for what he can "make of it."

Raeth, Claire J. "Henry James's Rejection of *The Sacred Fount*," *English Literary History*, XVI (1949), 308–324. Feels that the novel fails because the narrator becomes a protagonist.

Ranald, Ralph A. "*The Sacred Fount:* James's Portrait of the Artist Manqué," *Nineteenth-Century Fiction*, XIV (1960), 239–248. Sees the narrator as a sinister person.

Roberts, Morris. "Henry James's Final Period," *The Yale Review*, XXXVII (1947), 60–67. Stresses the suspense and excitement in the novel.

The Spoils of Poynton

Levy, Leo B. *Ibid*. (above, General Criticism). Sees the "significant evil" as Mrs. Gereth's.

Quinn, Patrick F. "Morals and Motives in *The Spoils of Poynton*," *The Sewanee Review*, LXII (1954), 563–577. Considers Fleda guilty of "the specific Jamesian villainy" of trying to shape the lives of others; unconvincing.

"The Turn of the Screw"

Daiches, David. "Sensibility and Technique," *The Kenyon Review*, V (1943), 569–579. Rejects Wilson's interpretation.

Edel, Leon. *Ibid*. (above, General Criticism, *The Ghostly Tales of Henry James*). Suggests that the story "may be studied by the biographer as a projection of Henry James's own haunted state."

Roellinger, Francis X., Jr. "Psychical Research and 'The Turn of the Screw,'" *American Literature*, XX (1949), 401–412. On a possible influence; rejects a Freudian interpretation and accepts the ghosts.

Willen, Gerald. *A Casebook of Henry James's "The Turn of the Screw."* New York, 1960. Gives complete studies by Kenton, Wilson, Fagin, Waldock, Heilman, Reed, Evans, Hoffmann, Cargill, Silver, Goddard, Lydenberg, Jones; symposium by Porter, Tate, and Van Doren.

THE MADNESS OF ART

Wolff, Robert L. "The Genesis of '*The Turn of the Screw,*'" *American Literature,* XIII (1941), 1–8. On the possible influence of a picture.

Watch and Ward

McElderry, Bruce R., Jr. "Henry James's Revision of *Watch and Ward,*" *Modern Language Notes,* LXVII (1952), 457–461. Notes that James pruned the rhetoric and made the phrasing more precise.

What Maisie Knew

Wilson, Harris W. "What *Did* Maisie Know?" *College English,* XVII (1956), 279–282. Treats the novel as the initiation of Maisie to evil.

Worden, Ward S. "Henry James's *What Maisie Knew:* A Comparison with the Plans in *The Notebooks,*" *Publications of the Modern Language Association,* LXVIII (1953), 371–383. Regards Maisie as having "innate, absolute morality."

The Wings of the Dove

Bersani, Leo. "The Narrator as Center in *The Wings of the Dove,*" *Modern Fiction Studies,* VI (1960), 131–144. Maintains that James saw human relations as "chaos" and found a solution only in renouncing "life in society for solitary integrity."

Blackmur, R. P. *Ibid.* (above, General Criticism). Strange interpretation: "The wings of the dove are still clean and silvery, but the sheepfold is fouler than ever; for the dove has created its dirt."

Hoskins, Elizabeth. "Henry James and the Future of the Novel," *The Sewanee Review,* LIV (1946), 87–101. Sees Milly as dying "like a kitten dressed up in doll clothes."

Krook, Dorothea. "*The Wings of the Dove,*" *The Cambridge Journal,* VII (1954), 671–689. Finds pride to be Maggie's tragic flaw.

Sandeen, Ernest. "*The Wings of the Dove* and *The Portrait of a Lady:* A Study of Henry James's Later Phase," *Publications of the Modern Language Association,* LXIX (1954), 1060–1075. Reads each in reference to Minny Temple.

on

INDEX OF JAMES'S WORKS